FOLK
LIKE
ME

FOLK LIKE ME

THE READ ALOUD BOOK OF SAINTS

k. m. lucchese

illustrations by
cathy rylander

maps by the author

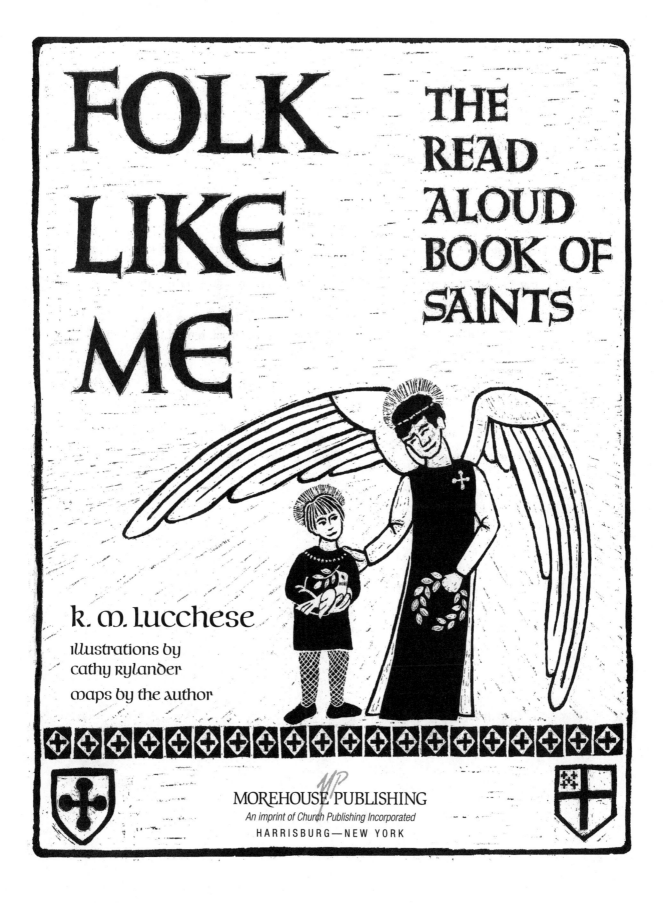

MOREHOUSE PUBLISHING

An imprint of Church Publishing Incorporated

HARRISBURG—NEW YORK

Morehouse Publishing, 4775 Linglestown Road, Harrisburg, PA 17105

Morehouse Publishing, 445 Fifth Avenue, New York, NY 10016

Morehouse Publishing is an imprint of Church Publishing Incorporated.

Cover art and interior illustrations: Cathy Rylander
Cover design: Laurie Klein Westhafer
Interior design by Beth Oberholtzer

Library of Congress Cataloging-in-Publication Data

Lucchese, K. M.
　　Folk like me : the read-aloud book of Saints / by K. M. Lucchese ; illustrations by Cathy Rylander.
　　　　p.　　cm.
　　Includes bibliographical references and index.
　　ISBN 978-0-8192-2289-3 (pbk.)
　　1. Christian saints.　I. Rylander, Cathy.　II. Title.
BR1710.L83 2008
270.092'2—dc22
[B]

2008009245

Printed in the United States of America

08　09　10　11　12　13　　10　9　8　7　6　5　4　3　2　1

dedication

James P. Spencer, 1932–2000

Once upon a time, there was a scientist who wore red socks. He was nearly deaf because he had stood too close to too many guns in the Navy. He liked hard candy, astronomy, Mickey Mouse, and Christmas. He wanted to teach and serve the little folks, and so he and his family and friends started a school.

Cruelty he did not tolerate, nor a lack of due order. He took prayer awfully seriously, but himself, rarely. He loved and served the Lord, and the Lord sent him the mighty and glorious Archangel Michael to shield him and his little flock, and to name his new school after.

At the scientist's school, each year brought new sheep to the flock. Some were sheep that did not know their master's voice, sheep who had been fed on slim pickings and thin air. But there were others already dear to the shepherd, who came sweetly and eagerly, knowing that the finest fodder was only to be reached in the highest and deepest places.

And though the scientist left them and walked among the spires and gardens of Paradise, his flock meanwhile grew tall and broad, and its united members resisted the powers of evil as best they could, clinging to that which is good and walking before the Lord in holiness and righteousness, all their days.

—*K. M. Lucchese*

To my best beloved student Jonathan,
who taught me more than ever I taught him.
Jonathan Aurand 1983–2004
—*Cathy Rylander*

contents

Preface
ix

Introduction
xi

YEAR ONE: **A Song of the Saints**
1

YEAR TWO: **Patient and Brave and True**
127

APPENDIX A: Maps
247

APPENDIX B: Extra Resources
273

Bibliography
285

FIRST INDEX: Saints Organized by Week
287

SECOND INDEX: Saints Organized by Characteristics
291

preface

The week-by-week format of this book might make finding your favorite saint a laborious process, especially if you cannot recall her or his saint's day. Please make frequent use of the two indices at the end of the book: one index lists the saints all in alphabetical order and then directs you to his or her specific date and thus their book location, and the other index—if even the saint's name escapes you—reminds you of the name by some memorable characteristic, like the fact that he was French and walked around with his head cut off (Saint Denis).

Do also recall that there are two sequential years of listings, so that people like me, who cannot remember which saint they told about in, say, October Week Two of Year One, can at least be certain that it *was* from last year and will be quite safe, by choosing one from October Week Two of Year Two, for example, from repeating themselves too often. Also note that each story begins with the saint's name, dates of birth and death (sometimes approximate), what their primary "job" was, and their feast day, that is, the day on which a mass might be celebrated in their honor; usually the date of their death, but often placed "over" an existing pagan holiday.

introduction

Salutation

These stories arose from a weekly "saint story" told in chapel every Friday at the Episcopal day school where I have taught for the past twenty years or so. They began with Saint Nicholas and Saint Lucy, then Saint Valentine, Saint Brendan and Saint Francis were added, until, for the past three years, there have been nearly weekly saints. The age range in our daily chapel is very broad: from Kindergarteners just barely able to sit through morning prayers to hardened Upper Schoolers, and in choosing which stories to tell I had to consider that some stories were too gory for the younger children or too sappy for the elder. The most successful stories were those with a core theme, or anything to do with animals, and upon the basic facts of each story I freely extemporized.

This book is a primer for children, and it is meant to be read aloud, ideally once a week in a school chapel, Sacred Studies or Sunday School setting, with as much feeling and emphasis as is possible. Although the most violent and disturbing aspects of the lives of the saints are for that reason left out or somehow softened, it is of course impossible and unwise to remove all sadness and brutality. After all, most saints sacrificed their worldly hopes on the altar of service and faith, hopes that often included good health and a family life, material wealth and physical security.

Children will always need to know that there is happiness beyond material wealth and in spite of poor health, that goodness is more important than beauty, and that beauty can be found in unexpected places … but most children know this already, and can easily spot the saint in a crowd! What they need is the fuel to keep that childhood gift burning, the light to keep that inward eye seeing, all their lives. Children want to be good, they want to be heroes and saints. As Lesbia Scott put it in our top favorite hymn (and the source of this book's title and subtitles) at Saint Michael's, "They were all of them saints of God, and I mean, God helping, to be one, too." Children need true stories of daring, kindly people, as well as a permanent stock of improbable—but well-attested—miracles to keep their minds open to mystery. I only hope that this little book will help to do that for them.

Definition *(for the kids)*

"What *is* a saint, and how exactly do I go about becoming one?" are two perfectly reasonable questions to ask at this point. There are *official* saint definitions and requirements, put out by the churches which have their own methods of "canonizing" people. That is not, of course, being shot from a large gun, but rather having your name added to a very long list of saints, the canon, which is read aloud from time to time as a sort of Roll Call of the Elect. Nowadays, it's a tricky business to be canonized: you must have so many miracles performed in your name seen by just so many witnesses and so on and so forth. You also need to be dead, but have a lot of living friends who are willing to do all the paperwork needed, *and* you need to be patient for quite a while. You might be what's called "beatified" first, a kind of Master's degree until you get your Doctorate, so to speak. But none of that concerns us here: I will work with the canon as it appears in commonly accepted texts, and only look on in sad wonder as saints like Mother Teresa of Calcutta make their long trek toward canonization, saints who in the Good Old Days would have been saints almost the instant they drew their last breath.

In the Good Old Days, it was hard in a *different* way to become a saint, or rather it was hard in the same old hard way all saints have earned the title: you had to die for your faith, and that was pretty much it—painful but quick, hopefully. As Jesus says in John 15:13, "No one has greater love than this, to lay down one's life for one's friends" (NRSV translation of the Greek or Aramaic). The truth is, most of these saints died for their faith, whether they were Early Christian Martyrs or not. They may have spent their whole lives doing it: giving up a little more of their sleep, a little more of their food, or working a little harder than anyone around them. They used themselves up in order to help other people find faith, or warmth, or food, or love, or whatever it was the people needed from them. Most of the saints seemed to draw from their faith the power to do incredible things, even if they *seemed* to other people

to be too small and weak or old and sick to do anything.

You will come across some words and names over and over that I should explain a little here. First of all, *Francis* with an "i" is always a man and *Frances* with an "e" is always a woman, at least in this book. You will hear a lot about *monks* and *nuns*: they are men and women, respectively, who have chosen to remain unmarried all their lives, live in groups, and dedicate their time to worship and serving God, more or less. They can live in a *monastery*, a *priory*, a *friary*, an *abbey*, a *convent* (that's generally nuns who live there) and be ruled by a prior, an abbot . . . all depending on the type of place it is. Feel free to do a little research to learn more about these details.

A *bishop* is a sort of priest-in-chief put in charge of a whole region and its priests, and *archbishops* can be in charge of whole *countries*. All these religious-type people who actually work for the church are known as *clergy*. *Hermits* are monks or nuns who live alone in the wilderness, trying to concentrate on God but invariably being disturbed by curious or troubled people looking for advice or a quick miracle. *Martyrs* are people who have died for their faith; the word is from the Greek, meaning "witness." There will be various possibly repetitious explanations in the text about periods of history when it was dangerous to be a Christian; this was the case in the Roman world from roughly the 40's until 313 A.D., with some particularly hot periods, depending on the emperor. The *Bad Old Days* are pretty much any time, as you will see, with the *Olden Days* reaching up until about the French Revolution or so, or about 1800. Historically speaking, the *Really Dark Ages* being full of Goths, ran from about 450 to 600, the *Good-and-Dark Ages* being loaded with

Norsemen, ran from about 600 to 1000, *Pretty Dark Ages*, seeing crusades and plenty of other hacking and stabbing—not to mention the Black Death and the Mongol Invasions—ran from about 1000 to 1400 but all of these dark times having some surprisingly bright spots. Oh, yes, and *theology* is the study of God, something most of these people did a lot of, in schools or wherever they happened to be.

Usually, all the folks around the saints could tell that they were saints—at least *eventually*—however long it took official canonization to arrive, if it ever did. So, even if you aren't dead or appear on any list, your friends might know *you* are a sort of a saint, because you're helpful and patient and full of faith, even if sometimes they make fun of you for it . . . which is also what happened to most of the rest of the saints. And of course, God will know, because after all, God already knows how many hairs there are on your head, for heaven's sake! If we *all* managed to be saints, the earth would be like heaven, only we'd all be much happier down here before going off up there. So that's why I'm reading you these stories: maybe if you see how some other people managed it—all *sorts* of people—you can pick up some ideas for yourself.

Suggestion *(for the readers)*

The first part of this book, *Song of the Saints*, constitutes one year of more "churchy," that is, saints who were mostly clergy. The second part, *Patient and Brave and True*, is a more mixed bag of saints, people who brought their love of God and fellow man into whatever work they did. You will notice that two and sometimes three saints are given for each week for each year, both so that you can choose and so that you can use the book two or even four years in a row without repeating. But you will have favorites, as will the children, and some just may have to be repeated every year, while others never see the light of day. I do hope that, however you use this book, it will *not* be as a chore, or something to be tested on!

You will add other materials as you see fit: a whole week devoted to the stories of Saint Francis, with an art show and animal-blessing, is not inappropriate, for example, given the number of beautiful books on the subject. We at Saint Michael's devote an entire afternoon to a pageant on "our" archangel, with time-honored skits and hymns, performed by the whole school. And, though I have repeatedly attempted to beg off, if a Saint Nicholas day or week were to go by without a reading of "The Boy Who Laughed at Santa Claus" (by Ogden Nash, included at the end of this book, and utterly disconnected from any sensible report on the saint), there would be trouble in chapel!

When you read these aloud, consider employing the old but successful teaching chestnut of having the kids repeat the name of the saint after you when you introduce her or him. It is also a good idea to have an "exit strategy," or way of closing, such as saying a prayer for the saint. In our chapel, I used to bring an index card to read key information from, on the front of which, in bold marker, was the saint's name and date. This I would then pin on a bulletin board in the chapel, filling the board by the end of the fall semester, then clearing it out for a fresh start in January.

When you read aloud to a group as large as a chapel full of kids it is really impossible to show any pictures without a projector, except to the front row; a large map held up by a volunteer is sometimes useful, if it is incredibly simple and enormously big. I have included some maps at the back of the book that could be enlarged, or copied and pinned to the bulletin board for students to look at later. The main thing is really to read with *vigor* and take your time, enjoying each bit of the story. Practicing ahead of time is no shame, and a quick internal prayer doesn't hurt. Try to learn the correct pronunciation of the names and places in each story before you tell it; this may take some doing! Some stories are longer than others, so you might consider planning ahead and having a coloring project for the small fry earlier in the week that you can show off with your story, or locate or commission an article or a poem for and by the elders.

Notice that dates of when the saints lived or at least died are sneakily inserted and should be used; a timeline stapled up in the chapel could be used, especially if you have a Sacred Studies teacher interested in such things. By year's end, certainly, the kids will have an instinctive notion of when the big persecutions were and when they ended, when the Bad Old Days were (these depend on the region) and generally who went where and when—the why you can leave for history class. As a geographer, I felt the need to make maps of where the stories took place, and you should feel free to use these to put saint-labeled pins on a big wall-map if you can find the wall space to do it. The importance of *time* and *place* in the stories of saints is sometimes overwhelming. The maps are also meant to encourage exploration, so that if one ever finds oneself near a saint's place, the means will be at hand to locate and visit key spots and so experience the link between past and present firsthand.

Finally, please note that, though there may be gentle irony and humor in these stories, there is never to be any sarcasm or snide commentary used in connection with them. If you have a rough audience, with lots of interruptions, simply smile, make up a comment on the spot related to their points and then say, "*speaking* of which…" and go back to the story, however un-connected the story may be to the point. It bemuses children and they listen, trying to figure out the connection. But then, as an educator, you already know that sarcasm and children mix like oil and water. Children are also literal-minded, which is why I have tried to keep metaphorical language out of my stories, and they need explanations for things elders think they already know, so please be patient with what seems to be all too clear to you. On the other hand, be careful not to pander to the gorier tastes of older children by adding back in the graphic detail that has generally been omitted. The world has graphic detail enough.

Elucidation

Many books could be and should be given over to examples of good people from every place, time, and faith: knowing where to begin or stop would be impossible. Due to its chapel context and goals, this book is unapologetically Christian in outlook, which also mercifully simplifies the choice of which stories to include. As part of this outlook I am assuming in my audience a certain level of familiarity with the core doctrines and liturgy of the Church and even an affection for them. It is to be hoped that those without that familiarity or affection may attain them.

In choosing the saints for this book, I have weighted my choices toward those from before the Reformation, a period which may be viewed as the common heritage of all Christian denominations. The truly monumental saints, such as Peter, Paul, Daniel, the Virgin Mary, Joseph, and the like, who are amply discussed in the Bible and who do of course have their own feast days, I have left to the Sacred Studies teachers and chaplains to discuss in homilies loftier then the stories here. Beyond those criteria, I have frankly chosen those I think will make a good story and a clear point. I am naturally aware that no ten-minute chat can hope to do any of these great-hearts justice. All the same, hearing even so little can spark the imagination of a child. Children are, after all, still building themselves up, bit by bit, out of all they see, hear, and feel; each moment is to them a day or month or year of adult life. So why not put before them some especially gleaming bits to build themselves with? They will be better people for it.

The arrangement of the saints is initially by their feast day, beginning with the month of August, since that is generally the first at least partial month of the school year, and ending with June, at the opposite end of things—although most school districts are unlikely to include both. We in Texas, for example, tend to start school in mid- or late-August and finish at the end of May. The saints of July are thus utterly left out, as are potentially those of parts or all of June and August. I have rashly taken the liberty of "larding" other months with key summer saints, particularly when some months are particularly lean as to really good saint stories. If, on the other hand, you would like to use the stories all summer, for Sunday School, you can track down the summer saints peppering the book over the rest of the year, or you could use summer to spend that extra time with favorite saints, with plays, skits, and art. Sometimes natural theme pairings present themselves, and these may shift around the locations of saints, as well. The dates for the saints' days' feasts are drawn from my

two chief sources (listed below), and, although have I noticed some discrepancies with some other sources, to these I will adhere. You will also note missing weeks at Christmas and Spring Break, which may be used to take either a saint rest or the magnification again of a favorite saint.

I have used commonly available sources, primarily the *Penguin Dictionary of Saints* and the *Oxford Dictionary of Saints*, cross-checked with standard Roman Catholic and general-knowledge references and informational websites, using common sense, onsite explorations and good research practice. When possible, I include knowledge of my own gleaned from research at the Vatican Library, booklets available from local places of pilgrimage, and the like. Any errors in information and judgment are emphatically my own; I have tried not to let my fancy carry me far from the facts as I have found them, but if I have done so, it is without malicious intention. Certainly, future hagiographers should not rely much on this book as a reputable source, but should return to the earliest accounts they can find and learn the details for themselves, possibly using my bibliography as a jumping-off place

Pacification

It may surprise readers to know that I am not a Roman Catholic, or even—outside of weekday mornings—an Episcopalian, but rather a member of a Congregational church, open-minded but Trinitarian and no heretic concerning any of the core beliefs of the early church. My background in classical languages excuses my antiquarian interests but does not mean I am a member of the clergy, and although I do hold a doctorate, it is in the mysterious field of cultural geography, not theology. What I do know about is how to teach—

how to grab and hold the attention of a roomful of kids—and so I must defend my stories as more or less tried and true.

I do want to apologize here for the preponderance of European saints, and at the same time note that I have taken one liberty with those African saints who *have* been included. Since I have chosen to focus on saints of the early church, this has meant most of the stories deal with people who were either citizens of Rome or early evangelizers of western Europe. The ethnicity of these people is generally a range from deep tan to beige to pinky-white. Anyone slightly darker irritatingly tends to be identified in the canon as "The Black." This is a foolishness I could not allow in my book; it is a bit like calling Clare of Assisi "Clare the Woman," or Francis of Assisi "Francis the White." Benedict the Black has been changed to Benedict of Palermo and Moses the Black is now Moses the Moor. East Asian saints, being late, are sadly underrepresented in the canon; I should have included Saint Paul Miki, but like so many of the martyr stories, it is simply too sad for small children. I hope to do justice to the martyrs of Japan in a future project.

I hope that there are no church officials who feel that the saints are their personal property and that they, as part of an official canon, may not be discussed by anyone considered to have the "unclean lips" of non-clergy. On the contrary, I am a believer in the Freedom of Information Act for church matters as for all others, and take it that, if it is published, it may be used by laypeople. As a prior example of such freedom, C. S. Lewis was certainly no clergyman, but has done a great deal, it seems to me, to propagate the faith.

K. M. Lucchese,
Summer 2007
College Station, TX

YEAR ONE

a song of the saints

I sing a song of the saints of God,
Patient and brave and true,
Who toiled and fought and lived and died
For the Lord they loved and knew.
And one was a doctor, and one was a queen,
And one was a shepherdess on the green:
They were all of them saints of God—and I mean,
God helping, to be one too.

They loved their Lord so dear, so dear,
And his love made them strong,
And they followed the right for Jesus' sake
The whole of their good lives long.
And one was a soldier, and one was a priest,
And one was slain by a fierce wild beast:
And there's not any reason—no, not the least,
Why I shouldn't be one too.

They lived not only in ages past,
  There are hundreds of thousands still,
The world is bright with the joyous saints
  Who love to do Jesus' will.
    You can meet them in school, or in lanes, or at sea,
    In church, or in trains, or in shops, or at tea,
    For the the saints of God are just folk like me,
    And I mean to be one, too.

Lesbia Scott, 1929

"Here we are at the start of another school year!" People are *always* saying that, this time of year. And here is another bunch of saints to hear about, one per week. Some have silly names, and some died in strange ways, but all of them have some gift for us to keep tucked away, somewhere in our memories. The song says, "they were all of them saints of God and I mean, God helping, to be one, too," and when the poet Lesbia Scott wrote that, she knew that we can all *mean* to be saints, but can't often manage it, and it's the "God helping" part that makes the difference. This year, with God's help, may we all come closer to being the saints we mean to be.

august

OSWALD, KING of NORTHUMBRIA
(605–642) king (August 9) *(see Map 1)*

You will need to know where Northumbria is, because it just keeps coming up in saints' stories, and part of the reason for that is today's saint, King Oswald. The borders of the actual *kingdom* of Northumbria changed with time and battles, but the general area is north of the Humber River in England, an estuary (that's a big river-mouth, actually) just above the old kingdom of Mercia, on the east side of the island of Great Britain and including, at the time of King Oswald, the region called Deira where the old royal cities of York and Bamburgh are, and as far as north as the Firth of Forth in Scotland.

Oswald was a Saxon, and he spoke a really old type of English, but the people to his north and west spoke a language called Gaelic, and they were generally grouchy with the Saxons since the Saxons had pushed them north to Scotland and west to Wales off their old lands. In fact, they even pushed other Saxons around, because when Oswald was just a boy, his father Ethelfrith was killed by another Saxon king (Saint Edwin, as it later turned out, whose story you can hear another time), so Oswald and his family themselves had to go off to Scotland to hide out.

There is an island off the coast of Scotland called Iona, and in those days there was a monastery there, run by Saint Aidan. From Aidan and these monks, Oswald learned Gaelic *and* he learned all about Christianity: so much, in fact, that he decided that when he

4 • *Year One: A Song of the Saints*

finally got back to Northumbria, he wanted to tell people there all about it. First, he had to get old enough and strong enough to defeat his enemies in battle, and finally did, near the old town of Hexham, when he was thirty-three years old. And he brought Saint Aidan and some of his monks back with him, but they all spoke Gaelic, and Oswald's Saxons couldn't, so when Aidan preached, King Oswald himself translated the sermons to his thanes—that is, his free-born, land-holding companions who had sworn loyalty to him—and men-at-arms, and they say it was a "pleasing sight to see." Oswald was a good king, and for a long time there was peace, and churches were built all over Northumbria.

But then the Welsh king Penda attacked. Now, Oswald was a mighty warrior, and they say that when he fought, two ravens went along with him as scouts, but he was defeated that day. What really made everyone sure he was a saint was that as he died, he prayed for the souls of those men dying around him. Penda, being pagan, chopped Oswald up and tacked the bits to a tree (at a place in Shropshire called Oswestry—"Oswald's Tree"—today) as an offering to his gods, but Oswald's ravens guarded the tree until his people came to bury him properly. Poor Saint Aidan was just about heartbroken, and the battle went on for Northumbria . . . as we'll see another time.

August: Week One

LAWRENCE (died 258)
deacon and martyr (August 10)

Toward the end of the third century (A.D., of course: all Christian-type stories happened after Jesus was marching about in the flesh, so they must be A.D., and that would be in the 200s since centuries work the way that they do), the Roman emperors at the time had just about *had* it with the Christians. The emperor certainly wasn't a Christian yet—that wouldn't happen until about 313

A.D.—and he was worried at how many other people in the Empire *were.* Christians refused to think that the emperor was a god like Hercules, and they wouldn't worship either of them, *or* Jupiter or even little Venus Cloacina, the goddess of the drains. Christians said they had this one God who was in charge of everything, and no one else mattered. They paid their taxes and ran poor-people shelters and seemed harmless, but the Roman emperor was *sure* they were out to bring down his government.

So the Roman government made it illegal to be a Christian, and every time the crops failed or there was a plague or a fire in the city, some Christians would be arrested and blamed for it, and if they were citizens they would quietly get their heads chopped off, and if they were not, then they would get killed in "fun" ways in the arena to amuse the rather bloodthirsty crowds during festival time. So one time, in the capital of Rome itself, there was a big round-up of Christians, and one of the people caught was a big, cheerful young man, Lawrence (or Laurentius, in Latin), who was a deacon—an assistant to a priest—but not a Roman citizen yet, so the city prefect (something like a combination of mayor and chief of police) decided to pick on him.

"Hand over all your valuables!" he demanded in a bossy, prefect-y way, and Lawrence smiled and said that would take awhile, so the prefect told him to take his time, but be back with the goods or else! So Lawrence came back the next day with a big crowd of people from the local Christian mission soup-kitchen and homeless shelter and said: "Here is the church's treasure!" Well, that did it. They decided to have some fun with Lawrence and grill him on a gridiron, but Lawrence was so brave—and I suppose he knew he was headed directly for heaven—that after awhile he said: "You can turn me over; I'm done on this side." He died, of course, and his friends buried him and missed him very much, but they all went on being Christians, anyway, whatever the emperor said.

August: Week Two

TIKHON of ZADONSK (1724–1783)
abbot (August 13) *(See Map 2)*

(They say we can also call him "Timothy," but Tikhon is more interesting, don't you think?)

When Tikhon was fourteen years old and living in Novgorod (that's in what's called western Russia today), he thought he would go to religious school and learn how to be a monk—that is, a man who never gets married and spends his life praying and working for the church and helping other people. Mostly Tikhon went to monk-school only so that he wouldn't be drafted into the Russian army, so he wasn't much of a saint yet! But he was very good at his studies and soon became a priest-monk who could preach and do communion and that sort of thing, and was so good at *that* that by the time he was thirty-nine he was a bishop (that is, a priest in charge of a big city and all its clergy of priests and churches and monks) of the Russian city of Voronezh.

Being a bishop is always a lot of work, and things in Voronezh were *bad*, so Tikhon had to work even harder than usual: the churches were a mess, the priests were doing everything wrong—and they *liked* it that way. By the time he had fixed everything, he was only forty-three years old but was completely worn out and had to retire to a little monastery at Zadonsk (now *there's* a great name!) to get to feeling better and to do some writing. They gave him a small retirement pension, most of which he spent on taking care of other people. He spent his time giving people spiritual advice, or helping them in other ways: it seemed as though he was almost as busy as when he was bishop.

People still remember some of the wise and funny advice he gave. For example, one time some men he knew complained that it was too hard to be good all the time, saying: "We're not monks! Why should we be expected to live like them?" Tikhon smiled as usual and gently reminded them that the Scriptures called people to love and serve one another "before there *were* any such things as monks or monasteries." Like most saints, Tikhon was almost always moderate, and forgiving, but also like many saints, he was quick-tempered about things that are really wrong: disrespect of God and cruelty to one another; he wouldn't stand still for either of *those*. And there you have the wise and funny Saint Tikhon of Zadonsk!

August: Week Two

MAXIMILIAN KOLBE (1894–1941)
missionary and martyr (August 14)

He is called "the saint for the twentieth century;" let's see why that might be true.

Grown-ups always think that the time they are living in is the worst, that it has never been so bad as this and that things were better in the "Good Old Days." Don't you believe it! There are good times and bad times, but some of the old days were really "Bad Old Days." The twentieth century will always be famous for all the amazing machines that were invented and the great new ideas that were thought up, but some of the machines turned out to be terrible, and some of the ideas were so incredibly bad that for centuries afterward people will still be suffering because of them. But there will always be good people who recognize bad ideas when they see them and will fight against them, and one of these people was Maximilian Kolbe.

Maximilian came from Zdunskawola (*such* a cool place-name and just off the left of map 2, south of Warsaw, near the big city of Lodz) in Poland, and became a priest in 1918, when he was twenty-four and all of Europe was tired out after the First World War and everyone wanted to be modern and happy, but many people were still angry and miserable. Maximilian thought that maybe this would be a good time to remind people about the big ideas of Christianity —brotherhood, peace, forgiveness, that sort of thing—but he felt that he needed to be modern about his approach. So, he started a printing shop, and then a radio show, and he went all over the world preaching and listening and learning and explaining. When he went to Japan, he studied Buddhism to understand its connections with Christianity, and he started more newspapers and study groups all over East Asia.

Maximilian began to tire himself out, the way saints do, and he had to go home to Poland for a rest in 1936. When the evil Nazi army of Germany took over his country in 1939, he and his whole congregation were arrested for awhile, but as soon as they were released, they went back to work saving people whose lives were in danger. They sheltered about three thousand Polish people, most of them Jewish (the people those crazy Nazis hated most of all, because of one of those incredibly bad new ideas added to a bad old idea). Of course, Maximilian was arrested again in 1941 when they found out what his church had been doing, especially after he wrote in his newspaper that "no one in the world can change Truth."

You may have heard of the terrible death camps where the Nazis sent people they didn't like, to kill them right away or work them to death more slowly . . . well, that's where they sent Maximilian Kolbe, to Auschwitz, one of the worst of those places. Maximilian did what he could to comfort his fellow prisoners, and finally, when one man who had a family had been chosen to die for some reason or other, Maximilian offered to die in his place. That very man lived to see Maximilian officially be made a saint, in 1982.

August: Week Three

LOUIS of FRANCE (1214–1297)
king (August 25)

Nowadays, we know that it is a bad thing to start a war over religion, but back in the thirteenth century or so, everyone was doing it, especially the Crusaders: European Christians who galloped off to the Holy Land (you know, where events in the Bible took place: mostly Israel, Jordan, and Egypt nowadays) on their great big horses and really heavy armor to save Jerusalem from the Muslims, only to discover that the Holy Land had been pretty peaceful up until then, and that the weather there was too hot for heavy armor and big horses, and that the Muslims not only had better horses and better manners but they also ate a lot of sherbet and wrote poetry. All the same, many serious people in France and England, Germany and Italy, thought going on a Crusade was a good thing. One of those people happened to be an excellent king and, in general, a very good man who did what he believed was right: King Louis I of France

Louis was the *ideal* king, so if you ever plan to be a monarch, listen up! He really had faith: he sincerely believed in God and that God was the boss, not Louis. In Paris, King Louis built one of the most beautiful churches anywhere, called La Sainte Chapelle. The walls are almost entirely made out of dark red and blue glass, and the ceiling is spangled with gold stars. He also knew it was an awesome responsibility to be in charge of all the people of France, and he did his best for them. As a judge, he was fair, whether you were rich or poor, and he was merciful, too, even when punishing people who did wrong. Louis insisted on preserving everyone's rights, no matter who they might be or what they looked like. In dealing with other countries, he was astute (meaning no one could fool him) and respectful, working for peace whenever possible, but he was a good soldier when he needed to lead his troops into battle. You could always trust him to do what he promised. And, like Joan of Arc and most saints, he hated dirty and blasphemous language (swearing by God and that sort of thing) and he wouldn't allow it around him.

Louis went off on one of those Crusades and—you guessed it—he died far away from France. But people never forgot what a good man he was, or how great a king he had been, so they made him a saint.

August: Week Three

CAESARIUS of ARLES (470–543)
bishop (August 27)

Back in the beginning of the Really Dark Ages of European history, also called the Early Medieval, the Romanesque, and so on and so forth, things were pretty rough, and they were about to get rougher. Attila the Hun had paid a visit to Italy as far south as Rome, and the Visigoths had followed him, grabbing everything they could grab, and then settled down and started fighting the other Goths for what *they* had. Things in France—or Gaul as it was still called—were beginning to look bad, too. The Roman emperor and his armies had moved east, way off to Byzantium, that is, Istanbul in the country of Turkey today, and all sorts of creepy bandits were loose in the countryside of western Europe. So it wasn't surprising that a few things started to slip: first, the water stopped running, because all the slaves who worked the plumbing had been stolen, killed, or run off because they hadn't been paid by the government in years and then—well, they couldn't lose electricity because that hadn't been discovered yet—but most of the schools closed, and pretty soon hardly anybody could read or write or add or subtract, so people got to be amazingly ignorant and easy to confuse.

Some people, thank goodness, hung on to their books and their wits, and helped out everybody else the best they could. One of these people—and an especially good one—was Caesarius of Arles, a citizen of what was left of Roman Gaul and a bishop, too. Arles was an important Roman city in the region called Provence, as you can see if you go there: you'll see the big Roman amphitheater left from the old days. Caesarius was a hard worker and a good preacher who used simple, logical language, didn't preach for too long, and got his message across. Another thing he did was start the first convent in Gaul: a place like a monastery but for *women* who wanted to pray and help people and never get married.

Caesarius had a sister named Caesaria (the Romans were always pretty unimaginative about names) who wanted to be in charge of the convent since she, like Caesarius, had managed to get a good education. They both decided that, since the nuns were going to be teaching children and helping out poor people who hadn't had much education, each nun should be able to read and write, and also that the nuns should be the *only* people to decide who was to be their abbess, that is, their nun-in-chief. So that's how they did it. Saint Caesarius was a broad-minded saint, for the Really Dark Ages!

August: Week Four

AUGUSTINE of HIPPO (354–430)
bishop and theologian (August 28) *(See Map 3)*

(Hippo, in this case, is *not* a large, grey, river-loving herbivore. Hippo Regius was a town in the Roman province of Numidia in North Africa, nowadays a town in Algeria called Annaba, not far from the Tunisian border.)

Back in the fourth century A.D., the coast of North Africa was a wetter place than it is today, with more trees and more crops, and it grew a lot of wheat for the rest of the world. Here Augustine grew up, with his pagan father and his Christian mother. His mother's name was Monica, and she later became a saint, too, and has her own story in another place. Monica, as I say, was a Christian, and she worried and prayed over her son no end! Augustine certainly did *think* about becoming a Christian, but meantime he learned public speaking and became good at it, thinking he might become a lawyer. Then he *thought* of becoming a philosopher, and he studied with all sorts of different religious groups. I suspect he was a little stubborn about his mother . . .

In his church in San Gimignano, Italy, there are wonderful pictures telling us the following story about Augustine, taken from his autobiography, called the *Confessions*. One day, he was *thinking* about picking up and reading a book of the Gospels that was lying there in the garden. Suddenly, a little boy who was watching him from over the wall of the garden called out, "Pick it up and read it!" Now, either that boy was an angel, as Augustine tells the story, or he was just a neighbor boy who was tired of watching him stare at the book. Anyhow, Augustine *did* pick up the book, *did* read it, and he felt as though all his questions were finally being answered! Later, he saw that same boy playing with pebbles on a riverbank, so Augustine asked him an important theological question about the nature of God. The boy gathered three pebbles together into one place, and that seemed to tell Augustine that God was indeed one being with three natures; anyway, it convinced Augustine and he spent years preaching about it and many other things. So I suppose the boy really *must* have been an angel, don't you think?

August: Week Four

PAMMACHIUS (340–410)
layman (August 30) *(See Map 4)*

The Caelian Hill in Rome, where Pammachius used to live, is a nice place to visit: very woodsy and peaceful, with a pleasant park, a roller-skating area, and several churches sprinkled all about. In fact, one of those churches (Saints John and Paul) used to be Pammachius' house, and you can go into the basement of the church and still see the old rooms. Pammachius was a wealthy Roman senator, and he used his nice big house to have prayer and worship meetings, because, even though it was legal to be a Christian at that time, there weren't many church buildings yet, and people were still used to worshipping at home. He also worked with other folks to help the poor and sick however he could.

Now, Pammachius wasn't a priest or any other kind of clergyman, or even a martyr "slain by a fierce wild beast," no, he was just a wealthy, married man with a family who did a lot of good things with his money to help people. He and another future saint, a wealthy Roman lady called Fabiola, put their money together and built a hospital and a place for travelers to stay down at Ostia, the port of Rome. He was also a good friend of Saint Paulinus of Nola, and he wrote helpful letters to Saint Jerome, who was living off in Bethlehem at that time. When Saint Jerome said that marriage was useless and distracting to a hard-working Christian, Pammachius totally disagreed with him. People are still arguing about important things like whether priests should marry and women should be priests even today, though you can tell which side Saint Pammachius was on!

When he died at the age of seventy, Pammachius had done a great number of good things that helped many people, and when the Visigoths arrived in Rome later that same year, and the Dark Ages really got started, people were glad they had someone bright and peaceful like Pammachius to remember.

september

GREGORY the GREAT (540–604)
pope and "apostle" (September 3)
(See Map 4)

Anytime some historical person is called "the Great," you can be sure that there have been just *oodles* of stories and even whole books written about him or her, and that is definitely true of today's saint, so I'll try to keep it simple. I wish I could tell you about the time Saint Gregory made Saint Michael sheathe his sword, or about when Gregory washed the feet of an angel at his supper-table, but there it is: he just did too many things!

Most of the important things Gregory did were while he was bishop of Rome. Now if you're bishop of Rome, you are also automatically in charge of the whole Roman Catholic part of the Christian faith, and you're called the pope. Back when Gregory was pope the Christian faith was still in one piece: there was no Eastern Orthodox church, Roman Catholic church, or Lutheran church, because none of those breaks had happened yet. It was all still catholic with a small "c", which means "universal."

Now, not only was Gregory bishop of Rome, he was a local boy: he grew up on the Caelian Hill there, in the house that is now underneath a church named in his honor. In fact, he lived across the street from Saint Pammachius' house, and he liked his former neighbor's ideas about organizing monasteries, so Gregory actually started a monastery in his own house. This will be important to remember, later in the story.

14

Gregory lived at the early part of the Dark Ages. Rome was still in bad shape from being invaded a hundred years earlier by Vandals and Goths, and now the Visigoths were fighting each other all up and down Italy. So Gregory didn't *just* have Church business to do like preaching, or organizing the money that came in from Church lands and offerings. No, he also had to continue to do the business of the prefect of Rome as well, which included making deals with barbarians, trying to fix the water supply, feeding and housing refugees, helping sick people, training troops, and more.

But the thing that those of us who speak English are *most* glad he did was to send some missionaries up to Great Britain to re-Christianize things there. Ever since the pagan Angles and Saxons had taken over from the Romanized Britons a hundred years before, people had mostly had to worship Woden and Thor and trees and things, or die, or move to Wales or to Brittany in France. But there were a few Christians here and there, and one of them was Queen Bertha of Kent, the part of England where Canterbury is and its own separate kingdom in those days. Bertha wanted a bishop and some monks very badly, and had sent a letter by way of her husband, Ethelbert, to Gregory, asking nicely for some.

Gregory had been pondering whether to send anyone when one day, they say, he was down near the slave markets in Rome (they still had such terrible things in those days), and he saw some boys for sale, probably stolen by pirates. Those boys had pale gold hair and pale blue eyes and beautiful rosy cheeks, such as Gregory had only ever seen in paintings, and he asked his friend what kind of boys they were. "They are Angles, your holiness," said his friend, meaning as in Anglo-Saxons, but Gregory wittily disagreed, making one of the most famous puns in history. "No, no, my friend, they are *angels!*" cried he, and Gregory made up his mind to send missionaries there as soon as possible: *forty* monks from the monastery in his own house (remember?) along with the monk Augustine whom we call "Augustine of Canterbury." So Gregory is called "Apostle to the English." (And I hope he bought those boys and sent them home to England along with Augustine, don't you?)

September: Week One

PETER CLAVER (1580–1654)
missionary (September 9)

About a thousand years after Saint Gregory the Great saw English boys for sale in the Roman slave market, people were still selling slaves in Europe, only now they were mostly from Africa. And many, many slaves from Africa, you know, were sent to work here in the New World: in North America, South America and the West Indies. Often the work was really terrible, down in the silver mines or out on the hot sugar plantations, and the poor slaves were treated like animals (or the way animals used to be treated in those Bad Old Days). Maybe other free people at the time didn't care how these slaves were treated, but the saint we're hearing about today certainly did!

Peter Claver was very stubborn about things he knew were right—"pig-headed," they used to call him—and he had to work hard to control his temper and not be rude to people whom he thought should know better. He was from Catalonia, in Spain, and they say that Catalans are just stubborn people, but they also say that they love music, and Peter Claver certainly did. Playing music helped to cheer him up when people were being really awful, as we'll see later. When he became a priest he decided that his mission would be to help the slaves as much as he could; maybe he couldn't change the laws all by himself, but he could start to make things better somehow, to be a servant in the service of others . . . as Jesus showed the disciples to do, at the Last Supper.

So Peter moved to Cartagena, in Colombia, South America, and spent the rest of his life there, meeting the slave ships at the wharf and serving the slaves any way he could to ease their suffering. He gave them food and water and made friends with them, learned their names, followed them to their various plantations, and argued with their owners to treat them better. He also visited prisons, and helped those miserable prisoners however he could: some of them were foreigners whose religious beliefs were different from those of the Spanish, but he helped them anyway. He also worked in hospitals with people who were sick or hurt. All those places were dirty, and dangerous, and smelly, and uncomfortable, for himself *and* for the people he helped, but he kept working at it, year after year, encouraging other people to help him with his work. Sometimes he was so tired or sad, even after prayers, that he would pull out his guitar or violin and play a little music, and that would always help to cheer him up, as we noticed before.

It's a strange thing, but many times saints become even more powerful *after* they die than before: it's as if their spirit becomes free to go everywhere, encouraging more people than ever. So, after Peter Claver died, poor and alone, it seemed as if all of Cartagena came to his funeral: all the people he had ever helped remembered what he had done for them, and they vowed that they would keep doing his work, and never let anyone forget him again. And we haven't!

September: Week Two

CYPRIAN (200–258)
bishop and martyr (September 16)

 I've mentioned before that for many years—about two hundred or so—the Roman emperors declared that Christianity was against the law because, even though Christians tended to be good neighbors, paid their taxes and helped the poor, they refused to pretend that the emperor was God or even *a* god. This worried some emperors less than others, so things would go along quietly for a while, and priests

would be ordained, bishops appointed, popes elected, church services would be held in people's houses, and more and more people would join the Church. But then an emperor would notice that there seemed to be fewer people coming to the big pagan festivals these days, and he would worry that the angry gods would withdraw their favor from Rome. Then the emperor would decide it was time to try to wipe out all the Christians at once.

One of these irritated emperors was called Decius, and after him Emperor Valerian was pretty crabby, too, so when they were emperors there was a period of what's called *persecution*, that is hunting down a certain type of person. Today's saint, Cyprian, was a Roman citizen living in Carthage, North Africa, when Decius "went ballistic," as they say. Cyprian was a classic Roman: a lawyer and an excellent public speaker, very refined and civilized, hair well-trimmed, chin smoothly shaven, the rest of him always dressed in a clean tunic, spotless toga and sensible sandals. He was also bishop of the Christian community in Carthage, as fine a preacher as he was a lawyer, well organized, generous, kind, and thorough. He never hid the fact from anybody that he was a Christian, so it was easy to find him when it came time to kill them all off.

He and the Proconsul were most polite to one another. The Proconsul told him to sacrifice some incense to the emperor's Divine Spirit and curse Christ or die. Cyprian politely refused, so the Proconsul regretfully informed him that he would have to be beheaded. They say that thereupon Cyprian gave the executioner a handsome tip (why? to be quick and accurate, I suppose!), knelt down, blindfolded himself, said his prayers and lost his head, just like that! A very civilized fellow, old Saint Cyprian, and someone who knew what he believed in.

September: Week Two

HILDEGARD of BINGEN (1098–1179)
abbess and mystic (September 17)
(See Map 5)

Note: It's fairly easy to find a recording of her music to play while you read her story.

These days, Saint Hildegard is pretty famous again, especially among music fans, because her music and poetry has been rediscovered. It is dreamy, mystical, and meditative. One of the interesting things about the Dark Ages is that there were definitely a few bright spots, especially before the Black Death arrived in 1348. People were building amazing cathedrals, they were traveling again (although of course *some* of that travel was Crusading), the wars were usually fairly small and local, and holy women and men were actually respected and encouraged, instead of laughed at. Of course, people also believed in fairies and dragons. But that's not so bad, is it?

Hildegard was a holy prophet, a wise woman, and really a little bit of a dragon herself, when she thought something important needed to be done for the Church, and quickly! She ran a big convent, or abbey (which makes her an abbess) and also advised local kings. Saint Hildegard certainly didn't believe that *fairies* were responsible for natural phenomena, no indeed! In her spare time, she used her sharp, *dragony* eyes to notice everything around her in good scientific fashion, and wrote books on all of it. According to *The Oxford Book of Saints* one book explained "the elements, plants, trees, minerals, how fires worked, types of birds, quadrupeds and reptiles," and there was another book on "The Circulation Of The Blood, Headaches, Hysteria And Giddiness, Frenzy, Insanity And Obsessions." Of course, she also wrote theological discussions on the Gospels, treatises about monastic rules and even some lives of the saints. She illustrated her mystical religious poetry herself and even set it to her own music.

More and more women joined Hildegard's abbey at Bingen (which is located at a bend of the beautiful Rhine River in Germany, just downstream from Wiesbaden), so that it became very big and famous. However, one time she broke the Church rules of those times and got in big trouble with her bishop: she allowed someone who had been thrown out of the church for shameful behavior to be buried in the cemetery next to the abbey. But by behaving very meekly and not at all in dragony fashion for a few years, Hildegard mended things up again. By the time she was a very old abbess, Hildegard had done so much and seemed to have helped so many people in so many miraculous ways and to have had such clear visions of the nature of God, that not long after she died, people around there decided to make her a saint, and a century or so later the official Church agreed with them.

September: Week Three

THOMAS of VILLANUEVA (1488–1555)
bishop (September 21) *(See Map 6)*

Here is a thought for you: have you ever been really sad or upset, but you didn't actually say anything at the time because you were *so* miserable, and then later your friends said, "Why didn't you *say* you were upset?" when, really, you'd hoped that if they were true friends, they would have just noticed, and asked you tactfully if anything was wrong? Well, today's saint understood all that. He knew that when people really need help or money, but they're not used to asking for help, they might prefer to starve rather than let people know!

Thomas of Villanueva (Villanueva de los Infantes, specifically, a town in Ciudad Real, Spain) grew up in a well-off family but was always giving his clothes away to the poor, so clearly he wanted to work for the Church or rather to be, as they say, "in holy orders." One of the reasons he worked his way up so quickly from being a monk and *prior* (a person in charge of a whole monastery) to being a bishop in charge of a whole region, was by being *tactful,* or sensitive to things that needed doing before they screamed out for action. He knew that if you pay close attention to things and to people, and you know all about them, you will know when something is wrong before it gets too serious. He used to say: "Anticipate the needs of those who are ashamed to beg." That's *tact.*

As a bishop, Thomas controlled most of the offering money that came into his churches, but instead of giving himself and all his clergy big pay raises when things were good, or of making his house the biggest one in town, he spent that money on the people in his *diocese* (his "whole region"). Like our good friend Saint Nicholas of Myra, he especially liked to help girls who couldn't get married because they needed dowries, because in Spain in those days, boys *definitely* didn't marry girls unless they brought some dowry money with them. He also liked to help abandoned children and orphans find homes. Sometimes, the other bishops thought he was giving *too* much money away, and then he got in trouble with them. Also, they didn't like it when Thomas was *so* tactful in dealing with parishioners or priests who had done something wrong. "Throw them out of the church!" they said. "That will show them!" But Thomas would always hint *tactfully* to the bishop that perhaps this was "throwing the first stone."

So Thomas of Villanueva was a reasonable man, generous, quiet, with a healing touch, straightforward, inspiring . . . and especially, *tactful*: in this case, the signs of a real saint!

September: Week Three

ADAMNAN (628–704)
abbot and innovator (September 23)

It seems like a strange idea, but most countries in the world have certain rules they've all agreed on about the right way to carry on a war. I mean, war is terrible, but people down the centuries have decided it doesn't have to be any worse than it already is. For example, even four thousand years ago during the Trojan War, the Trojans and Greeks agreed to stop fighting long enough at least to collect the dead soldiers and bury them properly, which is more than the British and Germans managed to do during World War I, not all that long ago. Customs seem to come and go, but today's saint started a custom during the Dark Ages that *tried* at least to make people a little more humane about warfare.

Anyway, in the Bad Old Days of the seventh century, when Saint Adamnan lived and worked as a holy man on the Scottish Holy Isle of Iona, someone needed to remind Europeans that people don't all need to turn into monsters just because they've gone to war. After all, in the early days, Christians had refused to fight at all because of their religious beliefs and were forced to leave the Roman army. Sadly, here in the seventh century there were men, all so-called quote-unquote "Christians," killing not only the soldiers in the other armies, but all the other side's women, children, priests, cows, donkeys, you name it, none of whom could very well fight off a big, supposedly Christian fellow in armor slinging a battleaxe around!

Saint Adamnan said: "If we Christians *must* fight each other—which I don't really believe we do, or anyone else for that matter—let us at least be merciful to defenseless people and creatures and save our swords to use on those who have them, too." He wrote this up in something that was to be called "Adamnan's Law" which everyone in Great Britain began to follow, a sort of law that made *chivalry* the rule in medieval times. Chivalry was the code that said that a knight was supposed to defend the poor and weak, spare the lives of priests and other unarmed folk, as well as to honor the ladies and open doors for them, write them poems, pine away for them, and so forth.

Once again, a saint changed people's lives for the better, partly because people realized he was right all along: that's Adamnan's Law for you! It's a bit like the story of Odilo of Cluny, whom you will hear about in January, and his "Truce of God," which was also thought up to make war at least a little less beastly, if not gone entirely.

September: Week Four

VINCENT de PAUL (1580–1660)
missionary (September 27)

I think you all may have heard of this saint, or of the group named after him that collects donations for poor people—sort of like Goodwill or the Salvation Army. *Somebody* needed to have the idea to do this in the first place, and Vincent de Paul was that "somebody."

You may also know that being a priest can be a nice, quiet, easy job: you can just preach, visit a few sick people from your congregation, do marriage and burial services, baptize people, and maybe run a Sunday School or Confirmation class. You don't have to get up before dawn every morning to do the milking, or wear yourself out plowing and planting, and then have a flood wash away your crop. Vincent knew all this, and he figured that being a priest was the job for him. He had grown up on a farm in Gascony, France, but he was a good student in school and was smart enough to become a priest and get out of farming forever by the time he was only twenty years old.

The funny thing was, though, that he discovered that he was used to hard work, and also that what he had learned in training for priesthood made him want to do much more than priests generally *had* to do. At this point he lost patience with people who wanted the easy life! As I say, he was a Gascon, and like Spanish Catalonians, French Gascons are known for being hard-headed; you may know that D'Artagnan, the famous musketeer, was a Gascon. Vincent was like that: hard-headed! Also, he was not particularly good-looking and a little abrupt in dealing with people who disagreed with him . . . but the people who knew him knew that he usually reserved his grumpiness for the unfairness of people to each other.

On the coast near where Vincent lived were things called "hulks." All of you who've read Dickens' *Great Expectations* will know what those are: horrible prison ships, anchored just offshore, where prisoners were kept in dark, filthy little cabins full of rats . . . *ugh!* Also, at the port, there were in those days galleys, that is, ships that didn't need sails to move because they were rowed by hundreds of rowers called galley-slaves. Vincent noticed that nobody much cared what happened to prisoners on the "hulks" or to the galley-slaves, and that they treated them the way a mean, thoughtless person might treat a dog.

This was *just* the sort of thing that made Vincent's Gascon blood really heat up, and he began spending all his time trying to make life better for these poor human brothers of his, including going around getting donations of clothing and anything else a person might need. Soon he had plenty of friends who believed in his work, and this was just as Vincent expected: he had great trust in *Providence*, that is, in God's ability to make people generous. He told his friends, who were Roman Catholic like him, not to make any distinctions about the people they helped: Catholic, Baptist, Jewish, Methodist or Muslim, all were to be helped the same amount. And they knew he was right, *and* that he was a saint!

September: Week Four

MICHAEL and ALL ANGELS (September 29)
and the
GUARDIAN ANGELS (October 2)

Angels, as most of us know perfectly well, are messengers of God, and they turn up throughout the Bible whenever God needs someone from heaven to take a message to earth. Sometimes they carry flaming swords and stand in the middle of the road, like Balaam's donkey's angel in the book of Numbers, or they might appear in the middle of the night with a huge number of fellow angels, like the shepherds' angels in the book of Luke. They are generally described as dazzlingly bright to look at, in robes too white to be washed by any human detergent, but otherwise have no particular color. There are whole long lists of different kinds of angels: Thrones, Principalities, Virtues, Powers, Seraphim, Cherubim, etc. We are told in the Bible that the ones who fly about the throne of God crying, *"Holy! Holy! Holy!"* have several pairs of wings, but the ones in Numbers and Luke aren't reported as having any wings. In most pictures, though, just to make sure that you know who's who—and maybe to show that they can fly from here to there—they are shown with wings.

It does seems as though, whenever an angel appears, the first message they have to deliver to us humans is "Fear not!" because we are always terrified by their stern, fiery faces and their dazzling glow. These are angels that make people jump whenever they appear, because if you don't believe what they tell you, you might end up like John the Baptist's father Zacharias, unable to speak until their prophecy came true! If they say: "Get up, Joseph, and take the child and his mother to Egypt," by golly, you get up and *go!*

Saint Michael and the other archangels, Raphael, Gabriel and Phanuel, each has had important jobs to do for God: Michael is supposed to have led angel armies against devils with the battle-cry

"Who is like God?" and protects those in danger or who have to go to war. Raphael helped a boy named Tobit find a wonderful fish and brought health and wealth to his whole family. Gabriel, we'll recall, was in charge of informing Zechariah that his son John would be something special, and of telling Mary something more important, still. Phanuel (also known as Uriel) is often shown with a censer, blessing everything around with the sweet scent of answered prayer.

Some angels, though, maybe because they don't always make themselves visible, are not frightening at all. These are what are known as guardian angels. Some people have felt protected on dark streets by the presence of such a spirit. Apparently, Saint Peter had a guardian angel, because when he miraculously escaped from prison, his friends thought it was his *angel* at the door, not him! Sometimes, if you are afraid of your enemies or of the dark, you might ask the guardian angels to watch over you, as in that beautiful bedtime song from Humperdinck's German opera, "Hansel and Gretel." When our little heroes are sleepy and lost in the woods, they sing:

> *When at night I go to sleep, Fourteen angels watch do keep: Two my head are guarding, Two my feet are guiding, Two are on my right hand, Two are on my left hand, Two who warmly cover, Two who o'er me hover, Two to whom 'tis given To guide my steps to Heaven.*

october

October: Week One

FRANCIS of ASSISI (1181–1226)
abbot (October 4) *(See Map 7)*

A lot of later saints were called Francis (like Saint Francis of Capistrano, for example) in today's saint's honor, but everyone has heard of the *original* Saint Francis, of course. People have little statues of him with a bird on his finger in their backyards, because he is the patron saint of animals, and once preached to the birds—who apparently paid close attention! But wasn't just animals that Francis loved, it was all of Creation: Brother Sun, Sister Moon, Brother Fire, Sister Water . . . even Sister Death. He appreciated all of God's gifts to us humans. Francis also knew that human beings can be like wild animals, if they don't keep their lives centered on God. He had been a soldier once, and he knew just how inhuman humans could become. Because Francis is like those "the Great" saints who have so many stories about them that they really do fill books and books, I can't tell you everything just now, except I recommend that you find those books: some of them have some pretty wonderful illustrations, for one thing. They called him the "Little Poor Man of Assisi," and I can't even tell you properly about the pleasant hill town in Italy he came from, Assisi, except that it's made of pink stone and has pastries that are worth crossing the seas to taste. But I will tell you the story of the Wolf of Gubbio, because it tells you a *lot* about why Francis is a saint.

Now, most of you are afraid of wolves, and you should be; they really aren't dogs, and even dogs are scary if they're in a pack. I know

I was really terrified of just the *idea* of a wolf when I was little . . . but this wolf they called the Wolf of Gubbio was really like your worst nightmare! He came down from the mountains behind the nearby town of Gubbio and developed a taste for people-flesh! Luckily, in those days all the towns had big walls around them, and stout gates that they could lock up every night and open up every morning— *and* they kept an eye on the gates in the daytime, so the wolf couldn't get into the town. This wolf was tricky, though, and his favorite thing to do was to pounce on people when they went out to the fields alone or when they went to get water from the fountain outside the gates. The people were terrified to go out at all: this wolf was like some kind of evil demon! Well, that made them think of Francis—he was a holy man, and holy men were good at driving out demons . . . maybe he could drive out this wolf for them. Francis heard about it and came to help, because he felt sorry for the wolf; he knew that animals, like people, are not really evil, they just do evil things.

So out Francis went, all alone out of the gate of the town of Gubbio, to meet the wolf. And there it came, racing at him with its mouth wide open, ready to eat him right up! But Francis didn't run away, he just put out his hands in front of him and called that wolf the way you would call a naughty dog, actually *told* him to "come here!" The wolf shut its big, ravening mouth and stopped short, then crept up to Francis' feet with its ears down, whining the way a dog does when it knows it's been bad, and crouched down.

Nobody knows exactly what he said to the wolf or what the wolf said to him, but when Francis came back to the people of Gubbio (who were watching all this from safely inside their walls), he told them that he and the wolf had made a bargain. If the people would give Brother Wolf a bowl of food every day, he would never hurt anyone again. He had just been hungry, after all, since they wouldn't let him eat their sheep. But first they had to forgive him—as Francis had—for all the terrible things he'd done. It was hard, but they did it, and Brother Wolf became so tame that even the children could play with him, all because he was forgiven and cared for. It's the sort of miracle saints are famous for, and one of the many, many amazing things that the "Little Poor Man of Assisi," Saint Francis, really did in his lifetime.

October: Week One

TERESA of ÁVILA (1515–1582)
founder and writer (October 15)
(See Map 6)

They say that Teresa of Ávila was "an eagle and a dove." She could be fierce and almost merciless, like an eagle, but also as sweet and gentle as a dove; it all depended. We notice this about many saints: they aren't all mushy and goody-goody, putting up with anything all the time. It is more as if they *are* kind when most people are *not*, but they take some things very seriously indeed that most people don't even notice. Now, the Little-Dove Teresa could tell you very kindly and with plenty of good humor where you went wrong in a little thing like stealing money, but if you had been cruel to someone or if you had joked around in church, her eyes would flash and you would be dealing with The Eagle!

Saint Teresa was just the person to be running a large church organization like the one in Ávila, Spain, which you can easily find on a modern map, in the Ávila mountains northwest of Madrid. She was good when you needed someone to write you a deep, poetical book guiding your spiritual life, like her *Interior Castle* book, or when you needed to figure out how to fix your plumbing or raise funds for a new building. Her bishop was wise enough to know this about her, and he put her to work reorganizing some convents that had gone wrong somehow. For example, when Teresa "reformed the discalced Carmelites" (which does *not* mean she slapped some squashed candies back into shape), her job was to convince some rather grumpy nuns to change their ways. She told them that they had either to go back to being holy *and* going barefoot (which is what the word *discalced* means: "shoeless") or just to go elsewhere, and leave holy orders. She did such a good job at this that more women than ever wanted to join the convent, because people generally know when they see a good thing, and want to help out with it.

So, the next time you are surprised when a friend loses his or her temper with you, remember Saint Teresa of Ávila, the Eagle and the Dove, and figure that maybe your *Carmelites* are no longer *discalced,* and you need some *reforming*!

October: Week Two

IGNATIUS of ANTIOCH (died in 107)
bishop (October 17) *(See Maps 3 & 11)*

Learning about Saint Ignatius is as exciting as finding the "missing link" in any history, only the best part is that he wasn't missing: he was really *there*, a living link between those who saw Christ in his original flesh, and those of us who come after and live on faith, visions and answered prayers. Listen, and find out how!

First, I should tell you that Antioch, now a good-sized city called Antakieh in the southeasternmost part of Turkey, used to be an even bigger deal in the Olden Days: it was capital of its own region, with half a million people living there (they were *not* all citizens) and its own port on the Mediterranean called Seleucia (generally pronounced by classicists as "Sell-you-*kye*-a"). It was a very rich and wicked city, a great place to start the first big Christian community after the one in Jerusalem. Paul and Barnabas started their missions from here, and Paul made it his headquarters. So to be the Bishop of Antioch back in those days was also a big thing, and also a *dangerous* thing for the first couple of hundred years or so, because of the laws of the time against Christianity, if you recall. So when Ignatius was Bishop of Antioch around 100 A.D., they were already on their second or third bishop.

Since he became a saint you can probably guess that Ignatius died bravely for his faith, which he did. But he did much more than utter some famous last words before heading off to meet the lions. He wrote letters of encouragement, the way Paul had done, to the early churches in Ephesus, Magnesia, Tralles, Rome, Philadelphia (yes, the first one was not in Pennsylvania) and Smyrna. In Smyrna, he met a young man named Polycarp (who became the hero of his *own* saint story) and he wrote Polycarp a strengthening letter when the guards came to take him, Ignatius, off to Rome for the last time. Ignatius called those guards the Ten Leopards, because he said that, just like wild animals, the kinder he was to them, the worse they treated him!

But the really spine-tingling, shivery thing about Ignatius' story is not so much his determination to die as Christ had done, no, it is this: people say that Ignatius was the *very child whom Jesus took in his arms* and put in the middle of the disciples, saying (according to the King James translation) "whoever therefore shall humble himself as this little child, the same is the greatest in the kingdom of Heaven, and whoso shall receive one such little child in my name receiveth me," thus making children more precious ever since. And to have *been* that child—wow! After that, Ignatius almost couldn't *help* becoming a saint.

October: Week Two

HILARION (291–371) hermit
(October 21) *(See Map 3)*

We know that hermits are holy men who hide out in the countryside to pray in peace, but also that other people always find them and pester them for advice; it seems to happen over and over in these stories. Some hermits are very patient about it, other hermits build columns to live on so they can rise above the herd. Today's saint just plain *escaped*, over and over again, from the press of people who came to see him do miracles. Because he certainly *could* do miracles, and everywhere he went, word would get out, and people were just hungry to see him, and first thing you know, he'd have to light out again for a new place. Jesus ran into the same thing, you'll remember: it seemed as if he really just wanted to preach, but he always felt sorry for some poor leper, and healed him but told him to keep quiet about it, and first thing you know, the leper had blabbed all over town and Jesus had to spend the whole next day healing, or he had to preach from a boat in the water so people wouldn't smash him or just keep touching him all over, hoping to get healed! It must have been maddening, but Jesus just kept at it, and he *definitely* had more patience than Saint Hilarion, which is really not too surprising, after all.

Hilarion's story starts in a little mud hut in the village of Maiuma, the ancient port of what is now the city of Gaza, on the far eastern coast of the Mediterranean Sea. Hilarion had settled down there as a holy man, living peacefully on figs and vegetables, bread and oil, and making for himself with his own hands whatever else he needed in life, which wasn't very much. The rest of his time was spent in praying, studying the scriptures, preaching once a day to people who came to hear him, then giving advice and maybe doing a little healing, if he could. But word got out that he seemed not only to be able to read peoples' thoughts, and see into the future, but also *change* the future with his prayers, just as Jesus had been able to do.

One day a charioteer named Italicus wondered if Hilarion could pray really hard so that his team of horses would win the chariot race the next day; it was almost a matter of life and death for him! Old Hilarion felt sorry for Italicus, promised that he'd pray about it and sure enough, Italicus won and then told everyone about it. Of course a lot more people became Christians as a result, so it was a *good* thing, but Hilarion just couldn't handle the crowds. He felt as if he had suddenly moved from little, sleepy Maiuma to the middle of the Roman Forum, and he just had to escape.

For the next few years Hilarion went from place to place—Sicily, the Dalmatian coast—but everywhere he went, someone would find out that he was the one who had helped Italicus, and the crowds would start to gather all over again. Finally a former disciple of his, Hesychius, found him, and helped poor old Hilarion find a safe place on the island of Cyprus where he could finally live and pray and die in peace, and be buried back home in Maiuma, safe at last from the interruptions of his fans. It's tough, sometimes, to try to make everybody happy *and* stay a saint!

October: Week Three

ANTONY MARY CLARET (1807–1870)
bishop (October 24)

Note: Yes, his middle name was Mary. Back in those days everyone wanted Mary as a middle name, even the boys.

Scientific inquiry and religious belief really *have* gone hand in hand in the open-minded parts of the world, as more than one saint story will show you. Some of the new discoveries that have so shocked scientists down the years were said to be against religion when they were just against the ideas those scientists had been publishing in their papers all their lives! The workings of the universe can be nearly as hard to fathom as the other mysteries of God, and some saints understood that *both* are fascinating to study, wherever those studies might lead. Antony Claret, for example, was as famous in his day as a great scientist and observer of nature as he was for being a distinguished bishop of the Church.

Antony Claret tended to inspire everyone around him to be as excited about things as he was, so he began his religious career by founding an organization of missionary preachers dedicated to the saint of his middle name—Mary. He was excited not only about the Church but about everthing in Creation! When he was made Bishop of Cuba, he spent a lot of his time trying to make the local bad folk, including priests, behave honestly and fairly while trying to avoid being murdered by irritated local bad folk, including priests. The rest of his time was spent studying the fascinating local *flora* and *fauna* (that's plants and animals) of Cuba. He loved to note down his observations in his laboratory notebook and to speculate as to their meaning, almost as much as he loved to study the scriptures.

When he was called back to Spain to be *confessor* (a sort of personal priest) to Queen Isabella II, Antony finally had the chance to start a science laboratory in the church school there, and then to found a natural history museum. He also thought that music and languages were important to study, and set up schools for them, too. It must have been sad for him to have to leave it all behind when the revolution of 1868 forced the Queen and her confessor into exile, and Antony never saw his schools, museum or laboratory again. But you can be sure that, wherever he lived, he continued his studies into the workings of the world around him . . . a true scientist-saint!

October: Week Three

JOHN of BEVERLEY (died 721)
bishop (October 25) *(See Map 1)*

There is an old Latin saying, *nihil ex nihilo fit*—"nothing comes from nothing"—meaning basically that everything we are and do has its origin in some earlier action or substance. For example, if people are kind to you, you may have *learned* how to be kind to others, or maybe you *read* something someone wrote long ago about kindness, and you can use that idea in what you need to do, now: that sort of thing . . . it happens all the time! This story is really for the teachers in the audience, for all of you older kids that the younger kids look up to; you are the ones who pass on the things that make other things possible.

Today's saint, John of Beverley, was certainly one of those "things that makes other things possible." He was a bridge between the good people who went before him and taught him, and the good people who came after, and learned from him. John came originally from a Yorkshire village called Harpham, and from there he went south to be a student of the great teacher Saint Adrian of the cathedral school at Canterbury, way down in Kent. Then, loaded with knowledge and holiness acquired from Adrian, he returned north to study at the double monastery (meaning it was for both men and women) at Whitby, ruled at that time by the great Abbess Saint Hilda. After his time there, John then went on to be bishop of the good old Northumbrian city of Hexham, where he was the man who ordained Saint Bede ("the Venerable Bede") as a priest, and helped to bring in the time of a great flowering of religious study in northern England. He retired to a place in Yorkshire's East Riding called Beverley, and spent the rest of his life at the monastery there (hence his name), where today is a great church, or minster. But isn't it interesting how they all inspired each other?

If those were good years for the growing of saints in England, Saint John of Beverley was one of those good "tenders of the garden." A later saint, in turn was inspired by John, a woman with the curious name of Saint Julian of Norwich, According to the *Penguin Dictionary of Saints*, she wrote of him that he was "a dear worthy servant to God . . . a full high saint in Heaven in His sight, and a blissful." Each one of *us* has a duty to pass on the good things we learn from those around us, and not to keep silent if we're inspired to speak up: whether or not any of us makes it to being "blissful," we can certainly work on the "dear worthy servant" part.

October: Week Four

FRUMENTIUS and AEDESIUS (died 380)
apostles to Ethiopia (October 27) *(See Map 8)*

The people of Axum, the northern part of what they call Ethiopia nowadays, have been Christians now for sixteen centuries, and they celebrate church very much the way people did so long ago. I would love to go to church *there* someday: they have amazing churches cut out of the solid rock, and a special shape of processional cross that they use, which is like five overlapping squares, a big one in the middle, set on its point, and the smaller ones set all around it and attached at the corners, also on their points: a simply beautiful design. They say that the Queen of Sheba came from Axum, and there is also the legend that, after the Romans destroyed the Temple in Jerusalem, the Ark of the Covenant came to Axum, and that if you go there, you can see copies of the stone tablets that are inside. But on to an important question: how did Frumentius of Tyre come to be *Abuna Salama* of all Axum? Let's see what that means and how it came to pass.

It all began like one of those ridiculous novels or plays that couldn't possibly happen, full of shipwrecks and harems and pirates. Frumentius and his friend Aedesius were on a sea voyage from Tyre to India with their adopted father, the Christian philosopher Meropius, and were sailing south along the Red Sea when they were shipwrecked, right there off the coast of the kingdom of Axum. The boys made it safely to land, but there was no sign of Meropius or of the ship's crew, so there they were, stranded in Axum. They were bright, good-looking fellows, and soon found work at the court of King Ella Amida, far up in the mountains of Axum: Frumentius became the king's secretary and Aedesius, his cup-bearer.

Frumentius was so good at what he did that, when King Ella Amida died, he was asked to rule as regent until Prince Ezana was old enough to rule for himself. When he *was* old enough, Frumentius and

Aedesius made the long trip north, down the Nile to Alexandria to ask the church there if they would send priests and stuff to set up churches back to Axum. People in Axum had liked what they'd heard from the two young men about this Christianity business, and wanted to know more. Saint Athanasius came back from Alexandria, with them, but it was Frumentius that the people there wanted to be their first bishop, or "Abuna," as they call bishops there. In fact, they called Saint Frumentius *Abuna Salama*, which means "Bishop of Peace," and no other Abuna ever had that title after him. So now you know how Frumentius of Tyre came to be *Abuna Salama* of all Axum, *and* a saint, besides!

October: Week Four

MARCELLUS the CENTURION (died 298)
soldier and martyr (October 30)

and **CASSIAN of TANGIERS** (died 298)
court stenographer (December 3)

(See Maps 3 & 6 for both)

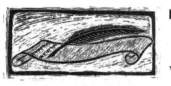

Today we're going to celebrate not just two brave men from Tangiers, but *all* people who just won't put up with evil nonsense any longer, even if they have to die for it. By the time today's adventures happened, a great number of people in the Roman Empire were Christians, even though it still happened to be illegal at the time. This particular incident began when Marcellus the Centurion, stationed in the then-Roman city of Tangiers in North Africa, threw off his special military belt. In those days, soldiers didn't just wear cloth uniforms the way they do nowadays, with different stripes sewn on the sleeve to show their rank. Instead they wore metal and leather armor over their cloth tunics, and a high-up officer, like for example a *cen-*

turion (that is, an officer in charge of a group of about a hundred men) would have insignia like a special helmet with a certain kind of plume, and a special belt with a big buckle on it and would carry a special swagger-stick. Whenever he was on parade, Centurion Marcellus had to wear his special belt of office, but on this particular day, he had been ordered to take part in the celebration of the birthday of Emperor Maximian, when everybody present was required to file by the altar to the emperor's Divine Spirit and offer some incense in worship, to show their loyalty.

This sort of thing disgusted Marcellus, who was a Christian, because he didn't believe *for a minute* that the emperor was divine. So, when he was informed of the reason for this celebration, he just his took off his belt and slammed it down on the ground in front of his tent, which meant he had resigned his commission rather than attend that festival! If he weren't executed for this right off, he would at least be demoted to the rank of a footsoldier. Naturally there were questions from the emperor, at the festival: here were his men; where was their leader, Marcellus? Why wasn't he at the festival? Didn't he respect his commander in chief? Emperor Maximian was embarrassed and angry, and demanded an immediate trial of this "rascal."

At the trial, the review of Marcellus's past record was very impressive: he had had a long and illustrious career in the army, led his men successfully into battle many times, never flinching at danger. He loved Rome and respected the emperor, but he could not worship either of them as a god; there was only one God, and he was without peers! Many people in the courtroom became very sympathetic to Marcellus, and thought maybe this Christianity was a good thing if such a brave fellow believed in it. But the emperor would only allow *one* verdict: guilty, with the punishment of death!

That brings us to our second saint for the day, Cassian. Cassian was the court stenographer that very day in the court of Tangiers, and he had been duly writing down everything that was said at the trial: all the questions and all of Marcellus's answers. And in all his years of experience, he felt he had never seen a clearer case for acquittal, even though he knew about the edict against Christians. So when he heard the verdict, he refused to write it down! Something just came over him, and his heart began to pound, and he stood up, his face all red, and heard himself say, "No! I refuse to take down that verdict! It's just not *right*!" And then the courtroom got really noisy, as you can imagine, and not just Marcellus, but Cassian, too was bundled off to prison, to await death in the arena—Marcellus in October, and Cassian in December of the same year. Some things you just can't stand for, even if saying so costs you your life!

november

November: Week One

HUBERT (died May 30, 727) bishop (November 1)

and **ULRIC of HASELBURY PLUNKNETT**
(died 1154) parson and recluse
(February 20) *(See Map 9)*

I'm sure that some of you have been hunting before, most likely with a parent or grandparent, so that you know what it's like: you get to wander around in the woods, maybe with your favorite dog, and sniff the fresh air, listening and watching carefully, and you quietly come up behind whatever it is you're hunting, but if it spots you first, then you have to chase it . . . pretty exciting! And it may take you all morning or even all day, especially if that day happens to be a thousand years ago and all you have to hunt with is a spear or a bow and arrows, because guns haven't been invented yet!

Well, both of today's saints started out as hunters, but I must tell you that they couldn't *stay* hunters and be saints at the same time, because the two things just don't seem to go together. Some saints kept being *anglers*, that is, they liked to go fishing with a rod and line in lakes or streams, but most of them gave up chasing and killing animals in the hunt. For one thing, their hearts got too tender when they got a little holier, so that they didn't enjoy it any more, and for another thing, it took up a lot of time that they could have been spending reading, or composing a sermon, or helping people.

Ulric of Haselbury Plunknett (*such* a great name!) had been a not-very-good *parson* (that's a preacher at a small country church) who spent much too much of his time hunting when he should have been reading, composing sermons, and helping people. He repented and gave it up, living ever afterward as a holy man out in the wilds of Haselbury Plunknett, in England long ago. I don't know whether he had a mystical experience that made him give up hunting like the one I'm about to tell you happened to Saint Hubert (and to another French saint, Saint Eustace, who later became the patron saint of coffee roasters due to being roasted in a bronze bull), but he may well have: it was certainly a very memorable hunting experience if it was anything like Hubert's!

Hubert, when he was a young nobleman growing up rather wild in France even longer ago than Ulric had in England, used to love to go out hunting stags. He would get on his fastest horse, and chase the stag all over the woods, and then spear it and have his servants take it home for dinner. He spent almost all his time hunting. But that all changed one day, when he had cornered his stag—a big, beautiful stag—and it turned and looked him right in the face. That startled him and his horse, too, a little, and Hubert looked back and saw an amazing sight that put him off hunting for the rest of his life, and made him become a bishop and a saint. Right in the middle of the stag's broad forehead, between the big branching antlers and above his staring brown eyes, Hubert seemed to see a glowing cross, so brilliant that it suddenly lit up the dark woods and dazzled his eyes.

Now, maybe Hubert had been hunting on Sunday, which was against custom, or maybe he knew he should have been doing better things with his life, or maybe this vision was a reminder that Christ had been an innocent victim like the stag, but it certainly made an impression on Hubert, as I've said. And although he never hunted any more, he still used to like to travel all over the big Ardennes forest where he was bishop, visiting all the people there, because the forest never frightened him; he felt quite at home, and his parishioners loved to have him visit. I'm sure the stags were glad to see him peacefully riding through the woods, too, don't you think?

November: Week One

WILLIBRORD of ECHTERNACH (658–739)
bishop (November 7) *(See Map 5)*

With a name like Willibrord, you know that this saint originally came from England in the Olden Days when all the Saxons were giving their children names like Willibald and Walburga and such, and when they sent missionaries all over Europe, which takes us back to the eighth century or so. Sure enough, our Willibrord came from Northumbria, the land of the Venerable Bede and other great scholars of the time, and he was sent to preach the Gospel to the folk of the Low Countries: to Friesland and Utrecht, and down into a town that is in Luxembourg today, namely Echternach.

It was difficult, dangerous work for Willibrord, because the local people still worshipped statues and trees and kept cows that were sacred to the god Frey (so they couldn't eat them), and that sort of thing. Once, while he was in that part of Denmark which bordered the Low Countries, Willibrord went to the slave market (as we have seen, they had such things in Europe in the Bad Old Days) and bought some thirty Danish slave boys and raised them as Christians. They helped him with his work in that part of the world. Another time, when a village was starving, he convinced the people there to go ahead and *eat* the sacred cows of Frey, and they did, and no angry Frey appeared to punish them. When Willibrord went ahead and burned the temple down, with the statue of Frey in it and all, and nothing happened to him, either, people began to think he had the right idea, and they became Christians, too!

Willibrord did such a good job of convincing folk and ordaining clergy and getting churches built and all that they called him the Patron of Holland, and after he died, his people built him a beautiful tomb in Echternach. Every year since then—for more than a thousand years, can you believe it?—the people of Echternach have had a festival in his honor, which, though it is solemn feels a little like Mardi Gras and New Year's, too! On the Tuesday after Pentecost (called Whit Tuesday on church calendars) all the pilgrims, local folks and visitors from miles around, along with all the clergy (bishops, priests and deacons), make one big procession through the streets of Echternach and all around the church where Willibrord's tomb is, and they do a sort of sacred dance-step as they go: two steps forward and one step back, called the "Echternach walk." Maybe it is meant to show the slow, hard work of being a missionary bishop, but anyhow, each group that comes brings its own brass band to keep them company, and they play and dance for all they're worth. Now *that's* the way to honor a saint, don't you think?

November: Week Two

LEO the GREAT (died 461)
pope (November 10)

As we've seen before, anyone called "The Great" generally has accomplished a lot in his or her lifetime: Charlemagne ("Charles the Great"), Peter the Great, Gregory the Great . . . and certainly Leo is no exception. He was the pope—that is, the leader of the western half of the Christian church—at a terrible time for the city of Rome where he lived . . . and remember: the pope is also the bishop of Rome. Leo was a local boy, like Saint Gregory the Great after him, and they say he "represented the best Roman character," that is, he was active, forgiving, and fair, with a strong sense of duty. Not surprisingly, since he *was* elected to be pope, he also had a strong faith in God's care and love. Leo's special favorite example of God's love was Christmas, that is, the idea that the Word that had set the universe spinning had come down to Earth as a little human child full of God's grace. They do say his Christmas sermons were particularly moving.

But to get back to our story: it really was a hard time to be pope. Not only did Leo have all the usual worries about people getting weird ideas about the divinity, part-divinity or non-divinity of Christ that required a constant flow of letters of explanation to various churches, but also he had the special worry that Rome was being attacked by various barbarian groups, and *he* was in charge of the safety of the people of Rome. So, he fixed up the old walls of Rome and built a new wall around the part of the city, over by the Vatican, called the Borgo today. Then when he heard that Attila himself, with all his ferocious Huns, was headed for the city, he went out personally to meet the army, north of Rome. With a *big* donation of gold and a lot of convincing conversation about a plague at Rome—*and* some powerful prayer—Leo persuaded Attila to retreat all the way across the Danube to Vienna. But when the terrible tribe called the Vandals came, all Leo could do was lock his new gates and try to get them to just loot and not burn and kill *too* much. But even today, Vandals are hard to deal with, as I'm sure you know!

Anyway, anyone who loves Christmas as much as Leo did and saves cities from barbarians (the best he can) deserves to be called "Great," *and* be a saint, don't you think?

November: Week Two

ALBERT the GREAT (1206–1280)
theologian and scientist (November 15)
(See Map 5)

November just has too many amazing saints, for some reason. Is it a big build-up to Advent? I'm not sure, but it's remarkable—they just stalk off the pages of the saints' books like giants, and here is another one: Albert the Great, the "Universal Teacher." Albert had this incredible mind and a great curiosity about the natural world that his Creator had brought into existence. Albert's worship of God was part of his hunger to understand how all of Creation *worked*. And back in Albert's day, there was not yet any conflict between the fields of science and religion, or between using your brain and using your faith.

At the great University of Padua (or Padova, as they call it there in Italy) Albert began his studies, then joined an order of preaching monks and got his Masters of Theology at the University of Paris in 1244. Yes, they did have universities back in those days! The oldest were at Paris, Oxford and Bologna—and that's no baloney. Padova was especially famous for its scientific studies, and reading the works of Aristotle while he was there really inspired Albert to organize his thoughts and be methodical when he studied nature. He returned to Cologne, in Swabia, the part of Germany he had come from, and one of his students there was Thomas Aquinas—another saint. Then Albert went off to Rome to teach *there* for a while, and to use his super-organizational skills to help out some monasteries. He tried being bishop for a while, but then resigned and went back to Cologne to teach for the rest of his life.

And what did Albert teach? Almost *everything*: Holy Scriptures and other religious studies, but also logic, metaphysics and ethics, and physical sciences, including physics, astronomy, chemistry, biology, physiology, geography, geology and botany. But maybe Albert's greatest gift was teaching his students *how* to learn, how to look at things scientifically, in other words, how to organize their thoughts, how to be careful and consistent experimentalists, how to trust their own senses and use them to study nature systematically, that is, to try to put living things into logical groups. *And* he was a saint, too. He really *was* Albert "the Great, The Universal Teacher!"

November: Week Three

MARGARET of SCOTLAND (1045–1093)
queen (November 16)

You've probably heard of the Norman Invasion. You may know that it happened in the year 1066 and that William of Normandy came and took away the throne of England from Harold, because William apparently had been promised it by King Edward the Confessor before Edward died. So the Normans took over England from the Saxons who had taken it over from the Britons, before that! Maybe you've wondered what happened to all the Saxon princes and princesses when the Normans took all the prince and princess positions in the government? This is the story of what happened to one Saxon princess named Margaret, the granddaughter of King Edward's older brother, the King Edmund Ironsides who died fighting the Danes.

Since life in England was now dangerous for Saxon princesses, Margaret went north to the kingdom of Scotland and there soon married Malcolm III, King of Scotland. They were very happily married, and had six sons and two daughters.

They say that Margaret was "every inch a queen," meaning she had a strong will—she was Edmund Ironsides' granddaughter, after all!—and she also had very firm ideas on the proper way to do things.

First of all, she insisted that everyone in the Scottish court behave in a *much* more civilized fashion than they had up to then: much more like the French or English courts, with gallantry and nice manners and all. Margaret was also deeply religious, and she suspected that the way they did church services in Scotland was *not* quite right, so she asked in experts from Italy to reorganize things. And she was positively ferocious about the way poor people were treated in Scotland at the time, so she took care of as many people as she could out of her own private funds, and made sure orphans had someone to take care of them. Margaret was also such a good mom that one of her eight children also became a saint (Saint David, King of Scotland) and another one, Matilda, became Queen of England by marrying William the Conqueror's son, Henry the First.

Now, Margaret may have had a strong will but she had a very tender heart, and when her husband Malcolm was killed by his enemies, that tender heart broke, and she herself died just four days later. But her people always remembered her as Good Queen Margaret, "every inch a saint!"

November: Week Three

GREGORY the WONDERWORKER (213–270)
missionary (November 17) *(See Map 3)*

This saint sounds a little like one of those performers in the circus, don't you think? You know: "Inn-tro-ducing . . . from faraway Neocaesarea . . . *Gregory the Wonderworker*!"—that sort of thing. He was a priest who did do a lot of miracles, but one of the most amazing things about Gregory is that he *didn't* wind up as lion-food in what the Romans called a circus, that is, a chariot-race stadium where they liked to kill Christians at half-time. When the soldiers came looking for *his* little flock of Christians, Gregory made them all hide in caves, while he and his deacon went off to the desert. The two of them, Gregory and his deacon, were standing there in prayer (people used to pray standing up, with their hands out and palms up) when the soldiers came looking for them, but all the soldiers saw were two trees out there, and went away without catching them . . . the first of *many* wonders Gregory worked.

When Gregory first arrived in Neocaesarea (that's the town of Niksar in north central Turkey nowadays) as a young priest, there were hardly any Christians living there. He spoke well in public, since he was trained as a lawyer, and so he got busy right away preaching and teaching. As it turned out, he didn't have time to write books about faith or any encouraging letters to other churches, because right after those persecutions with the caves and the trees, there was a *plague* in Neocaesarea, and *then* there was an invasion of marauding Goths, for heaven's sake! By that time, the local people had elected him bishop (local people could do that themselves in those days), and Gregory just kept thinking of new and interesting ways to convince the local pagan people to join the church.

One way he boosted church attendance wasn't really new, it was just doing miracles the way the apostles used to (the "wonderworking" part of the story). Gregory seemed to be just chock-full of the miracle-working Holy Spirit! Once, when two brothers were arguing about which one of them should get some land along a river, Gregory prayed and the river just dried up! Then there was his ability to heal people: folks would come from miles around to have him lay his hands on them, and they would get better, just like that. It also helped his ministry that Gregory was kind and patient and never lost his temper—imagine! That's rare, even in a saint. But his *really* new idea, one that caught on all over Christendom, was to celebrate saint's days not just with a solemn worship service but also with a great big party or fair: a festival sort of like the pagan ones, only harmless, with no animal sacrifice or wild drinking, just good food, games, music, booths selling souvenirs and local crafts, all that fun stuff. People loved it, and church attendance went *way* up.

A little while before he died, Gregory looked back over his work at Neocaesarea, and asked his deacon how many people in town were *not* Christians now. He was told, "seventeen," and Gregory just smiled and said there had only been seventeen who *were* Christians when he came, so now he could die happy.

November: Week Four

HUGH of LINCOLN (1135–1200)
bishop (November 17) *(See Maps 1 & 9)*

Really, I think it was Hugh of Lincoln who made me want to share saints' stories with everybody—after Saint Nicholas, of course, but he is a special case! No, right from the start I especially loved to read about the wild swan that adopted him as a master and liked to hide its head in Hugh's long sleeves. I also loved the fact that Hugh might be found playing with children if he was nowhere around his office, and that he called himself "peppery" because he had no patience with injustice. People said he was fearless as a lion because not only did he refuse to pay taxes for the war on France (Hugh was a Frenchman, after all!) but he also calmed down the several angry English kings he served with a joke or a kiss.

But you need to have a few details. You may know that King Henry II of England had a quarrel with his old friend Thomas Becket after Becket became Archbishop of Canterbury, and that Henry's men thought they would cheer Henry up by killing Becket for him, and did so, right there in Canterbury Cathedral? Well, afterward, Henry was very sorry, and he was also in big trouble with the Church, so he built a nice new monastery at Witham in Somerset, to make amends for what he'd done, and called in our Hugh from France to run it. But Hugh refused—*refused!*—to come until King Henry paid back *every cent* of its land value to all the people who had lost their land to make the monastery!

When Hugh became bishop of Lincoln, no one had been bishop there for sixteen years, so you can imagine the mess it was in. First, he started to rebuild the cathedral at Lincoln, which had become a ruin. There was also the fact that Lincoln was the largest *diocese*, or area served by a bishop, in all England, but that was all right: Hugh liked to travel all over it, visiting all the people who were lonely or sick. That is how he found out that the king owned all the forests in Lincolnshire so he could hunt deer there for fun, but wouldn't let the local people hunt there, even for food. Hugh went straight to the king and complained until that changed. Then again, when the people in the cities of Lincoln and Northampton decided they didn't like the Jews who lived there and started to attack them, Hugh stood up to the swords and torches, and sent all the angry mobs home.

Hugh lived through the reigns of several kings, and whenever he went to London to visit whichever one it was, he would stay at the old Lincoln's Inn, appropriately enough, and that is where he died, all worn out at last with helping people. The poor people of Lincoln certainly missed him, and they say his pet swan flew off into the wild again, never to return.

November: Week Four

ALEXANDER NEVSKY (1219–1263)
prince (November 23) *(See Map 2)*

One reason we love hearing stories about heroes is that it is really encouraging to know that someone was brave enough to do the right thing, no matter what. It's even better if there is a good movie about that person! Alexander Nevsky was a great prince and hero and had a wonderful movie of the same name made about him by Sergei Eisenstein, although the part with the Teutonic knights is too scary for the young folks. In addition to all the princely and heroic things Alexander did, he was also a saint.

Alexander was the Grand Prince of Novgorod, Vladimir, and Kiev, which were the most important cities of Rus, or what they called western Russia in those days. The first thing Alexander did to save his people made him unpopular with his noblemen, because he refused to fight. He made peace with the ferocious Mongols (or Tatars, as they were called thereabouts) who had come from the east, burning and pillaging, not long before. Year after year, Alexander would make the long journey east to the Golden Horde (Mongol headquarters) with tribute money to keep Russia safe, and some called him a coward. But Alexander knew that it was only money that the Tatars wanted, not land, and that the time to fight them hadn't come yet.

But when the Swedes attacked from the west, Alexander led his armies against *them*, because he knew they wanted land and couldn't be bought off with gold. He had a great victory against them at the Neva River, for which they nicknamed him "Nevsky." The third threat, from the Teutonic Knights of Germany, was the worst, because the Crusader Teutons wanted *not only* Russian land but also to kill off the people of Russia because they were a different kind of Christian from them! When the Russian nobles came begging Alexander Nevsky to help them, he was a little irritated: they had *just* been calling him a coward about the Tatars again! But again he went to war, and as always he was very clever so that as few of his men would die as possible. It was winter time, and he arranged it so that the battle took place on the surface of a big frozen lake called Lake Peipus. The Russians, on foot and in their lighter armor, fought safely, but the heavy Teutons, in full armor on horseback, fell through the ice and were drowned, poor fellows . . . and think of all those poor horses!

Why did Alexander Nevsky become a saint and not just a national hero? Partly because he saved his people from being killed just because the Russians were a different "flavor" of Christian from the Teutons, but also partly because he cared about the poor people of his country with real Christian charity—it was the poor farmers who would die if the Tatars weren't paid their bribe money, not the rich noblemen, who could escape on their horses, after all! He was essentially a peacemaker who made war unwillingly and, when he did have to fight, preserved as many lives as possible, and as such he makes a grand saint.

december

NICETAS of TRIER (died 566)
bishop and missionary (December 5)
(See Map 5)

and **GERMANUS of PARIS** (496–576) bishop (May 28)

Nowadays, the French are considered to be *so* civilized that you're really not fully educated unless you can pronounce and understand a few key phrases like *je ne sais quoi* or *voilá*, and when you're a grownup, you have to know a little about French wines, cheeses, and general cuisine or you're just nobody! But this was not always the case. Before the Romans took over what was then Gaul, the people there—*mirabile dictu*—didn't drink wine at all, just beer. And before Catherine de' Medici married the King of France in the early fifteen hundreds, French cooking wasn't so great either, or at least that's how the Italians tell the story. And then, of course, the barbarian Franks came in, after the Romans and before Catherine de' Medici, and sort of smashed things up until people like these next two saints came along and then Charlemagne got them all organized around the year 800.

No, the Franks were not a very nice bunch in those early days. Saint Germanus was bishop of Paris then, and believe me, Paris was no "City of Light" yet! He had his hands full trying to keep the people of one part of town from killing off the people of another part of town (actually, that continues to be a problem there, from time to time). But then, Germanus was also trying, apparently with little success, to

---

"curb the viciousness of Frankish kings." We will hear more about Germanus when we get to the story of his friend Geneviève.

Saint Nicetas, our official saint for the week, was bishop of the town of Trier. Trier is in the far west part of today's Germany, near Luxembourg, and has some terrific Roman ruins, but was definitely in the Frankish part of the world back in the sixth century. Nicetas was bringing, shall we say, the *niceties* of culture and civilization from his native Auvergne in central Gaul to the newly-arrived Franks in Trier, who were just barely Christianized. For example, on his way to Trier, Nicetas and his Frankish escort had stopped for the night, and instead of *buying* fodder for their horses from the local farmers, the Frankish nobles just turned their horses loose in a nearby farmer's wheatfields! Nicetas scolded the thoughtless men, and he himself drove the horses out of the fields. And that was before he even got to Trier. As both Germanus and Nicetas discovered, civilizing people and being a saint can be really hard work sometimes!

December: Week One

NICHOLAS OF MYRA (fourth century)
bishop (December 6) *(See Maps 3 & 23)*

Note: I have included a silly St. Nicholas play and an Ogden Nash poem at the back of the book: enjoy!

We know this saint as the patron saint of thieves, moneylenders and especially children—*Sinter Klaas*, as the Dutch call him—and we know that in Holland he arrives by boat, all dressed in his bishop robes, with his crosier and his mitre, and then goes riding a milk-white horse through the town, while his servants give out gifts to the children. We also know that he was eventually buried in Bari, on the southeast coast of Italy, in a wonderful old church there. So we think we know "Santa Claus," but there are many more good old stories to tell about Saint Nicholas of Myra, the *Thaumaturge* (or "Wonderworker")—and even some history!

They say that Nicholas was born in the beautiful seaside town of Patara in Lycia (on the southern coast of modern-day Turkey), and that he was a very bright boy from birth, really a genius, who was very good at his Sunday School lessons and had wealthy parents who loved him. He was only eight when his parents died and he took to the road, traveling up the coast, visiting churches and just poking along, intending to be a holy man, or at least holy *boy*, somewhere. As the story goes, he just walked into this church in the town of Myra and all the people there, who were gathered down at the altar in the church praying hard for a new bishop, pointed to Nicholas as he came in the door and said, "You're the new bishop!" That's certainly *one* way to decide things like that . . .

Saint Nicholas was at the Council of Nicaea (another interesting location in Turkey, now called Iznik, off in the west near the Sea of Marmara) back in the late 300s. This was where the Nicean Creed was first written up—the creed that starts: "We believe in one God, the Father, the Almighty, maker of heaven and earth, of all that is, seen and unseen". They also say that he had the sacred tree of the goddess Diana cut down, and did all sorts of other important deeds. He even had adventures after he died: the people of Bari on the southeast coast of Italy came and stole his body away from Myra and popped it into their own church, where he has managed to stay to this day!

But our favorite stories are the ones about children: the three boys he saved from being turned into pies by an evil innkeeper, and the three girls he saved from slavery by putting little sacks of gold in their stockings. And we certainly know enough to put our own stockings up on Christmas Eve, or our shoes out on Saint Nicholas' Eve. And *of course* we know what Saint Nicholas did to Jabez Dawes in Ogden

Nash's poem (or if not, find out by reading the poem, in the back of this book), for saying there wasn't any Santa Claus . . . . and it served him right!

December: Week Two

AMBROSE (334–397)
bishop and poet (December 7) *(See Map 14)*

and **VENANTIUS FORTUNATUS** (535–605)
poet (December 14)

Now I expect that each of you has at least *one* hymn that you like to sing, at least sometimes. If we had a "Hymn Sing" and you could pick whichever one you liked, what would it be? "Onward, Christian Soldiers" is fun to sing, even if people think it isn't very "politically correct;" then there's "Immortal, Invisible," with that great old Welsh tune, Hyfridol. Think what a quiet place chapel or church would be without any singing!

Both of today's saints are connected in most people's minds with hymns, although Ambrose did *other* important things, too: he was bishop so early in the history of the Church that he had all sorts of things to invent and get going. He was born in Trier, on the beautiful Moselle River, when it was still a Roman outpost and *well* before Saint Nicetias or the Franks arrived, or even the Vandals. After Ambrose became a bishop and moved down to Milan, in northern Italy, he really encouraged hymn-singing there, although only a few other people in the western half of the Church were already using hymns; the eastern half had been singing hymns since pagan days. But when *Ambrose* suggested a thing, people really listened and did it, so hymn-singing really caught on. He even wrote quite a few hymns himself.

To write hymns, you really need to be a poet, and that is how Venantius Fortunatus got to be *Saint* Venantius Fortunatus (actually Saint Venantius Honorius Clementianus Fortunatus, if you must know): by being a really good *hymnographer*, that is, a "hymn-writer" type of poet. Venantius was quite the gallant Roman troubadour, and dedicated all his poems to his benefactress Queen Rhadegunda of Neustria (which is the fancy Frankish name for the part of France called Normandy today). And he did write a lot of poems.

If you look under "Authors" at the back of your hymnal, you will find a lengthy list after his name, even though he lived fifteen hundred years ago and wrote in Latin. "Hail Thee, Festival Day," and "Welcome Happy Morning" are actually two different translations of one of his Easter hymns, *Salve Festa Dies*, though he didn't write the music: those tunes are by Ralph Vaughn Williams and Sir Arthur Sullivan, respectively, no slouches at writing good hymn-music. *Vexilla Regis* ("The Royal Banners Forward Go"), *Quem Terra, Pontus, Aethera* ("The God Whom Earth and Sea and Sky"), and *Pange, Lingua Gloriosi Proelium* ("Sing, My Tongue, the Glorious Battle") were also lovely, tongue-twisting Venantius originals. Like Ambrose, Venantius knew that a good hymn can teach doctrine and liven things up a bit, and that a really good hymn can almost stand in for a sermon . . . almost!

December: Week Two

THOMAS BECKET (1118–1170)
penitent, bishop and martyr (December 29)

 You may remember from hearing the story of Saint Hugh of Lincoln that Bishop Thomas Becket was killed in his own cathedral in Canterbury by the henchmen of King Henry II of England, and that because of this murder, Henry was in big trouble with the Church.

You might also know from reading Geoffrey Chaucer that Canterbury became a popular pilgrimage spot to visit "the holy blissful martyr" Thomas, maybe because it was good for peoples' souls or maybe just because of the beautiful April weather in Chaucer's *Canterbury Tales*. But you may *not* know that Thomas Becket started off as a bit of a rascal! He said himself that he went from being "a patron of play-actors and follower of hounds to being a shepherd of souls," meaning he used to go to plays and go hunting all the time before he was made Archbishop of Canterbury. Thomas had been a friend of Henry's ever since King Henry II was Prince Henry, and he had worked as a diplomat and a soldier for his king before becoming a man of God.

It is strange but true that sometimes we become better people when someone gives us a big responsibility. Maybe we really admired the last person who did that job, and we want to try to do as well, or maybe we had *meant* to become a better person and here is finally a chance to prove ourselves, but it has happened throughout history, and our friends are always surprised when it happens to *us*. They can't really believe that we could become different from the person they know. They do say that President Chester Arthur (the twenty-fifth president of the United States) surprised his cronies by thinking for himself once he was in office, rejecting all their crooked little ways. His friends were angry, but the rest of the country was mighty relieved.

So when Thomas Becket was made Archbishop of Canterbury, he knew that finally he was responsible to no one but God and his parishioners, and he certainly wasn't going to allow his old friendship with Henry to change that. Henry had thought he could use Thomas to make church folks do just as he, Henry, wanted them to (rather the way his descendant Henry VIII did), and Becket just wouldn't be used, and you know the rest: he was killed, right there in his own cathedral. You can still see the spot where it happened to this day. And you'll also notice from this story that by becoming a better person, you may lose your old friends and maybe even your life (if your old friend was King Henry II), but history will remember you as a better person, or even a saint.

The rest of December is hopefully a holiday for all of you, so let's have a Merry Christmas! Then it's on to the New Year.

January

ODILO of CLUNY (962–1048)
abbot and innovator (January 1)
(See Map 10)

What better way to start the new year than with the story of someone who thought up some new ways to do things, but who didn't look like the sort of person who could do much of *anything*, especially anything brave or important? Odilo was abbot (that is, the head man in charge of monastic things) of the abbey of Cluny, in the east-central part of modern-day France, just a century or so after Charlemagne, when the Franks were still getting civilized. Odilo was a little, pitiful-looking fellow, but he was actually tough as nails; he lived to be eighty-six years old at a time when that was particularly unusual. He also came up with some new ideas that made life better for a lot of people down through the ages; I'll tell you about two of them.

The first great idea Odilo of Cluny thought up—no doubt after much prayer and reflection—may not seem so big, but people all over the world are still doing it. He decided that, right after the big festival in honor of the saints, called All Saints' Day (which itself replaced a big pagan festival) on November 1, all the abbeys under his control should celebrate *another* festival, in honor of all their dear dead relations, called All Soul's Day, on November 2. This gave people a chance to clean away weeds from their grandparents' graves, have a picnic in their memory, bring fresh flowers: things that even the pagans used to do, but that were loving things to do, anyhow. The festival spread to the whole Church, and from this we get the *Dia de los Muertos* ("Day of the Dead") and all the celebrations that go with that, and the good memory of our relatives when we list their names and pray for them in church.

The second great idea Odilo of Cluny thought up—also no doubt after much prayer and reflection—was something called the "Truce of God." Now, back in ancient times, the Greeks had a truce or cease-fire every time they held a big sporting event like the Olympics, and they would also have a truce after a big battle to collect the dead soldiers and bury them properly. But the Franks didn't know anything about the Greek way of doing things and had barely heard of the Roman way of doing things, and their fighting manners were still very bad. Odilo figured that, since mostly Christians were fighting mostly Christians in Europe in those days, they could at least have a cease-fire for the Easter holidays, and for Christmas, so that everyone could take a break from fighting (it seemed as if everyone was *always* fighting back in those Bad Old Days). This would give them a chance to buy food, see their families, pray and whatnot and generally behave more like human beings and less like mad dogs. People seemed to think this was reasonable, and interestingly, it also made them think that maybe they could find ways of *keeping* the truce beyond Easter or Christmas: in other words, make peace; a very saintly thing to do.

January: Week One

GENEVIÉVE (420–500)
patroness of Paris (January 3)

You may remember that I mentioned in the first week of December Saint Germanus, the bishop of Paris who had such a hard time taming the wild Franks who had just taken over what had been Roman Gaul. Well we know they still needed more taming, centuries later. But way back when Germanus was bishop of Paris he met a Parisian girl named Geneviéve, who told him she wanted to devote her life to serving God now that her parents had died. Since there weren't any convents around Paris in those days that she could join, Germanus advised her to go on living in her godmother's house as she had been doing, but to devote herself and her time to good works and prayer. So that is what Geneviéve did.

Paris was indeed a wild place in those days, full of cruel and uncharitable people who made fun of Geneviéve every time she tried to make things better for poor and sick people, and called her all sorts of bad names. She helped her city, all the same, something like an early-times Joan of Arc. She saved Paris from the Huns by her prayers and her good advice: she told the panicky Parisians that they should not run away from the city, to have faith that Attila would not attack Paris. Not many of them believed her, of course, but sure enough, Attila turned aside at Orléans.

Another time, when Paris was blockaded by enemies down the Seine River and no food was getting up to Paris, Geneviéve led a convoy of boats past the blockade *herself*. She even tried to help Bishop Germanus tame the wild Frankish kings, who tended to behave any way they felt like at the moment. She did get King Childeric not to kill *all* his prisoners of war, and later convinced King Clovis actually to free some of his prisoners and be more merciful to the rest.

Geneviéve used to have a beautiful tomb in Paris, and after she died her spirit seemed to go on protecting the hapless people of Paris from wars and plagues. She slept there peacefully for twelve hundred years, until the Revolution of the 1790s, when the Parisians dug up her grave and danced around on her bones! Hopefully, Saint Geneviéve still watches over her city, however ungratefully it may have treated her at times.

January: Week One

SIMON STYLITES (390–459)
shepherd and column saint (January 5)
(See Map 11)

To say that this Simon was an *outstanding* saint would certainly be true, but it is also a big pun, because "Stylites" means that he lived on the top of a column! It was a big stone column with a broad platform on top, but still it was only about three-and-a-half feet square, really a tiny space to spend your life on, and it had no roof, so when it rained, he got wet, when the sun was out, he got burnt and when the wind blew, he got cold. There was a wooden enclosure around the top so he couldn't fall off, and a long, long, ladder leaning up against it so he could get his friends to send up food and water, but he lived on top of that column—really and truly—for thirty-six years. Believe it or not, other holy hermits saw this as a great invention, and copied him!

Simon started out as a shepherd in the Holy Land, so he was used to living out in the open, I suppose. Then he was in a monastery for twenty years, but he ate and slept so little and read and prayed so much that it really irritated the other monks: maybe they figured he was just showing off. So he moved out into the desert to a place called Telanissus, in Syria, to be a holy hermit there, but so many people came out into the desert to ask him for advice, watch him pray (he would bow toward Jerusalem as many as a thousand times a day) and hear him preach, that he set up a little platform there, about four meters above the ground, to escape the press of people a little. Gradually he got helpers to make it higher and higher until it was about the height of a normal column, or about fifteen meters tall. Now he could have his privacy and still be available to whoever chose to visit, preaching twice a day and taking questions all afternoon.

Although living on a column seemed like a really crazy thing to do, Simon wasn't really crazy. He gave helpful, sensible advice, his knowledge of scripture was sound, and he preached good solid sermons. He was quite an inspiration. The Bedouins of the desert in particular were converted to Christianity in large numbers, and this was a couple of hundred years *before* Islam appeared on the scene. It's true he ate and drank very little, and was used to it, but during Lent he really ate nothing, just drank a little water, so that by the end of Lent, he would preach lying down, and his voice was pretty weak. Simon Stylites is still remembered in that part of the world, as nowadays Telanissus is called Dair Sem'an: can you hear the name "Simon" in there?

January: Week Two

ADRIAN of CANTERBURY (died in 710)
abbot and teacher (January 9)
(see Maps 1, 3 & 25)

If you are studying a foreign language, you know that it can be hard work, and the younger you start working on it, the better. To become really *fluent* in another language, that is, to speak it like a native, to write it correctly, and even to dream in it, is even harder. So, when I tell you that today's saint taught his students so well that they could speak Greek and Latin as well as they could English (and they *were* English boys), that is really saying something.

For someone who ended up with a quiet job like teaching classical languages in a pleasant town like Canterbury, Adrian had a really adventurous early life! He and his parents escaped from North Africa just before the Arab invasion, and they moved to Naples, in Italy, where Adrian became a Benedictine monk, then he was abbot in charge of a little monastery on the tiny island of Nisida, in the Bay of Naples. There he became a great scholar but, like the Greek philosopher Socrates, Adrian was *so* wise that he realized how little he really knew about anything, so when Pope Vitalian asked him to go to Canterbury in England to be archbishop, Adrian said "no," because he felt he wasn't worthy. The second time Vitalian asked him to go, he still refused, but he did say that if his friend Theodore was made archbishop instead, he would be willing to go along to help. So, off they went, but that was still not the end of this classics teacher's adventures.

On the way to England, Adrian was arrested and put in prison in France for *two years*. The French had decided that having such a brilliant intellect go along with Theodore as a mere assistant was clearly an attempt to hide the fact that Adrian was a spy! When Adrian finally made it to England, Theodore made him priest of the church of Saints Peter and Paul (later called Saint Augustine, or "Austin" as the English liked to shorten it). As well as giving Theodore a great deal of excellent advice, Adrian started a school at the church, and also built several others around England, to train up young men to be priests. Aldhelm and John of Beverley were two saints in this book who studied with Saint Adrian. He taught Latin and Greek at Saints Peter and Paul for the rest of his life, even when he stopped doing other churchy things, and the boys were very fond of their old master. After he died, at a great age, his friendly spirit lingered on to help his students when they prayed for his intercession: he was especially helpful to schoolboys in trouble with their teachers . . . something to remember next time *you* forget to study for a test. Have a word with Adrian of Canterbury, the saint of schoolkids!

January: Week Two

PHILIP of MOSCOW (1507–1569)
metropolitan and martyr (January 9)
(See Map 2)

When Saint Philip of Moscow was still just plain old Theodore Kolyshov, son of a wealthy nobleman, he used to like to help his father in figuring out ways to drain their marshy fields. Even after he became Philip the Monk and then Philip the Head of the Monastery of Solovetsk Island, off the coast of Karelia in the White Sea, he used his knowledge to turn the chilly, swampy island a useful, busy place. His improvements allowed the monks not only to escape from the distractions of the mainland, but also to make enough money on their various farming and building projects that they could keep the themselves fed and the buildings from falling apart. With all the trees around there, they were able to fire up big kettles to boil away seawater and gather the salt, and to fire up big kilns to turn mud into bricks. So they sold salt and bricks, and the little island flourished. Philip loved to make soggy land useful *almost* as much as he liked helping desperate people find hope.

Unfortunately for Philip, though, he made such a name for himself in Karelia that the tsar of all Russia wanted him to come be *metropolitan* (like an archbishop) of the capital city of Moscow and the tsar's own private advisor—just as the Archbishop of Canterbury advised the Kings of England. The metropolitan would try to be the tsar's voice of conscience, like those little angels sitting on people's shoulders in the comic books. The trouble was that the tsar of all Russia just then was Ivan the Terrible, and being *his* conscience—at least, if you were a good advisor, and told him not to do terrible things—was guaranteed to get you killed!

Ivan had already killed his own son in a rage, and sure enough, it wasn't long before he grew furious with Philip's insistence that he,

Ivan, behave like a real Christian, and not like some wild animal. Ivan's bully-boys were so rough with poor Philip, trying to "teach him a lesson," that he died soon afterward, and even his beautiful island was later turned—by an even *more* terrible ruler of Russia, Josef Stalin—into a horrible prison work camp. But good really is stronger than evil, and now the monastery has been re-established on Solovetsk Island and Philip is once again remembered as the voice of conscience sitting on the shoulder of every good ruler, telling each one how to be less terrible, and more like a saint.

January: Week Three

BENEDICT ("BENET") BISCOP (628–690)
bishop and collector (January 12)
(See Map 12)

There were two things—besides God, his mother, and his dog—that Saint Benedict Biscop liked better than anything else in the world: his native Northumbria (north of the Humber River, on the northeast coast of England) and collecting books. Northumbria was a long way from anywhere else in the world, and books in those days were very expensive, since they were still all written out and decorated by hand. It wouldn't be until the printing press came along in the 1440s—eight hundred years later—that most people could afford them. Books were often very large so that several people could read them at the same time, and they were so valuable that they were bound with bronze loops built into their covers, and then chained to reading benches. It was partly through books that Northumbria became really important to the rest of the world.

When Benedict, or "Benet," as they called him in old England, went to work as a clerk for King Oswy of Northumbria, the king sent him off to Rome on church business, since King Oswy was already a Christian. Our enthusiastic Benet was so utterly dazzled by the beauty and antiquity of Rome and the *holiness* of it all that he decided he really wanted to become a monk before he went home again. Maybe he learned more about his own namesake, the original Benedict, while he was in Rome. He also met up with Saints Theodore and Adrian there, about to set off for Canterbury down in the Kingdom of Kent (when England was still made up of many kingdoms, you see). If you'll recall from their story Theodore was going to be archbishop and Adrian was going to start a monastery church of Saints Peter and Paul (who were the main saints of Rome). So of course, Benet decided that Northumbria *also* needed a monastery of Saints Peter and Paul.

Benet studied hard in Rome to be a good monk, and when he got back to Northumbria at last, he convinced King Oswy that they needed a really top-notch, cracker-jack monastery, definitely better than anything they had down in Kent. Oswy naturally agreed, and Benet really got down to work: he built an abbey church, of course, and places for the monks to live and work, but then Benet built the most fabulous library building ever seen in all of Britain. It was the sort of library you might find in Rome itself in those days, only there were no big books chained to the new reading desks, not yet.

So Benet went back to Rome with loads of money from Oswy and all the wealthy people of Northumbria, and he proceeded to buy all the best books he could lay his hands on: hundreds and hundreds of precious books, just as fast as they could be made. He also collected relics of the saints, and sacred paintings called icons, and charts and calendars for figuring the date of Easter, and, because he had great friends there, he convinced John, the archcantor of Saint Peter's Basilica to come all the way to Northumbria to teach the monks there *exactly* the correct way to sing the liturgy (that is, the service of worship) and to write in *exactly* the correct beautiful uncial lettering that was then all the rage in Rome. And for centuries thereafter people came from miles and miles around to study at the monasteries at Wearmouth and Jarrow, where they also became great makers of books, and a great light in the middle of the Dark Ages, thanks to the enthusiasm of Saint "Benet" Biscop.

January: Week Three

HILARY of POITIERS (315–367)
bishop and poet (January 13)

This Hilary is not to be confused with "King Hilary the Great and Good" from the poem by A.A. Milne in *Now We Are Six*, because he was not a king, and he came from Poitiers, not England, but he certainly was great and good, and also well-off and highly cultivated. Back when Hilary lived in Poitiers it was still called *Limonum Pictonum*, and France was still called Gaul. Hilary became bishop of Poitiers way back even before Saint Martin was bishop of Tours, and even before Saint Ambrose was bishop of Milan. Hilary advised Martin, in fact, as to what his duties were as a Christian, and even had the idea of putting hymns in the church service, before Saint Ambrose picked up on the idea and made it popular in the western Church.

Hilary had visited the churches in the Holy Land and all through the eastern Mediterranean, and he brought back these things called "metrical poems," or poems that rhyme and have a strong beat. These poems were already used for popular songs in Roman times, but then were put to use for religious purposes by the early Christians. Anyway, lots of saints "back east" were doing this, so Hilary wrote a few, and then Ambrose and the others got the idea and took it from there. This may have been just as well, since Hilary liked to write in a particularly precious and convoluted sort of Latin, and his hymns were as difficult to figure out as many of his other religious writings. But Hilary was gentle, and courteous, friendly and helpful, always ready to advise, and he never minded letting other people become famous for the idea he came up with, far, far back at the beginning of things.

Saint Hilary did become famous in *one* way: he was one of the very early saints who had whole seasons of the year named after him, particularly divisions of the school year back when most students went to university to become priests. There was fall term, starting on September 29, and that was called Michaelmas Term, after the feast of Michael the Archangel on that date. Then there was Hilary Term, which began on January 13th, Hilary's feast day. Last came the summer term named after the feast of the Trinity, which was rather shiftier in its date, being tied to the date of Easter, but starting in early June. So "great and good" old Saint Hilary really did make his mark, and very early on.

January: Week Four

HONORATUS of ARLES (350–429)
bishop and healer (January 16) *(See Map 13)*

By now, you must have heard in this book about some poor holy hermits, who tried to escape from it all by going to some deserted place, but then were bothered by all these people bugging them for advice or help or healing, and so on and so forth. Here at last is a saint who not only got away from it all, he *stayed* away from it all, and then he invited others to join him there at least long enough to refresh their spirits. The place he got away to is one of the beautiful, sunny Iles de Lérins of Cannes in the Côte d'Azur of France. In French, his name is Honorat, and he was a Gallo-Roman (early Frenchman) who became a Christian, then went on a pilgrimage to visit monasteries in Rome and Greece and came back with great ideas about starting a monastery of his own.

Honorat got permission to build on one of these little islands where, long before, the pagans used to worship other gods, and anyone could see there was *something* holy about the Iles de Lérins. On his little desert island, Honorat made a place where people could come for awhile if they were all burned out with life, and he would give them some pleasant task to do to help out around the place, so that they never became dispirited or sad. And since they came to him so worn out, he made sure that although there was always something for them to do, it was not too much. It was a very early "retreat center," where people could live quietly and pray, study, work, and refresh themselves. By the time people were ready to leave, they were full of peace, inside and out.

Wouldn't that be lovely: to go to a sunny island, full of the scent of pine trees and the sea, to work up a good sweat, then go sit under a shady grapevine and study about the amazing works of God? Even if we never get a chance to visit Ile St. Honorat, we can imagine we're there, any time we get tired and out of sorts, and maybe feel better and a bit more saintly.

January: Week Four

JOHN the ALMSGIVER (560–619)
patriarch (January 23)

This Saint John began as a churchgoing businessman with a wife and a family, who was asked to become patriarch of Alexandria, thereby controlling churches in a large part of Egypt and North Africa, just before its takeover by Islam. The church of Alexandria was hugely wealthy, and John used most of his years as patriarch—you guessed it from his name—*giving that money away*, one way or another. He began by building hospitals that had maternity wards, where moms could have their babies in a nice, clean place with plenty of help, which was a new idea at the time. He made sure his hospitals had wards for the sick and hurt, and separate old-people's homes, and also built lodging houses for travelers. He paid for many of these projects by taxing the clergy (that's priests, monks, and other employees of the church, remember)!

John also helped poor people—whom he called his "masters"— partly by making sure the measures at the marketplaces were fair so they wouldn't be cheated out of the little money they had, as well as by giving people gifts of money when gifts were needed. If people asked him for money again and again, he gave it to them again, and again! He was as generous with his own time and money as he was with church money, giving free legal advice, and helping people resolve arguments and disagreements with one another, even on small matters.

Just before he died, John the Almsgiver wrote a will in which he declared that he had done his best to "render to God the things that were God's," and that he had found the church treasury full and left it empty, used up in a hundred good projects that would keep helping people for years and years. Like Saint Nicholas, he knew that it's a saintly thing really to know how to give joy by giving help and money when people need it the most.

January: Week Four

POLYCARP (died 155)
martyr and disciple (January 26)

 It's really a shame that this saint's name is so strange, because more people should be named after him! Polycarp did a huge amount to help along the young churches in the early, dangerous days of the Church, giving advice on everything from understanding the Gospels to the need for members of the Church to pay bills promptly, and always to deal fairly with all debtors, whether Christian or not. He was an old man of eighty-six when he died, and he had known Saint John the Evangelist, Saint Ignatius (the first one, not the more famous one) and others "who had known the Lord." He was also one of the earliest saints after Saint Stephen with an honest-to-goodness story of his martyrdom, written down by someone who was actually *there*.

Smyrna, which is modern Ismir in Turkey, was a great port city that they used to call "the eyes of Asia Minor" because you could see as far as Athens from Smyrna's Mount Pagos on a clear day. They also say that the poet Homer came from near there, at a place on the Meles River. In Polycarp's time there was a pagan festival in Smyrna, maybe for one of the popular goddesses with temples there—Athena or Cybele or Roma—but whatever it was, the people wanted to teach the Christians who refused to celebrate with them a *real* lesson, this time! So the proconsul sent out his troops to round up some obvious Christians for execution at the games. They found Polycarp at home that evening and brought him in for the next day's big events. But when he saw him, the proconsul felt sorry for the old man, and urged him to just offer a little pinch of incense to the emperor's statue, curse Christ, say "Caesar is Lord," and he could go free!

But Polycarp gave the proconsul his famous, ringing answer (in Greek, of couse): *"I have served him for eighty-six years and he has done me no wrong. How can I blaspheme my Lord and Savior?"* So they took him away to be killed. When he had prayed and praised God and said "Amen," they tied him to the stake, but before they lit the pyre, the proconsul had him killed quickly with a spear, so Polycarp didn't feel the flames at all. They say that for a while the flames made a big arch like a sail over his head, and that he looked all golden in the light, like a loaf of bread, or like metal in a fire. It was a sight that made people who didn't know him begin to wonder if perhaps there had been something extra special about this old man, but all his friends already *knew* Polycarp was a saint, even before all that happened (and you see that people are still talking about him today)!

february

ANDREW CORSINI (1301–1373)
bishop and peacemaker (February 4)
(See Maps 7 & 14)

Maybe someday you will be lucky enough to go to the beautiful city of Florence in Italy. Florence, or *Firenze* in Italian, is the home of marvelous works of art, like Botticelli's *Primavera*, and the birthplace of many famous people, like the poet Dante and the artist Michelangelo. If you've read the picture book called *Michael the Angel* by Laura Fischetti, about Michelangelo growing up there, you know that in medieval and renaissance times, it was a rowdy, dangerous, violent place. Dante himself was banished from Florence forever, and the people of Ravenna refuse to give back his body to this day, even though the Florentines said they were sorry, and even Michelangelo was usually safer in Rome. Well, today's saint's family, the Corsini, were in the thick of all that quarrelling. Andrew Corsini started out as a typical Florentine: grouchy and troublesome, rich, and famous and even *bad*, but then something finally brought him up short.

One day, after being particularly nasty and rotten, Andrew came home to find his poor mother in tears, and saying over and over: "You are a wolf, you really are a wolf!" He was startled (because he really did like his mother and had never seen her like this before) and asked what in the world she meant. She finally told him about a dream she'd had, just before he was born, in which instead of having a baby, she had a little wolf that turned into a lamb when he went into a

Carmelite (that's a kind of monastery) church! She hadn't known at the time what the dream had meant, but now she thought she knew: Andrew had become as cruel and careless as a wolf, and only the church could save him. Somehow, that talk with his mother changed Andrew; he went to those famous Carmelite brothers for advice on how to straighten himself out. He tried to make up for his bad ways by being just as humble now as he had been horrible before. For example, he washed the feet of poor people to remind himself what Jesus had said about service to the poor, and then, when Andrew was finally made a priest, and his family wanted to make a big fuss and have a party in his honor, he wouldn't let them. And later, when he was asked to become a bishop, Andrew actually ran off to the middle of Sicily to hide!

What Andrew discovered he was really best at was making peace among the proud families of Italy, and also between these families and the poor people who served them. Because he himself was a Corsini, the other big families respected him, and because he had become such a holy man and friend of the poor, the poor people believed in him and trusted his judgment. So, when angry mobs of poor people attacked the houses of the rich folk in the city of Bologna because they had been treated so badly, the pope sent Andrew Corsini out there to make peace, and he managed to do it. They say it takes a thief to catch a thief, and maybe an old wolf like Saint Andrew Corsini was the best person to make wolfish people into lambs like his new self.

February: Week One

JOHN de BRITTO (1647–1693)
missionary and martyr (February 4)
(See Maps 6 & 15)

Sometimes you can do something good, but it gets you into tremendous trouble. How can that be, you ask? It certainly isn't fair, but it does happen. Maybe your friends don't want you to be nice to the new kid in class (even friends can be wrong sometimes) or maybe you made someone jealous of you without realizing it, or, as happened with John de Britto, sometimes you change the way someone behaves, and that makes someone else unhappy, and *you* get hurt.

Now, after the Jesuit (that is, a member of the Society of Jesus, great preachers and teachers) priest Saint Francis Xavier started leading missions off to India and Japan to teach people there about Christianity, many other Jesuits decided to do the same thing, and one of these was our Saint John de Britto. He originally came from Lisbon, in Portugal, and went all the way to Madurai, in the kingdom of Madras (now called Tamil Nadu State, in southern India) to do his work. In Madurai there is still a huge Hindu temple complex, with many shrines and sacred pools, but John knew that many of the poorest Hindus were badly treated by their religion, and lived miserable lives. This was because in those days, poor people were thought to be doomed to be poor their whole lives because of something bad they had done in another life, and they were called "untouchables," and wealthy people could treat them as badly as they liked. It was even believed that it was really doing the untouchables a favor to kill them, because maybe they would be reborn as a richer person next time!

So when John de Britto started preaching that everyone was precious in God's eyes, and that Jesus had died for the poorest as well as for the richest sinners on earth, many of these people became Christians very happily. John also did all he could to help anyone who needed it, and he dressed and ate and spoke as much as he could just like the people of Madurai, and people there really appreciated this. Even many of the wealthier people with good hearts listened to what John had to say, and they decided to become Christians, too. But when the local king became Christian and so kept only one wife and sent away all the others, one of the *other* wives became angry and complained to her uncle, who was another powerful king, and that uncle started a war against Christians, particularly against John de Britto. He was caught and had his head chopped off, just as in the Bad Old Days of the old Roman Empire. But you'll be glad to know that not all the Christians were caught, and there is still a church there where the people remember good Saint John de Britto to this day.

February: Week Two

SIGFRID (died 1045)
bishop and missionary (February 15)
(See Maps 1 & 16)

Back in the days when the north of England was a hotbed of sprouting Christians all eager to get out and convert the world, there was a Saxon priest named Sigfrid. He came from York, the main city there, which *had* been a pagan Viking settlement but now was Christianized and had a big important cathedral. Perhaps the connection between York and the Swedish Norsemen and the Saxons and Denmark (where Saxons come from) was still pretty fresh, because when the people of Denmark and the people of Sweden showed an interest in changing from the old Norse religion of Woden and Thor, to Yorkshire-style basic Christianity, they sent off to York for a missionary, and Sigfrid went to do the job. Some other good York folk came along to help, including his own three nephews,

Winaman, Unaman, and Sunaman (believe it or not), who hoped to become priests like their favorite uncle, and always helped him out.

Off they all went to Sweden, to the court of King Olaf. The king himself was baptized, but as usual there were people who were angry about this, who didn't want to be peacemakers but instead wanted to keep carousing like the heroes in the old tales and die happily in battle as they always had, *not* settle down and get Christianized! So a bunch of angry Thor-worshippers thought they'd get their revenge and one day when Sigfrid had left the mission church at Växjö and was off in the countryside, leaving his nephews in charge, the pagan warriors sneaked up and killed all three of them, cutting off their heads one-two-three! They also seemed to enjoy destroying everything they could and burned the mission buildings down. Sadly, Sigfrid returned to Växjö and, collecting his poor nephews' heads, returned to the court. Because he knew the Swedes at that time were very superstitious, he told the king and his court, with the murderers in the room, that the heads had told him who had killed them! The murderers jumped up to escape, and so they were caught.

King Olaf was all for executing the murderers there and then, but Sigfrid wouldn't allow it: in Christian places like Yorkshire, he said, they merely collected blood-money from the murderers, and even that, he said, he wouldn't accept (though he needed money to rebuild the mission). Everyone was *so* impressed with this whole new way of doing things that more people than ever left the cruel ways of Woden and Thor behind and became Christians like Sigfrid and his nephews. Poor old Winaman, Unaman, and Sunaman: At least they became saints along with their uncle Sigfried!

February: Week Two

FINTAN of CLONENAGH (died 603)
abbot (February 17) *(See Map 17)*

From the old books, we know that today's saint, Saint Fintan, was a handsome man as well as holy-looking, with shining eyes, a ruddy complexion and dark hair flecked with white. One of the reasons this is important is that his healthy appearance is almost a miracle in itself, because everybody *knew* that Fintan lived on nothing but stale barley bread and water from a muddy well, with the occasional vegetable added in as a treat.

Life at his monastery at Clonenagh ("Clo-*nee*-na"), in the middle of Ireland, was very simple, but Fintan never made his monks live as frugally as he did himself. They all farmed together without using any beasts of burden, so they pulled their own plows and used only simple tools to do all their work. Monks from other monasteries complained that such a life must be too hard for the men at Clonenagh, but Fintan, courteous and gentle as always, disagreed with them, and so did his men. Doing all the work for themselves not only taught them patience and just how much work is needed to feed and clothe a person, but it also taught them to be thankful when they saw how much of the work is taken care of by Providence: the sun, the rain, the growth of the seeds. So they kept at it!

As you probably know, most churches have cemeteries near them, where people can be buried and remembered, and certainly there was one at Clonenagh, and the monks were very careful to pray once a day that everyone buried there would get to heaven. This is why one day—in those tumultuous times of war—a band of soldiers galloped up carrying the heads of their enemies. Apparently they had duly chopped them off and shown them to their king and now didn't really know what to do with them. So Saint Fintan said his monks would be glad to bury them and pray over them every day, because logically, he said, the head was the principal part of a person, therefore, he was sure that, given long years of daily prayers, all the rest of the parts of these men would find mercy in the end!

Make the best of what little you *do* have: that was Fintan's saintly motto.

February: Week Three

PETER DAMIAN (1007–1072)
theologian and poet (February 21)
(See Maps 7 & 14)

Peter came from the nice flat northern Italian city of Ravenna, which even back in 1000 A.D. was full of beautiful churches loaded with glittering mosaics. You know what those are, don't you: pictures made by little pieces of colored glass, gold and precious stones? In those churches, lines of saints still march along on lovely green-glass grass under skies of lapis lazuli, while emperors and empresses look on, loaded with pearls and purple and gold.

But things weren't so glorious for our Peter, because both his parents died when he was a little boy, and he had to live with one of his older brothers, who was already married. This brother was either a weak fellow or genuinely bad, and either his wife was nasty or she couldn't control this bad man, but anyway, this unpleasant couple decided that Peter could earn his own way in the house by taking care of the pigs and living in their shed with them. What a life for poor Peter: no school, no friends, hardly any food, and only pigs for company!

Luckily, Peter had *another* older brother, a priest named Damian, who had been living out of town, but came back to Ravenna to discover this terrible situation. Damian rescued his brother Peter from a life of slavery and arranged to have him go to school at the finest schools in the area. There Peter learned everything he possibly could—and with him, that was a huge amount—and he was so grateful to his brother that he added his name to his own, calling himself Peter Damian from then on. Now, maybe because he had been raised so harshly and so he had no tolerance for bad people after that, Peter Damian became famous for making people in the Church shape up and stop doing bad things. If he heard about some bishop being lazy and not caring for the poor, he would *blast* that bishop out of his throne with a really stiff sermon, or sling a ferocious letter of reproof at him.

But the thing Peter Damian liked writing best was poetry, especially super-elegant Latin poetry. Here is a little piece of one his Latin poems called "Hymn on the Glory of Paradise," translated by me into English:

Here they live in endless being:
Passingness hath passed away:
Here they bloom, they thrive, they flourish,
For decayed is all decay.

And you see the same elegance in a hymn in praise of Pope Gregory the Great, which starts like this: "Once the apostle of the Angles {the English}, now the companion of the angels . . ." and goes on like this: "Your lips, sweetened with honey water, distill a heart; your burning, fragrant eloquence conquers violence." Peter Damian had some "burning, fragrant eloquence" himself, but it would have been hard to write such saintly poetry in a pig-shed, wouldn't you say?

February: Week Three

BENEDICT (480–547)
abbot and founder (July 11)
(See Map 18)

Today's saint, Benedict, left his twin sister, Scholastica, behind in Norcia, in the part of Italy called Umbria where they were born, and went off by himself to be a holy hermit in a cave in a cliff face near Subiaco, outside Rome. He had some *big* problems to solve in his cave besides the problem that his sister was irritated with him for becoming a hermit before she did. First of all, whenever he tried to concentrate on his prayers, his mind would wander. For example, even though he knew that his friends would remember to lower him his food basket from the top of the cliff, he still worried about it, and would start wondering when they were coming . . . or had they forgotten this time? And his stomach would start to growl, and he couldn't really keep praying, or even think straight. At times like these, he got his attention back on God by jumping out of his cave and into a nearby thorny rose bush, and then, by golly, he wouldn't think about food anymore: he could concentrate on the sufferings of Christ instead, and how painful they must have been.

Another big problem Saint Benedict had out there in the wild was that the local people hated him, and didn't want a bunch of sightseers hanging around their town looking for spiritual guidance from some guy in a cave. They thought the best thing to do was to get rid of him, so they nabbed his basket one day and poisoned his loaves of bread! But Benedict had some *other* friends who were too smart for them: the crows who lived at the top of his cliff and liked to come down and chat with Benedict. They flew down and snatched up that bread and threw it into the ravine before Benedict even touched it! (Luckily he had some spare crusts to chew on while he waited for the next batch to come.)

After a long time in the cave and after reading what people like Pachomius and Cassian and Basil the Great had written about monasteries, Benedict figured out a good way to organize them, which he called his Rule, or "School for Beginners," that many other people who wanted to start convents or monasteries followed, too. Late in life, one night after he had founded the great monastery of Monte Cassino—a steep hill that looks over the whole valley of the Liri River and the road from Rome to Naples—as he looked out over the valley, it seemed to Benedict that he saw a sudden vision of a beam of light, and in that one sunbeam were gathered all the places of the world . . . maybe to show how far and wide his Rule would spread. And it did, too.

February: Week Four

*(Only one: unlike January,
this month is thin on good stories.)*

MARTYRS of the PLAGUE of ALEXANDRIA
(died 262) (February 28) *(See Map 3)*

The title of today's saints tells you most of what you need to know: they died in a plague in Alexandria, Egypt, somehow dying for their faith, the way martyrs do. The date tells us that this happened before Christianity became legal in 313 A.D., so they *could* have died in an act of persecution, but did they? Were they fed to large, toothy furry creatures in the arena, while a plague was going on? All right, I'll tell you: they weren't!

Here's what happened: there were several big *epidemics* (that's when just about everybody in town catches the same disease, and a lot of people die) in the late Roman Empire. One after the other, measles, mumps, rubella, and all the other nasty diseases that you get inoculations for at the doctor's office nowadays arrived in Alexandria and all around the Roman world for the first time. It was popular to blame these diseases on things like sinful behavior or on people like Christians, but this time that just wouldn't work, because it was the Christians who were being the most helpful.

When everybody else was hiding out in their houses, hoping that the plague would just go away, too afraid even to visit their relatives to see how they were doing because they might catch the plague from them, the Christians were out and about, visiting sick people— even people who weren't Christians—taking them milktoast (which they called in those days *pultes tractogalatae*) and whatever medicines they had in those days.

Of course, a lot of these brave people caught the plague themselves and died, but at least they had done all they could for one another, and probably they would have been blamed for the plague anyway, so why not do the right thing, and die of the plague instead of lion bites? The good thing about all this was that the pagan folk of Alexandria, when they saw all that the Christians had done for people, began to think that Christianity was a pretty good thing, after all. So the next time the emperor sent out a memo that all local Christians were to be fed to the lions, they more or less ignored it!

march

seasoned with more July saints
who would otherwise never be heard
of during the school year.

March: Week One

GERASIMUS (died 475)
abbot (March 5)

If you'd gone out into the deserts of Egypt or Palestine about sixteen hundred years ago, you'd have found—if you looked hard enough—clusters of holy men, or just single hermits, living here and there in the wilderness just like John the Baptist (only I'm not sure they all ate locusts and wild honey). Anyway, sixteen hundred years ago being a desert monk was all the rage, but—being alone so much—they sometimes forgot a lot of the details of the Gospels and got muddled in their theology.

This was certainly the case with our Saint Gerasimus, before he met up with another saint, Euthymius the Great, who must have known what he was doing, with a name like that. Euthymius straightened out Gerasimus, for which Gerasimus was very grateful. They became good friends and decided to set up a *lavra* together (that's the official eastern Church name for a desert monastery) way out near Jericho in the Holy Land, on the Jordan River. Their *lavra* became a holy-man magnet, whether for people who wanted to stay and join them or for those who just needed a quick refresher-course before returning to be solitary in the wilds. Clearly the two saints were doing something right.

But the thing that really proved that Gerasimus was saintly was his friendship with Jordan. Now, some people are easily confused about names and think that Jordan was a friend of Saint *Jerome*, which is Hieronymus in Latin, and sounds a little like Gerasimus if you don't know what you're doing. Actually, it was like this: one day Jordan came up to Gerasimus, limping and holding out his paw—by which you may see that Jordan was not a river or a human but a beast, in fact, a lion. You guessed it, he had a thorn in his paw and Gerasimus pulled it out for him! Once Gerasimus had gotten the thorn out of Jordan's big paddy-paw, cleaned out the cut and bandaged it up, Jordan was his friend for the rest of their lives. They say that if the monks needed help moving something heavy, they would just hang it over Jordan's big furry sides and he would carry it for them. I'm not sure he would have liked the monastery food, but I suppose he ate fish from the river and was quite happy.

Unfortunately, Gerasimus died, and after that, poor Jordan refused to eat any more fish: he just lay down on his old friend's grave and died, too. Dear old Saint Gerasimus and Jordan the Lion: loyal to one another to the end!

March: Week One

PERPETUA and **FELICITY** (died 203)
martyrs (March 7) *(See Map 3)*

There are many more martyr stories than can be included in this book, because most of them are so gory and sad that the littlest people hearing the stories might have nightmares. Certainly the *whole* story of these two young women really is too heart-rending to tell, but you do need to know how important they were in showing how cruel the law against Christians was, back in the Bad Old Days. Also, their story was written down immediately at the time they died—in fact, part of it was Perpetua's diary—so we know a great deal about what really happened, which isn't always true of saints' stories.

Perpetua was a young mother with a little baby boy, living with her parents in Carthage. We don't know what happened to her husband; maybe he had already been killed for being a Christian. We know that her parents tried as hard as they could to keep Perpetua from being killed, too, when the authorities came around to get her. It broke her heart to see her father so upset: he begged her not to be so brave (if you can imagine a father saying that), but to worship the emperor, curse Christ and all the usual things, not to leave her son an orphan and not to leave her old parents alone. It was a terrible time for him, and for her too!

While she was waiting with the other condemned Christians for her day in the arena with the wild beasts, they all prayed together day and night. One night, in a dream like a vision, Perpetua saw a terrible ladder stretching up to heaven, and all along the edge of the narrow ladder were sharp weapons: swords, spears, pruning hooks, and all bloody and horrible. At the foot of the ladder was a dragon! In her dream, Perpetua tamed the dragon and managed to climb the terrible ladder without being hurt, just by keeping her mind focused on all she believed, and calling upon Christ to save her. Then she had a second dream-vision in which she was a young man, fighting in the arena like a gladiator against a sort of demon, and when she beat him in combat, she won the palm of victory from a very tall angel and was allowed to leave the arena in triumph.

Felicity was a member of Perpetua's group of Christians, and she was also a young mother with a very new baby, so both she and Perpetua were condemned to be attacked by a wild mother cow, since the Romans thought that was a funny way to kill them, a sort of customized punishment, or "let the punishment fit the crime," as they say in the operetta called "The Mikado." Well, the cow was pretty fierce and hurt them a lot, but certainly didn't kill them, so in the end a young man with a sword had to finish them off. Perpetua felt sorry for him, because his hand was shaking so badly, and she helped guide his hand to the right spot on her neck to kill her quickly. So, asking someone like Perpetua "not to be brave" was a silly thing to do, don't you think? She was the bravest of them all.

March: Week Two

PATRICK (385–461)
bishop and missionary (March 17)
(See Map 17)

We all know a little about Patrick: that he was the great apostle to Ireland, that he drove out all the snakes (supposedly, but zoologists say there never were any there, anyway), that he taught about the triune nature of God using a shamrock (one leaf, three parts), and that we are all supposed to wear green and eat corned beef and cabbage and soda bread on his saint's day . . . but I expect there are still a few surprises here for you.

First surprise: Patrick was embarrassed that he never got a proper education (his fellow bishops used to call him an "ambitious ignoramus," if you can imagine). But really, he couldn't help it. I mean could *you* help it if you were minding your own business on the coast of Roman Britain and one day some Irish pirates nabbed you and before you could say "Jack Robinson" had dragged you off to Ireland to be a slave minding the sheep while all your Roman-British buddies graduated from high school (or the fourth-century equivalent) and went off to seminaries to study to be bishops? Of course you couldn't, and neither could Patrick! It took him years to catch up on the education he'd missed while he was a slave in Ireland.

Second surprise: Patrick was a Man of Action! Yes, indeed, when he was twenty-one, after he'd escaped from Ireland and quickly trained himself to be a priest, he went right back to Ireland to de-paganize the place at the risk of his life. He had a *huge* show-down with the druid tree-worshippers on Easter Eve at the Hill of Tara where the high king lived. Patrick was so powered up by the Holy Spirit that he was able to confront and defeat the druids in the presence of High King Laoghaire, earning so much respect that the people listened to his preaching thereafter, without so much as an interruption.

Third surprise: Patrick wrote the words —in Irish, originally—to the terrific hymn we generally know as "I Bind Unto Myself Today." It has been put to a wonderfully strange tune and there is a special bit toward the end that has a completely *different* meter and tune. Patrick composed that special part back in the times when all the were druids were out to get him, and he got in the habit of muttering a special protection prayer to himself when he had to go through dark forests or along lonely paths. It's called the *Lorica*—that's the Roman word for breastplate, or the front part of your armor—and it starts, "Christ be with me, Christ within me, Christ behind me, Christ before me . . ." and it is mighty powerful stuff to know by heart if you're ever in a tight place, or afraid of the dark.

So there you are: three more reasons why Patrick is such a great saint.

March: Week Two

FRANCIS SOLANO (1549–1610)
friar (July 13—transferred to March)

You should know that a *friar* is a special kind of monk who wanders around preaching and begging instead of staying inside a monastery all the time, and that our Francis was actually called *Francisco* in Spanish, and was named after the original friar, Saint Francis of Assisi. This Francis had loads of what you might call *spunk*, which is the old American way of saying he was filled with the Holy Spirit. Back in the Bad Old Days of slavery, our Francis sailed to Peru to preach, but just before the ship got into port at Lima (the capital of what was then called New Spain) a storm caught them. Everyone abandoned ship, or everyone except the miserable slaves chained below decks and Francis, who was determined to save them. He unchained as many as he could before the ship broke up on the rocks. It was a terrible situation, and that was his welcome to Lima.

In those days, Lima was where everything was happening in New Spain, but Francis Solano was not impressed with Lima, no indeed, no matter how delicious their beans were. Even though the residents showed him their fine houses and fancy dinners, he already knew how they felt about the slaves who ran those houses, and soon he discovered how they treated the local natives, too, because he kept his eyes open and because he learned all the native languages he could lay his hands on: people thought it was a miracle of God how many languages he could learn!

When he did learn exactly how the white folks of Lima really treated their fellow man, Francis Solano was not at all happy with his countrymen. He went into the marketplace at Lima and into the beautiful big churches of Lima and he began lambasting those bad high-class Limans up one side and down the other until they were terrified of the wrath of God. He left them like that for awhile, and they were very, very good . . . for a little while. But the fact that they were good, even for just a little while, certainly proves that Francis Solano must have been a saint.

March: Week Four

(spring break took out Week Three.)

CUTHBERT (634–687)
bishop and founder (March 20th)
(See Map 1)

**C**uthbert is another name that is not used enough nowadays. If you read Tintin books, you will have heard of Cuthbert Calculus, the scientist on roller skates. This Cuthbert was also quite scientific!

There are several Holy Islands in the British Isles that we know were bright spots in the Dark Ages. Bishop Cuthbert built his church on the holy island of Lindisfarne, which is located off the coast of Northumberland, that part of England's northeast coast that seems to come up in a lot of these stories. Now, islands tend to have particularly interesting creatures on them: rare plants that washed there from someplace far away or birds that blew there in a storm and have evolved into very different sorts of birds than the sort they started out to be, and Cuthbert noticed them all, because he had a keen eye for noticing things, like a scientist, or like a good friend.

Cuthbert was a good manager, and his little group of monks and regular folk were well cared for and each had an important job to do, but more than that, Cuthbert was good at healing both people and other creatures. Maybe he knew where to find just the right herb for a medicine or just the most peaceful spot on the island or could tell just what was ailing the person or creature, but however people felt when they came to Lindisfarne, they left it feeling better, much as Honorat of Arles helped people with *his* little island.

Cuthbert had a keen eye for what was happening inside a person's heart, too, and what sort of spiritual medicine, what prayer or passage of scripture, might be just what he or she needed to hear or read. Maybe it was also his beautiful smile, or the charming way he had about him, just glowing with kindliness, that was good to be near. They say he could heal a sick baby with a mere kiss on its soft cheek: he was *that* sort of saint.

Lindisfarne is still a lovely place to visit and to go to for a spiritual retreat, but it must really have been something when Saint Cuthbert was in charge. But then, I suppose he still is in spiritual charge there, in the way saints generally are, if they're needed.

March: Week Four

BONAVENTURE (1218–1274)
bishop and theologian (July 15)

Have you ever known someone who always has his or her nose in a book, just loves to read all the time but maybe doesn't really know how to be a good friend or listen to your troubles? Well, today's saint was *not* like that! Yes, he loved to read and made sure that every church or monastery he worked in had a lot of books and a fine building to keep them all in, but he also loved to do simple things like cook dinner for guests or play in the dirt with children, and he was easy to talk to, even though he had written loads of books himself and could discuss logic and mysticism all day long with the rest of the experts.

When Bonaventure was studying in Paris to be a priest, his favorite professor was an English Franciscan monk, so naturally Bonaventure wanted to become a Franciscan monk, too. Franciscans tried (and modern Franciscans still do try) to behave just like their founder, Saint Francis of Assisi, but it was very hard to live as simply and faithfully as he had. When Bonaventure became the chief of the whole Franciscan order, he completely reorganized and revitalized it. He made a very good Franciscan, too, although he had been a brilliant student in Paris and could have been a wealthy cardinal or acclaimed professor of theology. But Bonaventure used to say that having the very simplest love and understanding of God was better than being rich and famous.

Just a little story to show you what Bonaventure was like: he had just been made cardinal bishop by the pope of that time—and cardinal is the highest position you can have in the Roman Catholic flavor of Christianity without being the top man, that is, the pope himself. Anyway, the official legation was coming over to his house in order to present him with his special cardinal's hat (which was a big red felt sombrero sort of hat in those days, with a fancy gold cord to go under the chin), and he should have been pleased and honored, but really he had no time for what he considered empty show. When the legation arrived with the hat, Bonaventure was out in the backyard washing dishes (he probably had just had some friends over for a nice summer supper outdoors, or maybe his cook was in bed sick) and he told them to hang the hat on that tree over there, since his hands were all wet and greasy! Typical Bonaventure, typical saint-type behavior.

april

JEAN-BAPTISTE DE LA SALLE (1651–1719)
teacher and founder (April 7)

This saint de la Salle was not a cruel man like the explorer René-Robert, Cavalier, Sieur de la Salle. No! But Jean-Baptiste was as brave as an explorer, in another way: he was . . . a *teacher!* He, Jean-Baptiste de la Salle, started out as a wealthy young priest who could have had a comfy life serving in some little church somewhere in France, but instead decided to teach poor children at a time when schools were not free and so most poor folk couldn't even read or write.

If you suddenly decide that *everyone* deserves to go to school, you will just as suddenly discover that you need a huge number of teachers you didn't have before. So Jean-Baptiste started by teaching teachers—a whole lot of them—and then sending them off to various free schools he'd set up in Reims, France. Unlike most church educators at the time, he made sure his teachers were not priests, just good teachers, but he called them the Brothers of Christian Schools, a kind of *lay brothers*, meaning they weren't members of the clergy. As you can imagine, teachers and schools that charged a lot of money for students were pretty grumpy about what he was doing, because some of their students wanted to go to these good new schools. But our saint kept at it, also started a Sunday School, and even was asked to teach for a while in Rome.

Jean-Baptiste put together all his new ideas about the way schools should be run into a book, which people are still using three hundred years later. A couple of important ideas in that book are that students should be taught in their "mother tongue"—that is, French, in his case—and not in Latin as they had been for centuries, and that the teacher should insist on *silence* and *attention* while he taught (what a novel notion). If it hadn't been for him, who knows? We might still be teaching in a noisy, one-room schoolhouse with nobody listening, plenty of spanking and all the classes in Latin ! Thank goodness for explorer-saints like Jean-Baptiste de la Salle.

April: Week One

GUTHLAC (673–714) and PEGA (died 719 in Rome)
brother and sister, hermits (April 11; Jan. 8)
(See Maps 1 & 19)

Guthlac and Pega were both of royal Saxon blood, but only Guthlac went off to fight for King Ethelred of Mercia. Pega, his sister, stayed behind with the hard job of keeping her brother safe with her prayers. Guthlac was what they used to call in Latin a *robustus depredator* ("mighty warrior"), but he finally hung up his sword and shield and joined the double monastery at Repton, run by the holy abbess Aelfrith. Repton is a smallish town in what is now Derbyshire but it was then capital of the kingdom of Mercia in central England, and a double monastery was an English invention: both men and women could be in holy orders there, living in two separate houses and ruled by one abbot or abbess. So Pega could join her brother there, too, and did so.

At first the other monks thought Guthlac was just *pretending* to be oh-so-holy when he wouldn't touch strong drink and slept very little and prayed a great deal, and that sort of thing. But soon they found that he really *was* holy, so they weren't so hard on him anymore. But Guthlac found that having all these other people around was very distracting and irritating, so he went off to be a hermit all by himself at a bend of the river Welland in the Fens of East Anglia to pray and contemplate God and give advice to any who came to visit him. There he stayed for the rest of his life.

The place was called Crowlands, because mobs of crows (big black birds, as you know) and magpies (big black-and-white birds, as you may not know) liked to live around there by the river. They also liked to visit Guthlac, who made friends with all the animals thereabouts. The magpies especially liked to steal anything he left lying around, especially shiny things like his candlesticks or his favorite little silver crucifix. Many a time he had to climb up a tree to the nest to fetch them back down again. People told him, "Get yourself a slingshot and kill a few of them, then they'll leave you alone!" But Guthlac said, "We humans ought to set an example of patience even to the beasts, not be as bad as them or worse." He was thinking of the marauding Britons who pestered him sometimes at his deserted hermitage, or the devils who appeared to him in his sleep and tried to tempt him to do evil, or maybe he was even remembering his old fellow monks, who had been so unfriendly to him for so long.

His sister Pega lived not far away, in a place named after her— "Pega's Church" or now Peakirk—and when Guthlac died, old and worn out with so much hard living, she was with him and buried him there at Crowlands, where a big church was soon built to honor his memory. Both of them became saints and were "mighty warriors" in their quiet way . . . and you know the crows (and magpies) must have missed having Guthlac to pester and be their friend.

April: Week Two

VALERIAN, TIBURTIUS,
and **MAXIMUS** (died 170ish)
martyrs (April 14)

Older kids will have heard in their Physics classes about something called a "chain reaction," when one explosion sets off another, and another, and another, like a string of fireworks at Chinese New Year. Well, sometimes people became saints in a sort of chain reaction. One person would get all fired up by the Holy Spirit, and then another would catch the excitement from *her*, and then *he* would inspire someone else, and so on. That is what happened with today's saints. Valerian "caught it" from his bride, Cecilia (who has her own story in November), then Valerian's brother Tiburtius wanted to be as blissful as Valerian and Cecilia, and then Maximus . . . we will see what happened to Maximus.

It all started in Rome, when Valerian married Cecilia, and she told him that she was a Christian and had already married an angel. Couldn't she and Valerian just live together like brother and sister? she asked. This confused him, as you might imagine, but all of a sudden he saw a vision of a big tall angel standing beside Cecilia, holding out two beautiful wedding wreaths of white lilies and red roses, one for each of them, so he decided that a heavenly wedding was fine with him. After a good deal of study and prayer, he became a Christian like Cecilia, and then his brother Tiburtius came to visit the young couple. When he entered their dining room, he said it smelled very sweetly of roses and lilies, though no flowers could be seen. Then Valerian just flamed up with excitement and told his brother how he should just believe in one God, stop worshipping stone statues—as if they could help anybody—and stop worshipping the emperor as if he were a god, then—*foom!*—

Tiburtius was all burning to be baptized and become Christians like them!

But it was still that time in history when the Roman emperor killed people for being Christians, and soon Valerian and Tiburtius were caught, and taken off to prison. Cecilia was locked up in her house. First, Valerian and Tiburtius were beaten up with clubs and told to sacrifice to Jupiter or die, but then Maximus, the man who was hired to kill them, was so impressed by how young and brave they were that he burst into tears. Maximus begged them to give up their belief and save themselves, but Tiburtius told him that their spirits would rise to heaven like a phoenix from its ashes. Then Maximus said, "Dang me, if I don't believe in your God!" He converted on the spot and was arrested too, just like that! Finally someone with a hard heart killed all three of them, and Cecilia buried them in a tomb with a phoenix carved on it. It was a good symbol for such a fiery chain-reaction of faith, don't you think?

April: Week Two

STEPHEN HARDING (died 1134)
abbot and founder (April 17)

and **BERNARD of CLAIRVAUX** (1090–1153)
abbot and theologian (August 20)

(See Map 10 for both)

Stephen Harding was a promising young priest from Dorset—which is in England, just southwest of London—and when he told his superiors he would like to help wherever he was needed, they sent him off to France. In a wild, swampy corner of the country near Dijon—and no doubt covered with wild mustard bushes—there was a new foundation of monks who seemed to be getting a little wild themselves. Stephen, cheerful, easy-going, good-looking and popular, seemed to be just the man they needed.

The place was called *Cistercium* in Latin (*Cîteaux*, in French, with a silent "x") and so the monks called themselves Cistercians, and they were supposed to be following the strict Rule of Saint Benedict in their way of life. Stephen found that they needed a total re-organization and a good stiff new Rule of their own, which he sat down and wrote himself. But, just when things were improving, his monks were getting old and sick and dying off, and Stephen began to worry that all their hard work would be wasted if no new monks joined them. Of course he prayed and prayed about this, and finally, he had a strange dream.

You should know that meanwhile, a brilliant young priest named Bernard (not the same as the mountain passes and dogs: he is in a different story) and four of his equally-intelligent brothers, as well as twenty-seven other friends, had recently decided to find some way to serve their church and heard that the swampy monastery near Citeaux was hurting for new members. Bernard had been studying at Châtillon dur Seine and was such a wonderful speaker that they called him in Latin *Doctor Mellifluus* ("the honey-sweet teacher").

Now, you may have heard that when bees want to move to a new home, the queen bee flies out and the other bees swarm around her in a cluster, and you can put that cluster in a new hive and they will settle down quite happily. Well, one night, as I say, Stephen Harding had a strange dream that a nice swarm of thirty-two golden bees came to live in a hive that looked a lot like his monastery, and the next morning when he woke up, there were thirty-two sturdy young monks, led by Bernard, at his monastery gate, saying they were here to join the Cistercians! Bernard of Clairvaux later took over Stephen Harding's good work, founded many more Cistercian monasteries—including a new one at Clairvaux that he was later named after—and wrote loads of good books on many religious subjects, all of them honey-sweet to read or listen to. So there you have a couple of sweet saints, Stephen and Bernard.

April: Week Three

GEORGE (died 303)
soldier and martyr (April 23)

There is no doubt at all that Saint George was considered to be a very important saint ever since long ago: early on, he was called the *megalomartyros*, which means a "really important witness" for the Church and against the powers of evil. They say he was a soldier who refused to worship the emperor, and so he was killed, and the Byzantine (Eastern Roman Empire) army later took him as their patron saint. His flag, the red Latin cross (meaning more or less shaped like a lower-case "t" or a crucifix) on a white background, is practically the flag of Christendom itself, and may be found on the Union Jack of Great Britain (along with the white cross *saltire*—meaning x-shaped—of Saint Andrew on a blue ground for Scotland and the red cross saltire of Saint Patrick for Ireland). That is because George is the patron saint of England, and "Saint George of Merry England, the sign of victory!" is a good old English battle cry. He went on to be patron of archers, of knights in armor, of armorers and—because his name puns with the Greek word for farmer—of farmers. You can tell him from Saint Michael in pictures because George has no wings, and is riding a horse, but both of them are often shown battling a dragon. Unlike in Asia, where dragons are quite popular and considered lucky, in Europe the dragon was a very early symbol of evil and darkness. The light-god Apollo fought darkness in the form of a huge snake, for example, and in Michael's case the dragon was none other than Lucifer the fallen angel, in dragon form.

But there is a fine legend—from that wonderful collection of saint stories called *The Golden Legend*—about Saint George's battle with the dragon that I can tell you here, though I warn you, the part about the dragon is rather sad, and not *all* of it may be the way it really happened. It may also remind you a bit of the story of the Greek hero Perseus, Princess Andromeda and the sea-monster called the Krakon. Here is how the writers of the *Oxford Dictionary of Saints* tell the legend:

> The dragon, a local pest which terrorized the whole country, poisoned with its breath all who approached it. Every day it was appeased with an offering of two sheep, but when these grew scarce, a human victim, chosen by lot, was to be substituted instead. The lot had fallen on the king's daughter, who went to her fate dressed as a bride. But George attacked the dragon, pierced it with his lance, and led it captive with the princess' girdle, as if it were completely tame. George told the people not to be afraid: if they would believe in Jesus Christ and be baptized, he would rid them of this monster. The king and the people agreed; George killed the dragon, and 15,000 men were baptized! George would take no reward, but asked the king to maintain churches, honor priests, and show compassion to the poor. He suffered and died under Diocletian and Maximian.

It's too bad about the dragon, I know, but I expect it's just some kind of *metaphor*, so hurrah for Saint George of merry England!

April: Week Three

MAUGHOLD (5th century)
penitent and bishop (April 27)
(See Map 1)

Today's saint is a treat for three reasons: first, you can pronounce his name "Muggle," if you like; second, he was a "prince, pirate and thief" before he became a saint; and third, he was bishop on the Isle of Man, which is a *very* curious place.

What do you know about the Isle of Man? You may know that people from there are called "Manxmen," and that Manx cats have no tails, but do you know that Man lies in the Irish Sea, about halfway between Dublin, Ireland and Carlisle, England? Or that they have their own parliament there called the Tynwald and a completely different legal system from that of the British, run by judges called "deemsters"? That they have minted some coins with Harry Potter on them? Or that their flag has a three-legged figure on it and that the motto that goes with it is: "However you throw me, I stand"? Well, now you do!

When Saint Patrick first met our future saint, Maughold was a pirate prince, operating out of his home base in the Orkney Islands, up north of Scotland. Patrick, as you know, was a man of powerful religious faith, and he convinced Maughold that if he did not immediately repent, his soul was well and truly doomed to fry in Gehenna, the lake of fire. So, to start paying penance for his sins, Maughold let Patrick chain him up and pop him into a little *curragh* (an Irish-type canoe) to let the current take him wherever it liked. And the place it liked was the south coast of Man, where Maughold then was rescued and released, and went to go live in a cave and get some faith. And as it happens, Maughold got *so* much faith that the people of Man came from miles around to be baptized by him at his holy well (which you can still visit today) and to get advice and finally to ask him to be their bishop, which he was glad to do.

Like any good Manxman, where Maughold (or "Muggle" as they call him there) was thrown, he stood, and I expect he managed to escape the flames of Gehenna, don't you?

April: Week Four

PETER CHANEL (1803—1841)
missionary and martyr (April 28) *(See Map 20)*

Now, if you've read the *Pippi Longstocking* books, you know that Pippi's father was king of the Cannibal Islands, and that cannibals are people who eat other people—although I don't think they did any more after Pippi's father became king. Today's saint went to help out a king of a Cannibal Island when the king had just decided that his people shouldn't be cannibals any more. The islands are nowadays called Wallis and Futuna, and lie in the South Pacific not far from New Caledonia, and the king's name was Niuliki, and on his islands his word was *law*.

Back in the early 1800s Wallis and Futuna were colonized by the French, and so it was a French Marist, Peter Chanel, who was asked to come there by Niuliki to teach his people about the Christian religion. Now, you may know that Jesuits are members of the Society of Jesus, and that they were determined to take knowledge of Jesus all over the world. Well, Marists belonged to the Society of *Mary*, and they were much the same as the Jesuits in many ways. Young Peter Chanel had started out as a French farmer's son, but he studied hard and became a priest and was eager to save the world starting with the South Pacific, so he joined the Marists and off he went to Wallis and Futuna.

Peter got along very well with the people on the island of Futuna, and they learned quickly all about Christianity. One of his Sunday school students explained to King Niuliki that he decided to become a Christian because of Peter Chanel: "He loves us. He does what he teaches. He forgives his enemies. His teachings are good." Peter even convinced Niuliki's own son and his friends to become Christians, but then things started to get tricky. Niuliki began to feel that his son liked Peter better than he liked *him,* and inside Niuliki a great jealousy and hatred began to grow, in spite of himself. Finally, one day when Peter's companions were on the island of Wallis, Niuliki's guards jumped on Peter and killed him. There on Futuna Island Peter Chanel was buried, but the people of Wallis and Futuna are still Christians to this day, so I expect Niuliki's son must have forgiven his father, and became a good king after him, don't you?

April: Week Four

CATHERINE OF SIENA (1347–1380)
mystic and reformer (April 29) *(See Map 7)*

I hope that someday you can visit the hill town of Siena in Tuscany, Italy, see how the streets go up and down and around and around the Y-shaped ridge it is built on, and then go to the big, shell-shaped open space, or *piazza* called *il Campo,* or "the field", which is paved with slender salmon-colored bricks laid in a herring-bone pattern. People like to sit on the Campo as if it were a beach, and there twice every summer for the past six hundred years the Sienese people have held the thrilling horse race they call *il Palio. Palio* means "banner," and the prize is a banner dedicated to the Virgin Mary. Maybe you will study at the Foreigners University there, but certainly you will eat some of the wonderful cakes they make there, or just sit on the sunny bricks of the Campo. . . . But at least once you have to go down one of those steep streets to the old fountain in the part of town called *Oca* ("The Goose") and visit the house of Saint Catherine, one of the two patron saints of Italy along with Francis of

Assisi. She is about the most famous person from Siena, along with a wonderfully crotchety old saint named Bernardino.

The summer after Catherine (that's actually Caterina, in Italian: C-A-T-E-R-I-N-A; people do spell Catherine so many different ways!) was born to a comfortable, big family of cloth-dyers, there was a terrible plague. It was called the bubonic plague, and in three months, more than half of the people in Siena died; it was like a scene from the most terrible nightmare you can imagine. All over Europe, people got the plague in the next few years, and they began to think that God hated them, or that God didn't even exist. They needed to hear that God still cared about them and that there was hope for the future, and saints like Catherine helped them to believe again. She had a very close friendship with God, whom she just knew as "Father." She prayed so much and ate so little that she would have visions of heaven and of the future and what to do next, and people believed in what she said.

Catherine drew a large group of priests and regular people around her from all over Europe, who called themselves the *caterinari*, after her; they would worship together and preach and give people hope. Catherine herself even gave advice to the popes, during the time when there were two popes and the Church was in turmoil. She was always energetic and cheerful, and did the best she could for everyone she came across, and even now, people like to visit her house, remember her and read all the useful things she said about faith. A saintly inspiration to all Catherines, however they spell their names!

may

May: Week One

BERNARD of MONTJOUX (996–1081)
archdeacon (May 28)

and PETER of TARENTAISE (1102–1174)
abbot (May 8)

(See Maps 14 & 21 for both)

For today's saints, I need you all to be thinking about mountains: real mountains, big ones with snow on top. Now, imagine you are on a little trail going up through those snowy mountains and down to the valley on the other side, but right at the top of the trail, at the head of the pass, that is, there are bandits who jump on you and take all the stuff you have with you, stuff you need to trade at the fair on the other side of the mountains in order to make a living. If you can imagine this, you'll have an idea what the passes through the Alps were like in the Bad Old Days. Now imagine you are *living* up in those snowy mountains and it is May, so the food you stored up to get you all the way through winter has pretty much run out, and you still have to save a few seeds to plant to grow more wheat for *next* winter. So maybe you attack the travelers who come through there, just to get some food. Life up there in the Alps of 1000 A.D. was really *rough*.

Both of the saints in this story understood about living in the snowy mountains, because they came from Savoie, in the French part of the Alps, and it is no accident that both of their saints' days come in May. Bernard came first: he was working as an archdeacon—that is a kind of an almost-priest—in the cathedral at Aosta on

107

the Italian side of the Alps. People kept coming into Aosta with terrible stories of the two dangerous passes on the roads near there: the higher one, on the road going north over to Swiss territories, and the lower one, on the road going west into France.

Bernard saw that action was needed, and we are told that he "cleared the passes of robbers," though how do you suppose he did it? Did he organize all the monks in town and go to the robbers and ask them nicely to stop? Or did he pray to God to bring snow down on their heads, or just to change their minds? Don't know, but he managed to clear *both* the passes, and keep them clear, too! Bernard also built permanent rest-houses at the top of each pass and staffed them all year 'round with monks to care for travelers. Later on, these monks started breeding a great big kind of dog to help with search-and-rescue in avalanches: you guessed it—Saint Bernard dogs. And the passes were renamed in his honor, too: *Petit Saint Bernard* and *Grande Saint Bernard.*

Saint Peter of Tarentaise continued Bernard of Montjoux's good work, rebuilt the hospices at the passes and added an endowment to pay for bread called *Pain de Mai* to be distributed to the hungry mountain people every May. This bread was given out every year for seven hundred years. Here were two mountain saints, who really acted on their faith, and gave people three things we love: safety, bread, and great big, helpful dogs!

May: Week One

LEOPOLD MANDIC (1866–1942)
confessor (May 12) *(See Map 14)*

Now you know that some people are much better at talking than they are at listening . . . blah, blah, blah, they tell you all about what they did, and never ask you about how you feel at all. Then there are other people who are good listeners . . . they really seem to want to listen to what you're worried about and what you think, and maybe they even have some good advice to tell you, once they've listened. This second person is what today's saint was like, a very good listener . . . but he started out wanting to be something quite different.

When Leopold Mandic was a little boy growing up in Croatia his name was Adeodatus, which means "given from God." He liked to dream of traveling far overseas to wonderful places he'd heard of, and of telling the people far overseas all about how much God loved them. Though Leopold's *huge* faith was a gift from God. Because of a childhood illness he was a tiny little fellow with a twisted back (he never grew to be taller than four feet five inches tall), he spoke with a terrible stutter and was often in pain from one ailment or another. With all his big ambitions packed into that painful little body, he felt like a great big eagle in a tiny iron cage, and for a long time he was very unhappy. But his family still encouraged him to go off to Italy and learn to be a priest, to do all he could for the God he loved so much.

So off Leopold went, preaching here and there the best he knew how and helping people any way he could, finally ending up in the great university town of Padua. He was a pretty good preacher, but there was *one* thing Leopold could do better than any other priest in town or even in all of northern Italy: he could hear confession, assure forgiveness and give good advice. Confession is part of every church service, because everyone does, as Saint Paul said, "the very thing they hate," and before we can worship God properly, we need to drop everything that is separating us from God and each other—that is, we need to confess what we've done wrong and be forgiven. In most places it is part of every church service, and in Roman Catholic churches there are little booths called confessionals where a person can go to a priest privately and do this.

Leopold discovered that he was a very good confessor because he was patient and he understood pain very well and he had a very generous and loving heart. In fact, he was a bit like a four-foot-tall Christ, suffering but loving and patient. For *forty years* he listened to confessions nearly all day long and gave people hope. He would say, "Have faith! Everything will be all right! Faith! Faith!" and people believed him and were comforted. Leopold died not all that long ago, but you can imagine he became an "official" saint pretty quickly.

May: Week Two

PACHOMIUS (290–346) abbot (May 14)

Do any of you have a messy friend or brother or sister that you would love to organize? Get all their stuff sorted by type and put into just the right containers and put away nicely? Or maybe *you're* the messy friend or sister or brother and you like to have things that way, because you know where everything is, even if nobody else does? Well, Saint Pachomius was the first kind of person: he thought it was a sad waste to have people doing things they weren't very good at or wasting their time arguing about how to run things when they could be doing their jobs. He was an organizer, and he made things *work*.

Pachomius spent thirty years as a soldier in the Roman army, seeing first hand how things could be efficiently organized to make the best use of men and supplies. When he finally retired from the army, it was now legal to be a Christian, so the first thing Pachomius did was go off into the Egyptian desert and live there as a hermit, studying and praying all day by himself. But pretty soon, he saw that living alone was no way to do the thing properly, and so he organized all the hermits in his neighborhood into a little community of the sort he'd read about in the Acts of the Apostles. This community was located in a ruined village on the east bank of the Nile, not far from the famous city of Thebes. He arranged it so that they would work at various jobs in the community and share what they earned from their work, and that they would have some people in charge (like him, for example) to organize things and write a Rule of Behavior for everybody in the community to follow (which he did). His rule was called "Tabennisial," after the little ruined village, Tabennisi.

It all ran like clockwork: the monks gave their superiors total obedience, the superiors could (and did) send off the monks to whatever front—er, monastery—seemed to need their help most. The monks were organized into houses by what their skills were: veggie growing here, making clothes there, baking bread over there, with all the profits going to support everybody in the monastery. Food and sleep were strictly regulated and there wasn't too much of either, but usually more than the single hermits had allowed themselves. They all worshipped together, memorized and repeated the Psalms and certain Gospel passages. By the time he died, Pachomius had started eight large establishments for men and two more big ones for women, and made a Rule that people like Benedict later used for part of their own monastery organizations.

Yessir! Saint Pachomius really organized those hermits into a going concern, and they have been "going" ever since.

May: Week Two

BRENDAN the VOYAGER or NAVIGATOR
(486–578) abbot (May 16)
(See Map 17)

Out in the green country of Killeedy in County Limerick, Ireland, many hundreds of years ago now, there was a school for little boys run by a saintly lady named Ide. She was in charge of a community of "dedicated women," back before convents were very official. Ide was a wonderful, miraculous person. She taught all her boys to have "faith in God, purity of heart, simplicity of religious life, and generosity in love." One thing she is famous for is writing a lullaby for the Baby Jesus, and another is for teaching Saint Brendan the Voyager. Brendan thought he could do all those things Ide taught him, although he had quite a temper at times, and by and by he did become a bishop. He was a good bishop, and even did some miracles with water and healing.

But when a traveler came up to Brendan one day, just back from overseas, and told him he had just come home from sailing to Paradise, Brendan's life became *much* more interesting. The man's clothes had the fragrance of fresh greenery and flowers that Brendan had never smelt before, and he told an amazing story of weeks at sea and the beauty of Paradise until Brendan was sure that he wanted to sail to heaven himself. So he took a big skin canoe called a *curragh*, got some supplies for a long trip and some men to help, and set out northwest from Ireland to find Paradise. Once, they came to a huge monster which hurled hot rocks at them, and once they saw a beautiful white castle, all made of glass, and another time they *thought* they had come to an island, but when then they gratefully stepped out onto it and started cooking their dinner, it turned out to be a huge fish, and swam to the bottom of the sea, leaving them and their dinner floating next to their boat!

Finally, they reached Paradise. It really was beautifully green, with fair lawns and trees and flowers, and grapevines loaded with fragrant grapes of the sort Brendan had smelled on the traveler back in Ireland. But soon, some tall beautiful dark-haired angels came through the woods, frowning and motioning them all back to their boat, clearly meaning that this was indeed heaven, and they were not allowed here, at least not while they still lived! They sadly sailed back to Ireland, seeing all the same marvelous things they had seen coming out. And Brendan was a good bishop for the rest of his life, but he did miss heaven and could hardly wait to get there again, when he died.

The strange thing is that some people recently took a little boat and followed the course that Brendan took west from Ireland, and they saw a volcano in Iceland (like a monster throwing rocks) and an iceberg in the Atlantic Ocean (like a castle of glass) and plenty of big whales that liked to sleep on the surface of the sea, and finally they came to America, to a green coast that once was covered with wild grapes—like those that Norwegian Leif Eriksson found hundreds of years later, when he took that route to "Vinland." The same tall angels threw out Leif and his men, only Leif fought back, but the Indians fought harder, and the Norwegians had to leave, too. But the Norwegians were certainly no saints, and I suppose that the Iroquois were no angels! So some people call Saint Brendan "the saint who discovered America."

May: Week Three

IVO of BRITTANY (1235–1303)
lawyer (May 19) *(See Map 22)*

People nowadays like to make jokes about lawyers: how nobody likes them, how they're tricky and only interested in making money, and all that sort of thing. It turns out that people have felt that way about lawyers for a long time. When people in Ivo's day wanted to describe him, and Latin was the language everyone used, they said about Saint Ivo, *Advocatus erat sed non latro, res miranda populo*—"He was a lawyer but not a thief, a thing that amazed people." But a good lawyer is really a helpful person and a downright peacemaker when you are trying to write a will or buy property, or solve a land dispute, and our saint was a very good lawyer, indeed.

Ivo came from Brittany in France and so he spoke Breton, a Celtic language a lot like Welsh, but he went off to Paris where he learned all about French law and about Church law, and so he also became fluent in French and Latin. He was very good at making his point, whatever he was talking about or in whichever language he spoke. He also studied how to be a priest, and how important it was to be fair, especially to the poor and helpless, so when he came back to Brittany, he became famous as a judge in Church cases. No one could make him change his mind by giving him money, so poor people knew he would judge their cases as fairly as he would a rich person's case. And he always tried to get people to settle their problems in a friendly way, outside of court, if they possibly could.

Later, Ivo became a preacher, and he used his lawyer skills to write great sermons, but he would still give free legal advice to whoever asked him. He could preach in three languages, which impressed important visitors to Brittany and made his people very proud of him. Ivo also helped people by building a hospital, and giving away his money and even his bed to people who needed food and shelter, and he liked to take care of sick people with his own hands. After all those years as a judge, Ivo believed very strongly in *pardon*, and remembered that Jesus had told Saint Peter he must not just pardon an injury seven times, but *seventy times seven* times. So Ivo started a Feast of Pardon in his town, and after seven hundred years they still celebrate it in Brittany: they start at the church in Treguier where he preached and they walk to Minihy where he was buried, and they take his relics along for the walk in his little coffin, every third Sunday in May. Maybe you can go along, if you're ever in France in May, and see good old Ivo, the saintly lawyer of Brittany.

May: Week Three

THE VENERABLE BEDE (673–735)
monk and historian (May 25)
(See Maps 1 & 12)

If you ever study any medieval history, you'll always hear "the Venerable Bede said this" and "the Venerable Bede said that," but he wasn't just a great historian, he was a saintly person, too. One of the main reasons Bede wrote his *History of the English People* was so that people could learn what was good and also what was bad in history, and to learn lessons from that about how they should behave. You know what they say: "People who are ignorant of history are doomed to repeat it." Certainly it is one of the best reasons to know your history, and to know about saints, too. Bede knew the importance of passing along knowledge, as he had learned at the feet of Benedict Biscop, the Northumbrian saint whose book-collecting habit and good connections with Rome had made the monastery at Jarrow the sort of place where an historian could really flourish, and Bede himself taught a boy who would grow up to be the greatest teacher of the age, Saint Alcuin.

Bede said of himself that "study, teaching and writing have always been my delight," and he did write a lot, although only his Latin writings have come down to us, not his works in Old English—alas, for he was the first prose writer in English! He was also the first historian, they say, to use *Anno Domini* ("in the year of our Lord," A.D.) for dating events in history. He also learned a great deal about the Earth: that it was a sphere, and that the moon affected the tides, and that sort of thing. Bede was a man of deep faith, and liked to write hymns, including two rabble-rousers still found in the hymnbooks: "The Hymns of Conquering Martyrs Raise," and "Sing We Triumphant Hymns of Praise." His students called him "our blessed Bede" and he is invariably called "the Venerable" not only to honor his saintliness but as the first historian of the English people, the only Englishman to be called a "Doctor of the Church," *and* the only Englishman to merit a place in the *Paradiso* of Dante. All this shows that Bede was a person clearly worth venerating!

May: Week Four

ALDHELM (670–709)
bishop, poet and clown (May 25)
(See Maps 1 & 9)

Aldhelm (whose good old Saxon name means "old helmet") did all the usual things to help you become a saint: he came from a royal Wessex family, became a monk, was taught by a saint (Adrian of Canterbury), became the abbot of a monastery at Malmesbury in Wilshire, and became bishop of Sherborne in the part of England called Dorset, around which he built a lot of churches. But we really remember "Old Helmet" because he was a poet and just a little bit *eccentric.* Eccentric really means "a little off-center," like an unbalanced ball that wobbles a bit and you really don't know where it will roll next, so you could say that an eccentric person is a little unpredictable, and sometimes being unpredictable is a good way to get people's attention.

Aldhelm was one of those famous students of Saint Adrian's who knew Latin as well as he knew English and, as one writer put it, "the Latin language went to his head," because Aldhelm loved writing ingenious Latin rhyming riddles. Anglo-Saxons, like hobbits, always liked riddles, or "kennings" as they called them, and his Latin sermons tended to be incredibly complicated just for the fun of it. But the most eccentric thing about Aldhelm, and maybe the *real* reason he became a saint, was that he would go into the marketplace and sing hymns, quote some Gospel lessons, and even make a few jokes and riddles, all to get people to come to church that Sunday to save their souls.

Aldhelm was a bit of a holy clown, and certainly nobody forgot him. In fact, when he died, he got a promontory (that's a piece of land that juts out into the sea) named after him in Dorset (often incorrectly called Saint *Alban's* Head, instead of Saint Aldhelm's Head). People also put up stone crosses at seven-mile intervals all along the road between Malmesbury, Wiltshire (where he was buried) and Doulting, Somerset (where he died) to remind people of "Old Helmet." Whether all those crosses are still there, you'll have to go see for yourself, and while you are there, honor the memory of Aldhelm, the humorous (and eccentric) bishop of Dorset.

May: Week Four

JEANNE la PUCELLE or JOAN of ARC (1412–1431)
shepherdess & savior of France (May 30)

You might know that Joan of Arc was famous and brave, that she led French armies into battle against the British, and that she was burned at the stake in the marketplace at Rouen. Here are just a few more details for you, and there are lots of books written about her, which you can read if you want to get the whole interesting story later.

Like most farm girls from the Champagne country of France back in the Olden Days, Joan hadn't been taught to read or write, but she was very bright, anyway. Unlike most girls, when she was about thirteen years old Joan began to have visions while she was watching her flocks of sheep out in the fields, visions of Saint Michael the Archangel, Saint Margaret of Antioch, and Saint Catherine of Sinai. These saints were telling her to go save France from the English, who were marching all over the place, winning the Battle of Agincourt and so forth, as if they had the right to run the place. When should a saint go to war? Perhaps only to defend people against invaders and sometimes that means pushing back until your people are safe.

So Joan (or in French *Jeanne la Pucelle*, "Jean the Maid") went to the court of the *Dauphin* (that's the prince of France) and told him and his bishops that she could lead them to victory. One way she proved her mystical power was to pick the prince out from a crowd, even though he was in disguise and she'd never seen him before, and then she also gave the bishops a secret sign from her saints. So they agreed to put her in charge of the armies, and gave her not only a special suit of white armor, but also a beautiful banner to carry, and a grand sword that she brandished in battle but never used to cut anyone. She led the French to two great victories so that the Dauphin was crowned King Charles VII of France, and then Joan should have stopped, as her voices had told her to, but she felt sorry for the part of the French army trapped at Compiègne, so she went to help them. But those rats, the Burgundians, captured Joan at that battle and sold her to the English, who put her on trial as a witch! And the new King of France was a bit of a rat, too, since he didn't pay her ransom or try to save her at all.

Joan was very brave and gave good answers to the bad questions at her trial, and she managed to keep her faith strong, even though they burned her at the stake in the end. During her life, she helped to bring an end to the terrible Hundred Years' War. She also performed miracles, showed pity for the people who trusted her even at the cost of her life, and refused to tell lies: more signs of a real saint.

june

at last!

June: Week One

EPHRAEM (306–373)
poet and theologian (June 9)
(See Maps 3 & 11)

They called Saint Ephraem "the Harp of the Holy Spirit," meaning, I suppose, that whenever the Holy Spirit inspired him, beautiful poetry poured out of him just like music pouring out of a harp. Ephraem was from Nisibis up at the northern edge of the Mesopotamian plain, then he moved to Edessa just west of there, into a cave in the hills, when the Persians took over Nisibis. Back in those days, many people in Mesopotamia and the Levant—that is, in that whole area which we are taught to call the Fertile Crescent—spoke a language called *Syriac*. In fact, Jesus himself spoke Syriac, so if Joseph needed some help in the carpentry shop and called to Jesus to come in and help, he would have likely called to him in Syriac. So all of Ephraem's beautiful poetry and hymns were written in Syriac, which the folks in the Syrian Christian Church can still sing without translation.

What Ephraem liked to do best was teach and write poetry, and he did a lot of both. All his sermons were written as poems, and maybe his classes were all given in poetry. Can you imagine having all your teachers speaking in poems all day long? And he wrote a lot, I mean

119

he really wrote a lot: one thousand books or a total of three *million* lines of poetry. And what did he write all that poetry about, you ask? Well, he wrote about the triune nature of God, the dual nature of Christ, the need for the Holy Spirit in prayer, the fidelity of the Virgin Mary, all about what heaven and hell look like . . . you name it, all the important stuff. He wrote so much good stuff that the higher-ups in the church wanted him to be bishop of Edessa instead of just a teacher and writer, so he had to pretend he was crazy to get out of it—just as the Greek hero Odysseus did when he didn't want to go fight at Troy—only it worked for Ephraem, he got to stay being just a poet and a teacher for the rest of his days, occasionally helping out the hungry and other needy folk, and dying happily in his cave: the perfect ending for a saint.

June: Week One

ANTHONY of PADUA (1193–1231)
preacher (June 13) *(See Map 14)*

 If you ever get to Padua—or Padova as they call it in Italy—be sure that you visit the huge *piazza* (plaza, or city square) there, called the *Prato della Valle* with the big, circular park in the middle and an island in it, all surrounded with canals crossed by bridges and a broad sidewalk where you can roller skate in circles around and around until you are dizzy. Like a spoke off of this big wheel of a piazza is a street leading to a tall church with three funny domes like knobs and two or three big cloisters (square porticoes built around gardens) each with ancient trees in its center. This is the church of Saint Anthony of Padua, who was almost as popular as his friend Saint Francis of Assisi. But Anthony did not build that big piazza *or* that church. He had no time for building, because he spent his life— used it up, even—in preaching.

When Anthony started out as a Franciscan monk, nobody thought much of him; he was a little bit sickly and very quiet. But one day, by some accident, when there was no one else who could possibly preach but he, he amazed everyone by having a big, strong voice, a persuasive message, and a fantastic knowledge of the Bible to back up everything he said. After that, he was in constant demand as a preacher. His big themes were right living and the truth of the doctrine. He wasn't afraid to tell rich, important people that they were misbehaving or to tell lazy clergy that they had better shape up. He spent a lot of time in the town of Padua, a university town full of professors, and he impressed the educated people as much as he did the regular country folk.

Anthony went all over the countryside preaching and healing people, and they say he had some kind of personal, spiritual magnetism: sometimes, people would just fall down at his feet and repent as soon as they saw him. Other times, when the humans didn't get the message, the animals would. For instance, once when he was holding communion out of doors the only creature that bowed when he held up the host (that's the big Communion wafer or piece of bread that represents the body of Christ) was a sensible mule nearby who immediately went down on its front knees. Another time, when no people wanted to listen to him preach, he went over to talk to the fish nearby, and they immediately popped their heads out of the water to listen. But in the end, it turned out that Anthony really *was* sickly and quiet on the inside, and he died when he was only thirty-eight years old, completely worn out with all that preaching, and most definitely a saint.

June: Week Two

HARVEY or HERVÉ (6th century)
bard, hermit and abbot (June 17)
(See Map 22)

Now, some of you theater fans who like old movies, or to act in good old plays, may think Harvey is a six-foot-tall white rabbit with a friend named Elwood, but I'm here to tell you that he was even more famously a saint from that part of France called Brittany (way out west in Finistère), and a very popular one, too. People still like to call their little boys Hervé around there, and in England the last name of Harvey came back across the channel with the Norman Conquest. I say "back across" because, like most Bretons, Harvey came originally from Britain, from Wales, actually, and his father Hyvarnion was a famous bard, or poet, there. People were leaving Britain for Gaul (as France was still called then) because those scary pagan Anglo-Saxons were taking over the area, even though King Arthur, Sir Gawain, and the rest did their best to keep them out. That's why in Brittany they speak a kind of language like the one people used to speak in Cornwall, in westernmost England, and why the two regions share some saints.

Harvey was a bard like his father, but, like the great Greek bard Homer and unlike his own father, Harvey was blind. When he was still a little boy, his father died and Harvey had to help his mother get by, so he found work, like the biblical bard David, as a shepherd. They say that like many saints, animals were attracted to him. At first he had a big white dog that helped him keep sheep, and later when he sang songs on the streets of town to make a little money, he had a sort of "seeing eye" *wolf* that guarded him from harm. When he was older, Harvey was taken care of by an uncle who was a holy man and who encouraged him to join a monastery school at Plouvien, and so after that Harvey made his songs into hymns or religious ballads, and helped to take care of the children at the school.

Harvey was good with children, as well as with animals, and there are some curious stories about both. One day, his pet wolf got into trouble when it started chewing on a donkey that was helping a little girl plow her mamma's vegetable garden. Harvey took the poor hurt donkey out of the harness, and put in the wolf, sternly ordering it to help the girl plow the rest of the garden, which of course the wolf did! Another time, when Harvey became abbot of the monastery, he was giving a sermon near a pond full of noisy frogs, and ordered them to be quiet, which *they* did!

Harvey's church at Cleder in Brittany used to have in it the very cradle he used to sleep in as a baby, and maybe because of that, or maybe because he was very good at singing lullabies, or maybe because he helped out at a school for little children, or maybe even because he tamed that wolf, and all children are afraid of wolves . . . Saint Harvey became the patron of babies, even though he himself lived to be a very old man, getting holier and holier the older he became, especially after he was abbot of a monastery at Lanhourneau (goodness, these placenames in Brittany can be a mouthful). So if any of you ever have to take care of a noisy, angry baby, remember to call upon Saint Harvey, the patron of babies who quieted the frogs and tamed the wolf.

June: Week Two

IRENAEUS (130–202)
bishop and theologian (June 28)

Have you ever been a member of a "secret club"? Secret clubs have passwords to get in, they meet in secret hideouts, and only *certain* people can get in, and no one is allowed to tell anyone else—especially not "you know who," who is usually you if you're new to class and nobody knows you yet—that the club even exists. It is a fun thing to put together, even though in your stomach there is a bad feeling when the new kid (if it isn't you) looks disappointed and left out.

Well, there used to be a kind of Christian—and maybe a few of them linger around even today—who liked to pretend that the Church was like a secret club, and who said that it wasn't God who ran things, secretly it was the *angels*, all of whom had mysterious tasks to do, and it was to the angels that you had to pray—in exactly the right, secret way—to get God's attention. If you didn't have the correct secret, mysterious incantation, you were just left out of Christianity, that's all. And they called themselves by the mysterious name of *Gnostics*, which just means "the people in the know." And of course, they were dead wrong, and regular Christian folks—and this was in the very early days of the church, even before Christianity became legal—had to work hard and fast to keep the Gnostics' ideas from taking over. Because the great thing about Christianity is that the most important part is very simple and out in the open, and that the only mysterious thing is just that the *simple* part is so amazing and hard to get your mind around. But it is all something you're going to want to read about for yourself, one day.

Now today's saint, Irenaeus, was just the kind of person who might have liked to be a Gnostic, because he was, as one ancient writer put it, "a curious explorer in all kinds of learning." You know how much fun exploring is, and that following your curiosity into all kinds of books and into the amazing places of your imagination is like exploring faraway lands. But Irenaeus knew the difference between exploring and making traps for other explorers, between high ground and quicksand, and he knew that Christianity is for everyone, not just for secret club members.

Irenaeus had patience with people who did things a little differently, as when there was a big argument as to the date of Easter, which he pointed out was not as important as keeping Christianity from becoming a closed club. But with the Gnostics, he was determined, as he said, to "strip the fox." He made his argument as simple as he could: all you need to understand about God, said Irenaeus, is that God has three parts: "The Father is above all, and He is the Head of Christ; Christ, the Word (Logos), is through all things and is Himself the Head of the Church, while the Spirit is in us all, and His is the living water which the Lord gave to those who believe in Him and love Him, and who know that there is one Father above all things and through all things" (as quoted in *Butler's Lives of the Saints:* June; full edition).

Irenaeus learned all this when he was a little boy from another saint, Polycarp, whose famous story of martyrdom is earlier in this book and who himself had been taught by John, the "disciple whom Jesus loved." Irenaeus used to say that he knew what Polycarp taught him not on paper, but in his heart, because (as he is quoted in the *Penguin Book of Saints*) "the things we learn in childhood are part of our souls." I hope some of these good stories become part of you, too.

YEAR TWO

patient and brave and true

Another year gone past, and another begins, with a new chance to make something better of ourselves! This part of the book is particularly full of your everyday type of saint: saints who were nurses, moms, doorkeepers, or had jobs in government. It is rather as you may have sung, in the old hymn "Teach Me, My God and King" derived from the poem "The Elixir," by George Herbert (1633): "All may of thee partake. Nothing can be so mean, Which with this tincture, 'for thy sake,' Will not grow bright and clean . . . Who sweeps a room as for thy laws makes that and the action fine."

august

JEAN-BAPTISTE MARIE VIANNEY ("the Curé d'Ars")
(1786–1859) priest (August 4)
(See Map 10)

There was a sort of simpleness about Jean-Baptiste that clever grown-ups took for stupidity but that everyone else recognized as goodness. For example, they say that when he felt very strongly about something, he wouldn't talk on and on about it, he would just smile . . . or burst out crying! He was so straightforward, when everyone else was being polite and complicated and never admitting to anything, that people said he was "deranged," that is, crazy. His bishop told those people that he wished more of his priests were "deranged" that way!

In religious school, people said Jean-Baptiste was "slow," since it seemed to take him so long to understand perfectly straightforward things like Incarnation, Resurrection, and Transubstantiation. It's true that he didn't know a clever way to avoid being put into Emperor Napoleon's army and marching all over Europe, killing other soldiers and other people's cows, burning their crops and then freezing to death in Russia, so he just decided to hide until he could think of something better . . . and hiding seemed to work just fine.

When he finally did become a priest (or *curé*, in French), Jean-Baptiste was sent to a sad little out-of-the-way village called Ars-sur-Formans, just north of Lyon in the Dombes region of east-central

France, and there he stayed for the next forty years, that is, the rest of his life. He gave the people in his village all of his time and attention, whenever they needed him. Like little Leopold Mandic and a few other saints, he became famous as a confessor, listening to people's problems and giving them good advice on life and faith. He was such a patient listener, and seemed to somehow see into people's hearts, that he wound up spending *eighteen hours a day* listening to confessions of people from all over France who had heard of the saintly "Curé d'Ars." He barely gave himself enough time to preach or eat or sleep.

Sometimes Jean-Baptiste got so worn out with his good work that he tried to go hide in a monastery, but always he felt sorry for his poor villagers when they begged him to come back and always he returned. Other priests—those clever grown-up types—said he was only pretending to be so good, and that he worked so hard just to make them look bad. But everyone else said he was a saint, and that's why we are still talking about him today.

August: Week One

CLARE of ASSISI (1194–1253) abbess (August 11)

There are *so* many stories about Saint Clare, but first you should know that she was from Italy, from the same town as Saint Francis, and so we should call her Chiara, Santa Chiara. Her name comes from an old Latin word meaning "bright," or "famous," and she was both bright *and* famous.

Clare was not only very bright but also very wealthy, and her friend and neighbor Francis was the same. After Francis went off in his shiny new armor to fight the boys from the city over the hill, she thought he was very brave, but after he gave away his armor and told his father he would rather serve God, Clare thought he was braver than ever. Then, when Francis gave his father back everything he'd given him, including his clothes, and a kindly priest gave him a scratchy brown gardener's robe to wear, Clare was proudest of all of him, and she wanted to go and wear a brown robe, too, and live in complete poverty and do God's work, too. Of course, her parents wouldn't allow that, so she ran away from home and Francis helped her start her own group of woman hermits, to pray and teach and help poor people. Today, those nuns are still called Poor Clares, and they still live very simply: some I've heard of even raise miniature horses and sell them to have just enough money so the rest of the nuns in their group can pray all day long if they want to.

They say that Clare once scared an army away from Assisi by her holiness, which is an impressive thing, and that she used to fly mystically—rather like Mary Poppins, but without the help of an umbrella—around from place to place, but there is a simpler story I like best about her. People say that when she was "mother" of her convent, she used to go around at night, tucking the sisters into bed, and that she told them not to be too hard on themselves when they fasted and stayed up late praying. "Our bodies are not made of brass," she would say. She was bright and famous, but kind, too, and *quite* the saint.

August: Week Two

ROCH or ROCCO (14th century)
healer (August 16), and **RESTE**, his dog

You can see churches of San Rocco all over Italy, especially where they had trouble with the plague: there's a very beautifully painted one in Venice that you should visit, if you ever get the chance.

Back in the Bad Old Days when there were hardly any doctors, and what doctors there were had hardly any medicines that worked, people who got sick were in big trouble. And if people had some really catching disease, then just about everyone would catch it and a lot of the oldest and youngest folks would die. Or some really incredibly bad disease like the *bubonic plague* (also known as "The Black Death") would come through town, and nearly every single person would die, and the people who didn't would all blame each other, especially strangers who came from some other town. If you were that stranger, they would say to you, "*You* brought that plague; it's *your* fault!" and then if you didn't die of the plague you would really be in trouble.

That's sort of how Roch—let's call him Rocco, the way they do in Italy, because it's easier to say—got to be a saint. He planned to go a pilgrimage from Montpellier in France to Rome in Italy to see all the churches there and all the holy places on the way. Unfortunately, it was during the Really Bad Old Days of the bubonic plague in the 1300s, and when he arrived in Lombardy in northern Italy, the plague had arrived there before him. Apparently either Rocco knew what medicine to use to help people, or he was specially blessed by God, but he was able to help people and make them better, so he went all over Lombardy helping sick people.

But one day Rocco himself started to feel sick, and he hurried off into the forest so that he wouldn't make anyone else sick. There he was discovered by a big dog—they say her name was *Reste*, which means "stay"—belonging to a local nobleman, and she took care of Rocco, stealing bread from the kitchen to feed him and licking his sores to make them feel better. Some say that the nobleman (named Gottard) followed his dog and brought Rocco into the house to get well, and others say that he put Rocco in prison because he thought he was a French spy who made people sick, until the villagers explained that he was a healer. Then Gottard let Rocco have Reste for his own, and they went off healing people together.

Rocco and Reste became famous and, as with Balaam's donkey, we see that sometimes an animal shows more sense than humans, when it comes to recognizing holiness.

August: Week Two

ALIPIUS (360–430) bishop (August 18)

You may have heard in another story about Augustine of Hippo, that great preacher and writer from North Africa back in Roman times; well, a good friend of his from back home in Thagaste, who studied alongside Augustine and was baptized with him, was Alipius. Alipius became a bishop, too, and visited the Holy Land, and did all sorts of good, churchly things, but he is famous because of a terrible habit that he had as a young man, and that, through a lot of prayer and hard work, he overcame. So he could be thought of as the patron saint of people who have trouble with addictions to smoking or eating too much or whatever.

When Alipius was a law student in Rome—and he was quite a notable student—he was already going to church, and he knew that some things were really bad, and that Christians just shouldn't do them, and that one of the worst of these things was going to watch the gladiatorial games. At those games people would go to the arena (the big one in Rome was called the Coliseum, or the Flavian Amphitheater) all day long and watch people kill animals, or animals kill people, or even people kill people or be executed as criminals, all for "fun," and in honor of the pagan gods . . . it was like a bullfight where they kill the bull, only much worse! Alipius had friends who liked to go watch the games, and they made fun of him when he said he shouldn't go, just because he said that killing was wrong. "Just come along to talk," they said, "you don't have to watch."

So Alipius told himself, "I'm strong, I just won't look." But you can guess right away what happened—he took a tiny peek, and then a longer look and next thing you know, Alipius was yelling for blood, like everybody else. In fact, he became completely obsessed, and had to go to the games all the time, whenever there was a festival. It was all he wanted to do; he didn't want to pray, or eat or sleep, just watch the games. It took him years of effort and all his prayer and faith and confidence, and help from his Christian friends to turn away from it all, to spend his time helping other people and not just sitting around watching people die in interesting ways. But finally he did it, and his victory was part of what made him a saint to people. If Saint Alipius could do it, they figured maybe so could they . . . and they did.

August: Week Three

GENESIUS of ARLES (died 250)
martyr (August 25)

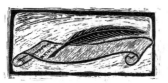 You may remember hearing the story of Cassian, the court stenographer who refused to write down the sentence against Marcellus the Centurion, but do any of you know what a "court stenographer" is? You can probably figure out it has something to do with writing, and indeed it does: it's someone in a courtroom who, when the judge and jury are trying to decide if this person who was arrested really did something wrong or not, writes down everything everyone in the court says—unless the judge says "strike that from the record"—and then types everything up so that people can check later to make sure of what was said. They have to take notes in a special fast way called "shorthand"; it's like a different alphabet for writing sounds quickly.

Now, courtrooms have been around for thousands of years, and so have official court stenographers—since Roman times, for sure—although they didn't use a typewriter until fairly recently; it was all written out in pen and ink. Besides doing courtroom proceedings, the Roman courtroom stenographers had to copy out many, many times—again, by hand—any official notices from the emperor or prefect or whoever was in power, since there weren't any copy machines or printing presses or televisions or radios in those days. Then they would have to glue the notices up at important places in town for people to come and read them. People were supposed to go find the notices and read them, because otherwise they might get in trouble for not knowing the new laws.

One day, in the Roman town of Arles in southern France, an official stenographer named Genesius was handed a set of official wax tablets with an edict on them from Emperor Decius to copy out for immediate posting all over town. So Genesius sat down at his desk, got out his poster pen with its great big nib, some pieces of sturdy parchment, and his big bottle of ink, and broke the seals on the set of tablets. It was a new law saying that "all Christians must be found and killed if they did not give up their faith and worship the emperor's Divine Spirit"! Genesius was a Christian himself, and so were a lot of good Arlesians, and he refused to copy it, just as Cassian had refused to write the "guilty" verdict for Marcellus the Centurion.

Whack, crash! Then and there, Genesius threw down the tablets, tossed his poster pen in its water jar, and ran out of the court building, intending to warn his friends. But the soldiers at the courthouse knew what was in that message, they saw what he'd done, and they set after him hot-foot. They chased him all the way to the banks of the Rhône River, and when they caught him, they arrested him and chopped his head off then and there! Genesius became known as a martyr, because he refused to do what he knew was wrong. So . . . then and there Genesius became a saint.

August: Week Three

MONICA (331–387)
mother (August 27) *(See Map 3)*

In California—where lots of cities and towns are named after saints because that was the custom when the Spanish ruled California—there is a town called Santa Monica, right on the beach by the Pacific Ocean. It is the perfect name for this town, because today's saint spent her last days very happily in the beach town of Ostia, in Italy, just downriver from Rome.

For most of her life, Monica was not so happy. She lived in the little Numidian town called Thagaste, married to a man who hardly spent any time at home with her and their three children, Augustine, Navigius and Perpetus. Then there was the fact that although she was a Christian, all the rest of her family still worshipped Hercules and Venus and the whole pantheon, and went to the big, gory games at the arena. Monica was just *sure* they would never get to heaven if she couldn't get them baptized as Christians. She was so depressed that she even started drinking too much wine to cheer her up, and that just made things worse.

Monica was especially worried about her son Augustine, and followed him over to Italy when he went there to study. Her big worry was that even though he was an intelligent boy and capable of great things, he was living with a girl he wasn't even married to, and now they had a little boy, but Augustine didn't seem to care how sinful they were being . . . she wept about it so much that her priest finally told her, "Monica, it is not possible that the son of so many tears should be lost," and she calmed down a little.

When Augustine's girlfriend died, he seemed to get more serious about things, and finally started reading the Gospels and studying with the famous Bishop Ambrose from Mediolanum (that's Milan, in Italy), and finally he and that no-goodnik friend of his, Alipius, were baptized. Monica was *so* happy, she was finally ready to sail home again to Africa. So she and Augustine went to the port city of Ostia, and while they waited for the boat to be ready to leave, they spent hours talking about everything: about what heaven was like, and the nature of God, and all the other important things. Monica said she felt that her work was over, and later in the week, she died in her sleep, just before her ship was going to sail.

Years and years later, someone came across her grave there in the fields near Ostia, and brought her little coffin up the road to be buried in the big church in Rome that is dedicated to Saint Augustine, where you can see her tomb today. It seems only fair that the woman who did all she could to make her son a saint should be honored as one, too.

August: Week Four

MOSES the MOOR (330–405)
penitent and monk (August 28)
(See Map 3)

They *could* have called this saint "Moses of Egypt," but that might have confused him with the Old Testament Moses, so instead they use a description of how he looked. In the vague way that Europeans describe them, Moors were people from the Sahara in Africa who had fairly dark skin, darker than the people who lived along the coast of the Mediterranean, and Moses certainly looked different from the other monks in his monastery, or the old books wouldn't have brought it up. But another thing about Moses was a gloominess and angriness about him that he had to fight all his life. He himself called it being "dark on the inside," and it was part of why he started out his grownup life as a bandit chief, the leader of men who attacked travelers along the Nile Valley in Egypt.

One time, though, the travelers Moses's band attacked in the desert near Alexandria turned out to have guards with big swords, so most of the bandits were killed and he himself badly hurt. Moses woke up in a monastery nearby, where some kindly monks had patched him up and were taking care of him. As his wounds slowly healed, Moses started helping out around the place, and soon he felt at home among these men of all shades of brown skin in their long white robes.

Moses began to work on his anger and sadness, replacing it with the patience and kindness and cheerfulness he saw around him, and he vowed never to kill or hurt another human being as long as he lived, and to dedicate himself to this God he was learning about. He officially joined the brothers, and soon he was ordained priest, and afterward wore the white robe with the rest. And one day, when another band of robbers attacked their little monastery, Moses was one of the first monks who died, because he would not raise his hands to fight those men. All his dark-inside anger was replaced with a light that even the robbers must have noticed, and perhaps they saw that he was a true saint and were sorry later for what they'd done, just as Moses had been.

August: Week Four

WILLIBALD (700–786) bishop
(July 7, transferred; Walburga's day is May 1)

This Willibald is like a few other saints you may have heard about who came from a whole family of saints. How does that work, do you suppose? Is it because when everyone around you is acting like a saint, it is easier to be one yourself, or maybe (as they say in biology class) there is a gene for saintliness? Or was it something they ate? Anyway, Willibald, his brother, Winebald, and their sister, Walburga, were all saints. Even their father Richard, though he did *not* spell his name with a "w," was revered by some people as a saint. Willibald and his brother and sister came from Wessex (definitely beginning with a "w"), in England, where they had all gotten a good education, but all three of them wound up in Germany, where people were just getting out of the habit of worshipping trees and starting to set up churches and they needed young Christianized folk to help out with all the work.

Their adventures really began when their father decided to take the boys on a pilgrimage to the Holy Land and to Jerusalem in particular. Apparently their mother, Winna, had died and Richard had promised her he would take them. Walburga had to stay home because she had no proper chaperone now that their mother had died. Doesn't *that* sound unfair! Father and the boys got as far as the town of Lucca in Italy when Richard took ill and after some weeks died. The people there had gotten to like Richard, and they called him the "King of the English," gave him a fine funeral and told all sorts of wonderful stories about him. But Willibald and Winebald went on to the Holy Land, and after many adventures they returned to Europe. They collected their sister, then worked on quite a few worthy projects, including a double monastery (meaning for both men and women) at Heidenhelm, where Winebald and Walburga were abbot and abbess, while Willibald became bishop of Eichstatt. And they all were great teachers and preachers and became *worthy* and *wonderful* saints together!

september

September: Week One

GILES AEGIDIUS (sixth century)
hermit (September 1)
and **PETROC** (sixth century) hermit (June 4)

These two saints both lived in France during the sixth century (that is, during the 500s, which we know were the Really Dark Ages) and both did what a lot of saints did in those days: they became hermits and lived in the wilds close to nature and God and far from material temptations of what is called "the World." As we've seen with other hermits, they spent most of their time studying the scriptures and praying and contemplating the mysteries of the faith. As usual, people with all kinds of worries and troubles and sick children would come to them for advice and, they hoped, healing, which of course distracted the hermits from their contemplations. As it happened, one of the mysterious things they were contemplating was how the Lord of the Universe had lowered himself to wash people's feet, so they helped everyone the best they could.

The other thing these two saints had in common was their choice of pets: they both had pet deer! One of the interesting thing you'll discover, next time you go off exploring in the woods, is that if you stay very still for just a bit longer than you usually do, and just patiently look around for a while, a strange thing happens: the birds and beasts who were there just before you came crashing in will relax and start to go about their business. Suddenly you find out there are really a lot of other creatures in there besides you. And if you decide to settle down in that spot for a few months, the creatures will even begin to get curious, come over and check you out, and the less you scare them, the braver they will become until, the next thing you know, they are living in your tent with you or perching comfortably on your arm! This happened to hermits all the time, and our two saints today, as I've mentioned, developed special favorites among their beasts, and people said it was a proof of what holy men they were.

Giles Aegidius—who lived in the south part of France near Arles—had a beautiful pet hind (that's the same thing as a doe, "a female deer"), just as sweet and delicate as you can imagine, with big innocent eyes and long sensitive ears. Petroc's pet—and *he* lived off in Brittany, in Northwest France—was a handsome big stag, a "daddy" deer with a big rack of antlers. Now you know that people have always liked to hunt deer and make venison pies and sausages out of them, and in those days, it was the same, and you guessed it: one day near Arles, King Wamba the Visigoth—a godless heathen!—with his pack of hounds was chasing Saint Giles Aegidius' beautiful doe through the woods, when suddenly the hounds fell silent. Wamba thought maybe they'd found a wild boar, so he shot an arrow through the bushes ahead . . . and there he found Giles Aegidius, his arms around the neck of his doe, an arrow sticking out of his arm and the hounds all silent and amazed. Of course, King Wamba knew this was some kind of holy man, and became a Christian on the spot (and then, I expect, he took the arrow out of Giles Aegidius' arm).

Petroc's story is much the same, only instead of a single king there was a whole bunch of hunters with spears, and Petroc very bravely stood in front of his friend the stag, and they were all so impressed by this that he converted them all right there. But Petroc, they say, also "converted" a dragon that had been terrorizing the neighborhood: I suppose that means he convinced him to be a kinder, gentler dragon henceforth. Good old Petroc and Giles Aegidius!

September: Week One

CIARAN of CLONMACNOIS (516–549)
abbot (September 9)

and CUTHMAN of STEYNING (ninth century)
hermit (February 8)

Two saint stories bunched together usually means we don't know much about them but they are too good to leave out, and they have something in common. That is all true of these chaps . . . I say "chaps," because that is a rather British thing to call people, and these were both rather British people, or nearly: Ciaran (that's pronounced *KEER-ahn*) was actually Irish, from the Shannon River area, and Cuthman was an Englishman from Sussex.

Both of these chaps, I say, started out as wanderers, each finally settling down and building a church, or, in Ciaran's case, a big monastery: Ciaran was the bigger wanderer *and* the bigger builder. He started out as a lad, wandering on the roads of Ireland, driving along his brown cow in front of him. She kept him in milk and butter, which he sold to other wanderers for whatever else he needed. Ciaran went from monastery to monastery, learning this and that, but they always sent him away again because he gave away too much of their food and goods away to the poor. "We cannot suffer you here with us," the monks would say (obviously they were not saints). Later, he settled with Saint Enda, who taught him all he wanted to know and who didn't mind his generosity. Finally, Ciaran himself started a monastery at Clonmacnoise, near Shannon in

County Meath, Ireland, with a fine library and school, where everyone went who wanted to study, and he never sent anyone away.

Cuthman, our second saint, didn't have a cow to drive and he didn't have Saint Enda, but he did wander around, and he did have his dear old mother, who was always good company, and who gave him good advice. As a child he kept his father's sheep and got some religious training at a nearby monastery, but when his father died, he had to sell the sheep and try to make a living on the road, preaching a little and doing odd jobs to make ends meet. His mother was a little bit feeble, and couldn't keep up with all his fast walking, so he made her a sort of wheelbarrow-couch, and fitted it out with handles to guide it and a rope to go around his shoulders and take most of the weight, and off they went together down the road, quite happily really, because they had each other for company.

When they came to the little town of Steyning, the people there took such a liking to Cuthman and his dear old mother that they begged them to stay and that he be their priest, and they even built him a little church and a house for him and his mother (sorry, his "dear old mother"), and there they stayed in peace and contentment the rest of their days. The people of Steyning (a little town just inland from Shoreham-by-the-Sea in Sussex, east of Brighton) are still proud of "their" Saint Cuthman, as you can see when you happen to visit there. Two saintly wandering "chaps," Ciaran and Cuthman.

September: Week Two

PULCHERIA (399–453)
empress (September 10) *(See Map 3)*

Pulcheria was the empress of Byzantium (the entire Eastern Roman Empire) and she lived in the capital city of Constantinople. Her name—as any Latin students can tell you—means "beautiful lady." I think that many women and girls would like to be named "Gorgeous," and to rule a huge empire, but the truth is that to do it well is a huge amount of work. The easy way to go about it would be to get all your servants to do everything for you while you sit in your throne room eating cakes all day long, ignoring everyone's problems until everyone is so angry with you they break into your palace and chop you into small pieces. But, you know what they say, "pretty is as pretty does," and Pulcheria ruled the *hard* way: she made sure all her governors were treating all her subjects fairly and that her generals were keeping the borders safe from barbarians, and even more . . . Since Byzantium was now the capital of the Christian Roman Empire and bishops had to consult with her, she also had to make sure that her *Church* officials were behaving properly. Then there was the fact that for a long time her baby brother was officially the emperor, and she had to take good care of him, make sure he had a good education, and see that his empire was kept safe.

What helped Pulcheria deal with all that pressure was what is generally called a "strong religious faith," which means that when she needed extra patience or strength, she prayed to God for it, and got what she needed to get along. One time she needed all her faith and her sharp mind to solve a problem: her counselors insisted that she should get married, but she didn't really care to. She had actually always wanted to be a nun and spend all day quietly praying in a convent far away from men, for one thing. And she also knew that if she got married, she couldn't count on her husband taking as good care of the empire as she did herself, and if they had children he might want *his* children to rule, instead of her baby brother. So Pulcheria did the next best thing: she married the man she trusted most in the empire, her best general, Marcian, on the condition that they live separately like brother and sister, but rule jointly. They actually ruled "very harmoniously" we are told, and Marcian certainly helped her bear the load of ruling everything, while keeping her brother safe. With a trusty husband helping to keep the empire going, Pulcheria even had extra time to build a bunch of churches, help the poor and continue to be a good judge in her law courts. She definitely *earned* her sainthood!

September: Week Two

NOTBURGA (1265–1313)
servant (September 13)

Nowadays, when a farm girl grows up, she might go off to the city and get a job. In the Olden Days, there weren't many cities, so peasant girls (that's "farm girls" of long ago) would start by going to the nearby castle of the local Lord So and So to get a job working in the kitchen. It was a hard life: you had to wake up earlier than anyone else in the castle to light the fires so that when everyone else woke up there were warm rooms and a hot stove to cook breakfast on, whenever Lord So and So felt like having breakfast. And then, no matter how late the lords and ladies stayed up at night, the kitchen maid had to stay up later, to do their dishes, and finally to put out the fires for the night. That's the way it was when our Saint Notburga worked as a kitchen maid for Count Henry, in the castle of Rattenberg (which sounds like "mountain of rats," so I wonder what the kitchen was like) up in the snowy mountains of the Tyrol of Austria, about a third of the way to Salzburg from Innsbruck. But Notburga was just the girl for a hard job like that:

cheerful, quick, dependable, but on the other hand very serious about going to church services on Sundays *no matter what.*

Sometimes Notburga got into trouble for her Christian generosity. Once, for example, the cook told her to take the leftover food from the count's feast to feed the pigs in the pigsties, and instead Notburga gave it to the poor people who were waiting around outside in the cold. When the countess found out, she was furious! "Do you want our pigs to starve?" she demanded. Notburga knew from her years on the farm that pigs could be taken out into the forest to eat acorns, but that people could not, and she told the countess so. Naturally, the countess sent Notburga away *at once*!

So then Notburga went to work on a farm belonging to the count, and there she worked hard, too, cutting more wheat at harvest time with her sharp little sickle than anyone else, but she would *not* harvest on a Sunday: "The Sabbath is a day for rest and reading my Bible," she insisted stubbornly. When the foreman insisted that she get out there and cut wheat, they say that her little sickle flew miraculously up in the air out of reach, and refused to come down until Monday! Meanwhile, at the castle, the countess was sorry she had sent Notburga away, as nobody else wanted to get up so early or to stay up so late. She asked Notburga to come back, and if Notburga was willing to take the pigs out to the forest to forage for acorns, the poor people could have all the leftover food. Notburga was glad to come back, work hard, and do good things for the rest of her life at Rattenberg, so that today she is the favorite saint of people thereabouts. She is also respected by farm workers and kitchen maids everywhere, as you may imagine.

September: Week Three

JOSEPH of CUPERTINO (1603–1663)
mystic (September 18) *(See Maps 7 & 23)*

You know a little about Saint Francis of Assisi already, and his special day is coming up in October. You may have also seen paintings of the Franciscan monks in their scratchy brown robes, their funny shaved heads (with the O-shaped ring of hair left on top) and plain sandals, wandering around preaching. You may even know that many of them came over from Europe to the Southwest of the United States when it was Spanish territory, and founded mission churches called San Antonio, San Francisco, and San Diego, which later became cities. One of those missions, in California, was called *San José de Cupertino*, which gave its name to the two cities of Cupertino and San Jose, was named after the mysterious Franciscan monk I'll tell you about today.

Nobody would have thought that Joseph—or Giuseppe, as they called him where he came from, in Italy—would ever have even one city named after him. His family came from the little town of Cupertino near Brindisi in southern Italy, and was so poor that Joseph was born in a stable, just like Baby Jesus, but he was an unhealthy child, and seemed stupid. In Italy, they have always loved giving people nicknames, even if they are sometimes a little rude, and they liked to call Joseph *Bocca Aperta*, "the gaper," because he would suddenly seem lost in thought, and stared off into space with his mouth open. But what was happening was that he was seeing heavenly visions, and his spirit seemed to fly off elsewhere. He got some work at the stable of a monastery called *La Grottella* ("the little cave"), and although he couldn't read or write, Joseph had a natural ability to pray, and continued to have more and more amazing visions.

Soon, even more mystical things began occurring: just like some Buddhist monks, Joseph had the ability to actually *lift off the floor into the air* when he was gripped by one of these visions: apparently there are some well-documented instances of this happening! This, added to his ability to foretell the future, soon brought hundreds of curious people to the door of the monastery, and the monks of La Grottella soon got tired of him, even though when he was on the ground he was always a hard-working, unselfish monk who never complained. Finally, he was hidden away in a little monastery on the coast of Italy far to the north, near Ancona, where he could live out his life in peace. Joseph of Cupertino: a mystery, but definitely a saint.

September: Week Three

PHOCAS (third century)
gardener (September 22) *(See Map 3)*

All we have for this story is a definite church at a definite place, and a charming but sad legend that connects a name to that place, but the date and the details are a bit vague. I happen to believe the legend about today's saint: it explains everything, and it really could have happened like this . . .

There is an ancient town on the southern shore of the Black Sea, called Sinope in Greek times, and Sinop today. It stands on a triangular peninsula of land that juts out into the sea, and it has been important to sailors and to sea trade ever since the Greeks founded it, three thousand years ago or more. Back in the time of our story, this part of what is the modern country of Turkey was known as *Cappadocia Pontus*, in the eastern part of the Roman Empire back when it was still against the law to practice Christianity.

In Sinope back in those days there lived a quiet man named Phocas. Later, he would become famous and even have a Christian Roman emperor named after him, but then he was just a market gardener: that is, he had a nice piece of rich land that overlooked the sea, where he planted all sorts of fruits and vegetables that he could sell to the markets in town, or straight out of his garden, at a little stand by the road. He grew lettuce, and celery, and cucumbers, onions and even some flowers to sell—but no peppers or tomatoes: those hadn't come from America yet. He particularly liked digging in the rich black soil, making furrows in it for water to run off and hoeing it to keep the weeds down.

Another thing Phocas was good at was praying and reading the scriptures, because he was one of those secret Christians the emperor was always after. One night, some troops from far away came to the little house where he lived on the edge of town, next to his fields. They were tired, hungry and angry. They told him that they had heard there was a Christian in this town by the name of Phocas, but they had asked all over town and no one could tell them—or *would* tell them—where he lived. Could he possibly help them?? "Well," said Phocas, "actually I do know him and can easily help you find him in the morning. But wouldn't you like to have some dinner and bed down in the storeroom for the night?" He seemed so helpful and sympathetic, and they were so exhausted from searching the whole wretched town, that they were glad to take him up on his offer. Phocas gave them a good dinner of eggs, onions, and figs from his own little farm, and a loaf of fresh bread from the baker in town with a little fresh olive oil to mop up with it, and then pulled out some spare straw that he used to keep the weeds down, and got them bedded down for the night. He spent the rest of the night digging in his garden.

In the morning, Phocas regretfully told them that *he* was their man, and that he had saved them some trouble by digging his own grave. They were embarrassed, but thanked him very courteously for his help and then sadly killed him on the spot, burying him in that grave in his garden. Later, a big church was built right there, in his memory, and people could see it from far out at sea and all over the coast. So this is why he became the patron saint of both gardeners and sailors (something that has confused people, apparently)—our saintly Saint Phocas!

September: Week Four

SERGIUS of RADONEZH (1314–1392)
abbot (September 25)

By now you all know what hermits are, so you won't be confused when I tell you that, when he was twenty years old, Sergius and his brother Stephen went off into the woods to become hermits. Once upon a time their family had been wealthy, but not any more, and when their parents died, they took to living in the nearby woods. After three years studying scriptures and living in the wild, they took vows to become real monks, and started their own religious community there in the Christmas-tree and birch woods of Russia, getting closer to God and nature, and building up the place with their own hands.

Sergius was the leader of their little band, and as new men joined it he had more and more work keeping everyone at peace with one another, keeping them from arguing and being selfish. As always, Sergius didn't mind doing all kinds of work around the monastery—sometimes he was a cook or a baker, oftentimes when there was wheat to be ground he was a miller, too. At other times he was a tailor, making clothes for the monks, and always a carpenter, helping to build whatever was needed at the monastery. Soon they moved to an old ruined monastery and fixed it up, calling it *Troitsa Lavra*, or "Holy Trinity Monastery," and then founded more monasteries after that.

When he got to be so well known it became Sergius's job to try to keep peace between the crabby and selfish princes of Russia, and to try to keep them from being cruel to their people and to give them good advice. When Prince Dmitry of Moscow asked him, in 1380, whether to go ahead and fight the Tatars, who had occupied Russia for more than a hundred years, Sergius told him to do it; their power was fading and clearly the moment had finally come to throw them out. Sure enough, the Russians were victorious, and Sergius became not only more famous, but something of a hero, too. Like most saints, Sergius (or Sergey, as the Russians call him) was kind, helpful, and humble. Like just a few other saints, Sergius also experienced a mystical state in which his face would be transfigured, as Christ's had been, actually radiating a dazzling light! An authentic saint, our glowing Saint Sergius, who did all he knew how—and that was a lot—to help those around him.

September: Week Four

LIOBA (700–780) abbess (September 28)

Back in the eighth century, things were really hopping in England, religiously speaking. Through the hard work of the missionaries who had been sent from Italy by Pope Gregory the Great a hundred years earlier, along with that of various kings, bishops, and everyday-folk since, the Anglo-Saxons were now exporting saints back to the rest of northern Europe. One of the most successful and accomplished of these saints was Lioba of Wessex.

Lioba was in charge of a bunch of what one book delightfully calls "well-domesticated women" (*Penguin Book of Saints,* 226). These were the sort of women who, when faced with an enormous challenge, would just size it up, roll up their sleeves, put on their aprons, and start cooking enough food for three hundred, or organize enough bedding for an entire village, then sew enough blankets for an entire territory and then, because they knew how to read and write and speak Latin and Greek, they would help out the local priest with his paperwork! They were sent by their boss, Abbess Tetta of Wimborne, to help future saint Boniface of Crediton (another English sort) do ministry work among the Germans.

Everyone should name their girls after Lioba. She was not only beautiful, always smiling and patient and sweet and generous, but nothing ever seemed to upset her. She was wise, too, and learned, always freshening up her faith with some reading from the scriptures. Everyone for miles around knew they could count on Lioba absolutely, to help them out of any difficulty; bishops and princes came to her for advice. When she was a very old lady, letting younger folk do most of the bustling about and mostly staying at home in the abbey herself, sometimes the young wife of the future Emperor Charlemagne would come to visit and give her a kiss on her soft, rosy old cheek. No doubt she asked Lioba what a future empress should know about the business of ruling a country and encouraging people's religious faith. And no doubt Lioba told her, which may have made all the difference to the future of Europe, if you know your history. A "well-domesticated" saint, Lioba, fit to turn medieval chaos into a homier place.

october

BAVO ("ALLOWIN") (died 653)
penitent (October 1)

Brabant, as anyone from Belgium knows, is the rich territory right in the north-central part of Belgium, combined with the south-central part of the Netherlands. It is famous for a special kind of powerful horse, called Brabant after the place, good for carrying knights in full armor or pulling big, heavy loads. It is also famous as the place that Saint Bavo came from, long ago.

Bavo was a young nobleman, who started out his life in Brabant being called Allowin, but he got the nickname "Bavo" from his friends. Now, I don't know what "Bavo" means, but if it means "selfish, lazy, good-for-nothing, interested only in hunting and enjoying himself" then it is the perfect name for him! He had lots of beautiful clothes and great hunting hounds and ate only the finest food. The result was that he ran out of money fairly often, and when he did, he would just *sell some of his servants* to his neighbors to get more. He had a good wife, and a sweet little daughter, but he would much rather go out to parties than stay home with "boring" people like them.

Then his wife died, and he suddenly realized that nothing he could do would bring her back; he couldn't sell a servant, or chase her down with his dogs or get her to come back to his wrist like his falcon . . . she was gone forever, and he felt that he'd hardly had the chance to get to know her. He could try to be a better father for the little girl she'd left behind, though, so Bavo finally started to do the things his wife had always tried to get him to, but he hadn't listened to her in those days. He started going to the church in the nearby town of Ghent along with his little girl, and after he heard a really super-duper sermon from Saint Amand there, he decided to give away all his fine clothes and possessions to the poor, and spent his time helping Amand any way he could. Once he had earned enough money to set his daughter up comfortably, he retired from the world and became a monk, spending the rest of his life trying to make up for the first part of it.

They say that one day Bavo met one of his former servants in the marketplace, someone he had sold into serfdom to pay some debt. He asked the man to help him make amends for what he had done by having the former servant lead him, Bavo, around the marketplace on a rope like a slave, to show what an evil man he had been in those days. Saint Bavo became such a good man that people called him a saint during his lifetime, and they almost forgot what he'd been like before.

October: Week One

EDWIN (585–633) king (October 12)

Here is a bit of English history: Saint Edwin was king of Northumbria before that place was famous for its saints, he being one of the first. How ironic that it was he who took over the lands of Ethelfrith, thus banishing young Prince Oswald (and future saint—see August, Week One of *Song of the Saints*) to Scotland. Edwin wished to marry a certain Ethelburga of Kent, sister of King Edbald of Kent, and all those Kentish princesses were flaming Christians, who wouldn't budge without at least one bishop and great numbers of monks at their side. Edwin himself was a pagan, but he saw no difficulty in asking Paulinus, bishop of York, to come to his court at Yeavering as a chaplain to Ethelburga. He even hinted that he might become a Christian at some future date . . . so that was all right, and Ethelburga became his queen. There was the not-so-small problem that he had to divorce a previous wife, a princess of Mercia, to do this, and that her family was furious and her cousin Cadwallon would want revenge . . . but that comes later.

Meanwhile, after many victorious battles, Edwin sat down in his great hall at Yeavering with his thanes (those are, as you may recall from elsewhere, freeborn, landowning companions) and chief men to discuss whether to convert to Christianity. It seemed to him that Paulinus's prayers had given him many of his victories and that over-all it was attractive faith that explained much about life and the here-after. It was at this point that a very famous conversation took place, recorded in the English History of the Venerable Bede (drawn here from the Internet Medieval Sourcebook of Fordham University). First, the chief druid priest, named Coifi, spoke up:

> "I have served the gods of the trees all my life, and they have certainly not rewarded me with fame and riches as your god has rewarded you; I feel as if all my years of service have been wasted, and would gladly follow a different faith, if it seemed to be the true one."

One of Edwin's chief men stood up then, and added that:

> "The life of man is like the flight of a sparrow, in and out of the win-dows of the great hall at Yeavering: outside all is dark and wet, and then briefly here is a place of warmth and light and then out it goes into the dark again. So this life of man appears for a short space, but of what went before, and of what is to follow we are utterly ignorant. If, therefore, this new doctrine contains something more certain, it seems justly to deserve to be followed."

The rest agreed, and they all determined to become Christians, and Coifi undertook to destroy his old temple and images with his own hands. And, although King Edwin later had his head chopped off in battle by his rival, the ferocious King Cadwallon of Wales (remember him from two paragraphs ago?), and Edwin's poor head was guarded by his pet wolf until his friends could find and bury it, he had already begun a tradition in Northumbria of faith and good government that would help establish it as foremost in Christian studies during the Dark Ages of Europe, outside Rome. Good old King Edwin!

October: Week Two

MARGUERITE d'YOUVILLE (1701–1771)
wife and foundress (October 16)

Not all saints get to go off to religious school and then become bishops and preach happily ever after. Some would really like to, but they have to leave school early to help their parents and brothers and sisters get by, and then, if they are girls, they are strongly encouraged to get married and have another family to take care of . . . then it is extra hard to find time to serve God, too. But if they do manage it, that's what makes them saints, as I think we've seen before.

Marguerite went to convent school—an Ursuline Sisters school—for just two years before she had to leave school to help her mother to raise their family after her father died. This all happened in old Québec city in the times when it was a French territory, which is why they still speak French in that part of Canada. You may have read about Québec in that great Willa Cather book *Shadows on the Rock,* so you can imagine what it was like there in those days. Marguerite married a man named François who treated her very roughly and spent all their money on wine. Then he died, and left Marguerite with two little sons and a terrible debt to pay off to the bank.

So Marguerite set to work running a little shop to pay the debt and support her little boys, and she did it *so* neatly that soon they were living fairly well, and it was time for her to take on a new project. For a long time—even while her husband was alive, and it had made him very angry with her—Marguerite had been helping her even poorer neighbors, washing their clothes and even washing *them* when they fell sick and needed care. She discovered that she wasn't afraid to ask rich people to give money to her neighbors if they needed help, and that the rich people trusted her to do the right thing. When she also discovered that there were condemned criminals who weren't even buried properly, she asked for money to help with that, too, and people were glad to give. She took into her own house children that had been abandoned by their parents, and then started the first orphanage in all of North America for them.

When her little boys grew up they became priests, and Marguerite was finally free to become a nun herself, and start an organization called The Grey Nuns of Montréal to continue her work with the poor, including a big new hospital that is still helping people today. She believed that if you really needed something, "Providence provides for everything." But she also worked and prayed really hard while she waited for Providence, like any good saint.

October: Week Two

BERTILLA BOSCARDIN (1888–1922)
nurse (October 20) *(See Map 14)*

It seems as though the people around many saints think they are foolish or weak to have such simple, strong faith, and certainly Bertilla had trouble with that. The grown-ups didn't seem to appreciate how wonderful a person she really was, but the children could tell, because, as all of you know, it is very hard to fool children about something like that.

Bertilla didn't do very well in school as a child: they said she was not very bright, her mind was not on her classwork and she always seemed to be daydreaming. But she wanted very much to help people, and so she went to work as a nurse with the nuns at Vicenza, near where she grew up in northern Italy. Since she was so quiet and gentle, they put Bertilla in the children's ward of the hospital. Back in those days, the medicines were especially nasty, and the cures didn't often work, and everything they did to you in the hospital seemed to hurt a lot, but Bertilla always made the patients at the hospital feel better, somehow, in spite of everything.

During the First World War, in 1917, Vicenza was bombed, but nothing could frighten Bertilla away from her sick children. After the war, a rather foolish matron took over the hospital and decided she didn't like all the fuss people were making about how wonderful Bertilla was, so she sent her off to work in the hospital laundry for a while. Bertilla went very patiently, and did a good job there, but the children missed her so terribly that even the doctors began to notice that they weren't getting well so quickly. So, when they decided to open a ward for children who had to be kept in special separate rooms (because their illness was so catching), they sent for Nurse Bertilla to be in charge. Immediately, things began to improve.

But then Bertilla herself got sick, and they had no choice but to operate on her right away. Back in those days, these sorts of things were much more dangerous, and Bertilla died. But the strange thing was that the children found that if they just *thought hard* about Bertilla, they would get to feeling better, and that is one reason that she was officially made a saint, fairly quickly for modern times: miracles always speed these things along!

October: Week Three

SEVERINUS BOETHIUS (480–584)
philosopher and martyr (October 23)

If today's saint seems to have a long, complicated name to you, then you need to know that his full name was much longer: *Anicius Manlius Severinus Boethius,* a proper old Roman name for a proper old Roman, at a time when the most proper Romans had at last become Christians. Boethius was not a priest or a bishop or a monk; he was a lawyer, a married man, and a great scholar, writing about everything from religion to music, mathematics to geography to scientific engineering (he liked to design clocks, especially). He also translated the works of Plato, Aristotle, Pythagoras, Ptolemy and Euclid from Greek into Latin, which is how he learned about all those things he was interested in, and which was why, for the rest of the Medieval period, even people who knew only Latin could still read what these old Greek philosophers had written, thanks to Boethius.

Boethius also became an important political leader in Italy when Emperor Theodoric was in control there. Theodoric was a good leader, most of the time, but also a bit of a barbarian, and he practiced a different sort of Christianity (called Arianism) than Boethius did, so he was already a bit suspicious of our saint. Theodoric's people, the Visigoths, had conquered Italy, and they still didn't quite understand the old Roman way of doing things. So, when Boethius *defended* a man in court who had been accused of plotting against Theodoric, the emperor was furious! Nowadays, we know that everyone deserves to have a lawyer, whether he or she is guilty or not, but according to Theodoric's view of things, anyone who would dare to defend this evil spy must himself be guilty of treason, and he threw Boethius into prison. The only person who dared to speak up for Boethius was his father-in-law, but the emperor wouldn't listen to him; he decided to kill Boethius in the most horrible way he could think of (I don't know what that way was, and I don't care to find out).

While he was waiting for that horrible day to come, Boethius had some time in his prison cell to think. He collected his thoughts about his faith, and then his thoughts about all the amazing things he had learned about the world and all the people in it, and wrote his famous book, *The Consolation of Philosophy*, in good, complicated Latin, and which later was translated into English by everyone from King Alfred the Great to Geoffrey Chaucer to Queen Elizabeth the First. As a good Christian dying for justice at the hands of a semi-Christian Arian, Boethius was considered a Christian martyr, but he is really most famous as a philosopher, after writing that book—if a very saintly philosopher.

October: Week Three

FELIX of THIBIUCA (died July 15, 303) martyr (October 24) and the SCILLITAN MARTYRS (died 180) (July 17)

As is usual with early Christian martyrs, we don't know too much about these saints beyond how they died, where and why. These particular martyrs died because they were so attached to the Holy Scriptures that they carried secretly about from house to house, which is where they held church in those days. Copied out carefully by hand, these scriptures generally included the four Gospels, the Acts of the Apostles, and the letters of Paul, Peter and some of the other apostles—basically what we call today the New Testament of the Bible—and people would defend these scriptures with their lives.

Since Christians had to meet secretly for worship in those Bad Old Days, the elements of the Eucharist and the Gospels had to be carried secretly from place to place. They would use the living room for the sermon, the garden fountain or bathhouse for baptism, and the dining room for their communion meals. At some point in every service, there would be a reading from the scriptures, brought along in a leather satchel from the last house of worship.

The Romans, who were trying to get rid of all the Christians, had heard how important these writings were to them, and were always on the watch to confiscate and destroy the scriptures if possible. Unfortunately, when our earlier batch of martyrs were captured in a little town near Carthage called Scillium, their leader, Speratus, was caught "holding the bag," literally. The Romans asked him what these writings were, and he told them that they were "the sacred books and letters of a righteous man named Paul." The Christians were given a month to think about whether to repudiate all knowledge of those books, at the end of which, when the Scillitan martyrs (as they're called) all refused to, Speratus said "Thanks be to God!" and they all went happily off to die.

Bishop Felix of Thibiuca also died at Carthage, about one hundred twenty years later, but he had carefully *hidden* the books and refused to hand them over to be burned, preferring to be burned himself, saying, "It is better to obey God rather than men!" These saints have given us something to think about next time we handle a Bible, don't you think?

October: Week Four

CRISPIN and CRISPINIAN (died around 285)
cobblers and martyrs (October 25)

Today's saints were cobblers, that is, they made and mended shoes for a living. We know they were particularly popular among cobblers of Medieval times and that they seemed to have lived in Soissons, in France, since they were even more popular there. People said they were brothers who came to France from

Rome during the Bad Old Days of the persecutions of Christians, and when they were caught, they were kept in a cave for a little while and then had their heads chopped off.

But the reason most English-speaking people are familiar with this pair of saints is that their day marked one of the Great Days of English History, to wit, the Battle of Agincourt, part of the Hundred Years' War Joan of Arc helped to end. This battle was fought on French soil by a smaller English force armed with longbows against a much greater number of French knights on horseback and their crossbowmen. So incredibly large were the French losses and so amazingly few were the English that English King Henry V declared that the victory was God's, not theirs, and had the prayer *Non nobis domine, sed nomini tuo da gloriam* ("Not To Us, O Lord, But To Your Name Give The Glory") sung to the stirring tune now called Agincourt in honor of the occasion. (This tune is now generally sung with the words "O Love, How Deep, How Broad, How High.") Before the battle, when his brave but frankly dubious captains stood around him, Henry gave a famous speech to hearten them, and Shakespeare's version of it (with "Crispian" instead of "Crispinian" because it scans better) has roused rabble ever since! *(Note: Consider asking older student volunteers to read the following excerpt.)*

> *This day is called the feast of Crispian:*
> *He that outlives this day, and comes safe home,*
> *Will stand a tip-toe when the day is named,*
> *And rouse him at the name of Crispian.*
> *He that shall live this day, and see old age,*
> *Will yearly on the vigil feast his neighbours,*
> *And say 'To-morrow is Saint Crispian:'*
> *Then will he strip his sleeve and show his scars.*
> *And say 'These wounds I had on Crispin's day.'*
> *Old men forget: yet all shall be forgot,*
> *But he'll remember with advantages*

What feats he did that day: then shall our names.
Familiar in his mouth as household words
Harry the king, Bedford and Exeter,
Warwick and Talbot, Salisbury and Gloucester,
Be in their flowing cups freshly remember'd.
This story shall the good man teach his son;
And Crispin Crispian shall ne'er go by,
From this day to the ending of the world,
But we in it shall be remember'd;
We few, we happy few, we band of brothers;
For he to-day that sheds his blood with me
Shall be my brother; be he ne'er so vile,
This day shall gentle his condition:
And gentlemen in England now a-bed
Shall think themselves accursed they were not here,
And hold their manhoods cheap whiles any speaks
That fought with us upon Saint Crispin's day.

King Henry V, Act IV, Scene III, Lines 43–70

October: Week Four

GERARD MAJELLA (1726–1755)
porter (October 16) *(See Map 23)*

and **ALPHONSUS RODRIGUEZ** (1531–1617)
porter (October 30) *(See Map 6*

 October has two porter saints, and there is at least one other, besides, in a different month. It's interesting, but maybe not entirely surprising when you consider the popular image of Saint Peter at the gates of heaven. I

think that this kind of porter is not the gentleman who helps you with your bags, but the old-fashioned kind of porter, a servant stationed at the front door. In the olden days a lot of houses didn't have locks, or at least the big front doors were kept unlocked and wide open during the daytime, so there was a servant who sat in a little room by the front door to see who went in or out. It was a low-paying job, you were often cold and lonely, and you couldn't really leave the house, but perhaps you can imagine why this is a good place to be a saint: you are humble, you let in some people because you think the master of the house ought to see this person (whether the master thinks so or not), and you are always available to listen to people's troubles, either from the street or from inside the house.

Saint Gerard Majella, from Muro Lucano near Potenza in southern Italy, was one of those holy innocents considered to be too dreamy-eyed to have any wits. Many of these "witless" folks became saints when people realized that their "dreams" were really vivid visions of heaven, and that they had other-worldly powers of perception, prayer and healing. Before Gerard became porter of a monastery, he had been a good tailor's apprentice, but it seemed as though he would *never* concentrate hard enough to manage to be a tailor. As a porter, he listened carefully to all those who came to the door with their troubles for the monks, and sometimes he was able to solve their problems before they even got past the door: he seemed to be able to look right into people's hearts and see exactly the trouble there.

Saint Alphonsus Rodriguez, our second porter, seemed to be just an unlucky fellow who had lost his wife, his two little children and his business all in one year. He retired from the world after that, to help out at a Jesuit college on the island of Majorca, off Spain. Alphonsus always seemed to have time to listen to all your problems, helping when he was asked to help, whatever needed doing. He spent some of his long hours at the front gate in prayer and study, and even wrote a few books on his spiritual life. When young Peter Claver came to Alphonsus for advice as to where to go and what to do with his burning desire to help people, Alphonsus suggested that instead of going to Morocco to become a martyr for his faith, he should go to America and save slaves from their fates, instead. So he did just that, and became a saint in his turn, as we've seen.

Gerard Majella and Alphonsus Rodriguez: both porters, both saints!

November

MARTIN de PORRES (1579–1639)
porter (November 3)

For those of you who like stories of porter-saints, here is another good one. We have noticed that porters seem to have a lot of time on their hands, guarding the front door and all, and can use that time for reading or praying or chatting. This porter did all that, but he also did odd jobs, whatever needed doing at the monastery where he worked, so perhaps he was a little like that *other* kind of porter who carries things for people, like luggage porters at the airport.

Today's saint was also a barber, a farm-laborer, a hospital nurse, and an almoner (that's someone from the monastery who would deliver money or food to needy people—one of Martin's favorite jobs). Saint Martin de Porres lived in Lima, Peru; his father was a Spanish landowner who didn't marry his mother, a local Indian girl. So most people looked down on Martin and called him a "halfbreed dog." But Martin kept a cheerful outlook: "Dogs are useful," he used to say, "and pretty smart, too." When he was old enough, he went to work at the Dominican friary (or monastery; the Dominicans were called "friars" but they were still monks), doing—as I said—whatever needed doing that they'd rather not do themselves, or couldn't.

At the gate of the friary, Martin met a lot of sick people and beggars who needed help, and he would bring them into the little hospital they had there at the friary and find them a bed, give them a bath and a meal. Martin would also stand at the gate and look out at the animals in the street, and if there was an overloaded donkey or a limping horse or a sick dog or cat, he would go out into the street to try to help them out, to bandage them up . . . you can imagine that he ended by having a lot of pets in his little guard-house! Also, while he sat there, people came up to him for advice: he was always sensible and kind, and never gave away a secret. A shy girl might come to him to see if he could help her get a dowry together, so she could marry, and he always seemed to know a rich person—to whom he had *also* given delicate help and diplomatic advice—to ask, very privately, for a donation.

Like many other saints, porters included, Martin had visions of heaven as he sat there praying in his little guard-house, and sometimes he was so rapt in these experiences that he wouldn't hear what you were saying. By the time he died, he was old and beloved, and everyone called him *Padre de Caridad*, "Father of Charity," and they all asked the Church to make him an official saint. But naturally, Saint Martin de Porres just called himself "Old Mutt," and "I'll do whatever needs doing!" was always his motto!

November: Week One

The FOUR CROWNÉD ONES (died 306)
stonemasons and martyrs (November 8)
(See Maps 3, 4 & 24)

This is a fairly straightforward story, but there is an interesting twist to it: in the beginning there were five in the group, not four. Their names were Simpronian, Claudius, Nicostratus, Castorius and Simplicius. They were all arrested as Christians, but only four were "crowned;" why is that? Actually, it's not much of a mystery, since a perfectly good legend explains exactly what happened . . .

These five men lived long ago in the town of Sirmium (modern Sremska Mitrovica, in Croatia), in the Roman province of Pannonia on the plain on the west side of the Danube River, which, if it existed today, would include a little of Austria, Croatia, Hungary, Serbia and Montenegro, Slovenia, Slovakia and Bosnia and Herzegovina—which just goes to show how much history happened there after it stopped being Pannonia! Anyway, in those days, Sirmium was an important Roman town and a big building project was started to prove just *how* important. A huge temple was being built there in honor of the Roman god of health, Aesculapius, by orders of Emperor Diocletian.

Diocletian was worried because there were so many of those illegal Christians on the work site, and he was certain they hated his favorite gods, and would try some funny business. So he kept an eye out, and sure enough, he heard that these five men—all of them top-notch stonecutters—had been engaged to do the columns and decorations, but absolutely refused to work on the statue of the god! What nerve! So he had them dragged in and told them they had better hurry up and curse this Christ of theirs and get back to work or you could be sure some horrible deaths were coming their way.

Now is where the "four" thing comes in: it turns out that *one* of the men, Simplicius, had no problem with cursing Christ at all. He had heard that the other four were the best in the business, and he figured that if he wanted to join them he'd better say he was a Christian, too, so now he was happy to swear anything the emperor pleased! The other four just crossed their big stone-cutting arms and looked pretty stubborn, so they got sealed up in lead caskets and tossed in the river Sava, where eventually they died, of course. Some friends gathered up the caskets and took them to Rome, where—as soon as it was legal to do so—a church was built over them, and they became heroes to stonecutters and masons all over Europe. There is still a newsletter put out by the British masons called *Ars Quattuor Coronatorum*, and you can still pay your respects to Simpronian, Claudius, Nicostratus and Castorius (but *not* Simplicius) at their church, *Santi Quattro Coronati*, in Rome: it's a little beat-up but worth a visit to honor our stubborn saints.

November: Week Two

MARTIN of TOURS (315–397)
soldier and bishop (November 11)
(See Map 24)

Saint Martin's Day is also Armistice Day, the day on which in 1918 the armistice was signed that ended World War I and, in a way—as historians will tell you—began World War II. The armistice was signed on the eleventh hour of the eleventh day of the eleventh month both to show that the twelfth hour—the end of the world—had almost come as a result of that terrible war, and to honor the Christian soldier-saint, Martin. In Martin's day, as maybe in any time, to be a soldier and a Christian was a difficult combination, and soon after his baptism he quit the army. His father had been a soldier, stationed in the province of Pannonia, and Martin was born there at Sabaria (modern Szombathely, Hungary). As a teenager, he was conscripted (drafted) into the Roman army, which didn't suit him at all. But it was as a soldier that Martin had his big encounter with Christ.

First, I need to explain about the *sagum*, the big red wool cloak that Roman officers wore on duty and to war. In peacetime, Roman knights wore their huge *white* wool toga wrapped around them like a nine-yard-long security blanket, but in war, when they put on their armor and got onto their horses, it was time for the sagum, a big *red* wool cape. The sagum was so huge that you could use it as sort of a tent when you were on duty, it covered the back of your horse when you rode (so it got covered with horse-hairs, of course), and you could use it as a bedroll, if necessary. It wasn't a silly, Disney-prince little cape; it covered your back from neck to heels.

But why the fuss about the sagum? Well, during one of the coldest winters in memory, Martin came across a nearly-naked beggar-man at the gate of the town of *Samarobriva Ambianorum* (modern Amiens, a big city north of Paris, France) where he was stationed, and he decided to cut his sagum in half with his sword and wrap the man in it. Even cut in half, the sagum provided a goodly amount of warm red wool for the poor man to wear, and he was truly grateful for it. Of course, now Martin looked like a silly Disney-prince, and his friends laughed at him a little, but there was a strange look on Martin's face: when he had looked at the naked old man, he had a vision of Christ standing there, you know: "when I was naked, you clothed me . . ." and he couldn't get the image out of his head. It was after that he became serious about his Christian calling, and soon he was baptized, and gave up the army, and studied to be a priest, and became in time a great bishop in the city of Tours in France. He was good friends with other saints, like Paulinus and Ambrose . . . but he always kept that half-a-sagum to remind him how it started.

The funny thing about the half-sagum is that he called it by the name that was given to those little mini Disney-prince capes that ladies sometimes used, or in Latin, a *capella*, meaning a "little cape." The little room at the church in Tours where they kept the cape after Saint Martin died, where people could come to see the cut cloak of the story, also got to be called the Capella . . . and, well, you guessed it, although it is almost unbelievable, that's where we get the word "chapel," where you may be sitting today! All from Saint Martin's "little cape." Cool, eh?

November: Week Two

FRANCES CABRINI (1850–1917)
foundress (November 13)

 **Y**ou know, white people don't think about it much any more, but they used to make a huge fuss about people with skin any darker than a snowbank. When people from southern Italy first moved to the northern part of the United States, the super-pale-pink people apparently

acted as if they'd never seen anyone with dark hair and tan skin before, and as if that tan was some kind of baked-on dirt, and treated the people like dirt, too! And people in that part of the country were suspicious of Catholics, but even the pale-pink Irish Catholics didn't like the Italians. It was hard enough having to leave their homes for a new country in order to find some work, but then to be treated like *that* was pretty rotten for the Italians. That is why today's saint came over to America all the way from Italy, even though travel, especially over water (and there were only boats for going overseas in those days) terrified her. It was to help out these poor, homesick, heartsick folk!

Frances (or *Francesca* in her native Italian) had started a series of French-style Sacred Heart Schools in Italy, and was ready to take them to the Far East and convert children there, when her bishop told her: "You're needed in the West!" So she went off to New York City with sixteen teacher-nuns and started a school and an orphanage there, mostly for Italian-American kids. It was *very* hard for Frances Cabrini at first for about a zillion reasons, even besides her fear of traveling. She had a hard time learning English, first of all, and then she had been taught that Protestants weren't really Christians and that you couldn't trust them, and then there was the problem that she was sometimes completely stubborn about getting her way, and that the people she was trying to help were so sad, and so poor and so unpopular.

But Frances was not about to let a few zillion things stop *her*. She kept right on working to improve herself and the general situation, visiting prisoners at Sing Sing prison, setting up schools all over. She would always say: "Who is doing this? We, or our Lord?" And so she took on all her problems and solved them, one by one. She was so hard-working and efficient that all those hard-working, efficient Americans—Protestant and Catholic—were happy to help her out. By the time she became an American citizen and retired to Seattle, Washington, she was well on her way to becoming the first citizen of the United States to become canonized (that is, you know, officially get listed as a saint). *Bravissima, Santa Francesca Cabrini!*

November: Week Three

GIUSEPPE MOSCATI (1880–1927)
doctor (November 16) *(See Map 25)*

One was a doctor, and one was a queen, . . ." says the song. Here is one of the doctor-saints! Saint Giuseppe Moscati was like so many old-fashioned doctors who made very little money and worked very hard, but he went even further: his strong faith led him to look for God among the poor people in the grimy backstreets of Naples, Italy. He tried to treat each patient as a whole person, not just as a sick lung or a broken leg, and to care *about* as well as *for* his patients. He seemed to get power from more than just food and sleep and shelter; he drew strength directly from his church life and his private prayer time.

But Giuseppe Moscati was also a really top-notch doctor. By the time he was twenty-three years old, he had earned honors in medicine and surgery from the University of Naples and started work at the hospital there. He helped everyone he could, charged no fee at all for the poor, and also visited and made friends with his patients whenever he could. He continued to study his craft, earning the Chair of Chemical Physiology at age thirty-one, and the University of Naples became famous throughout Europe because of the quality of his research.

Of course, all this hard work and caring and studying is really exhausting to a human being, no matter how saintly he might be. Doctor Moscati was only forty-seven years old (that may sound old to some of you, but it really isn't!) when one day, feeling a little unwell after morning rounds, he went up to his office to sit down, and died quietly in his chair. Of course, everyone who had ever known Giuseppe Moscati insisted that he become an official saint ASAP, and I expect he still inspires doctors everywhere who get up at all hours to help us when we're sick, God bless 'em!

November: Week Three

ELIZABETH of HUNGARY (1207–1231)
princess (November 17) *(See Maps 1 and 5)*

and **MILDRED** (seventh century)
princess (July 13)

We have all heard tales of fairy princesses, and these stories tend to be very romantic and make it sound as if it must be wonderful to be a princess, to be beautiful, wealthy, generous, kind, to spend one's time visiting the people and making sure they're treated fairly. While there really are such things as princesses, they rarely lead such simple and idyllic lives as this. You may have heard of Princess Diana of Britain, who helped people but had a sad story. Today's saints were also both officially princesses, and the first one has a very romantic, if tragic, story.

Elizabeth of Hungary was very happily married, living in a beautiful castle with her little children. But then her husband died very young, and she was completely overwhelmed, and ran screaming though the castle in very dramatic fashion. Then, even more dramatically, her brother-in-law turned Elizabeth and her children out of the castle, into the snow, they say, and she finally took refuge in a convent in Marburg, in her husband's home country of Germany, after sending her babies off to live with relatives. After that, life was still hard for Elizabeth: the priest in the convent who acted as her confessor was a pretty harsh fellow, making her do all sorts of penances and things, but she always just bounced back, as she put it, "like a blade of grass after a storm." That is when Elizabeth began to be like a real, saintly, fairy princess. She used the wealth she still had to help her people when they needed it. She would go and serve hungry people with her own hands and even went fishing to feed them, if necessary. They loved her very much, and folk around Marburg still talk about the kindness of Elizabeth of Hungary.

Another saintly princess was Princess Mildred of Minster in Thanet, England, way back in the seventh century. She was never thrown out of her castle; she went of her own accord to run the convent that her mother, Queen Ermenburga, had started. Mildred was a good abbess, and people remember her as being gentle and kind, "a comforter to all in affliction."

So even if you are not a real princess, you can always act like one, like Elizabeth, or Mildred: never stuck-up or irritating, always kind and helpful.

November: Week Four

BERNWARD (960–1022)
artisan and bishop (November 20)

Saints are generally creative people: they start things, think up good ideas, write important things, get things done, and use their talents for all they're worth. They are sometimes also really good with their hands, as painters, blacksmiths, apothecaries or wood-workers. In the olden days monks often made a living for themselves by specializing in certain crafts and selling them, so monasteries would be good places to train apprentices. Today's Saint Bernward was the official monastery blacksmith and painter, and he even did fine metalwork in silver and gold. But he also studied hard and preached well, and soon enough became bishop of Hildesheim, in northern Germany, just southeast of Hannover and southwest of Braunschweig, where liverwurst comes from. It turned out that the monastery there needed a big, new church to be built, because the community had become so big and prosperous.

This was the perfect project for someone like Saint Bernward. From near and far he called in workers in stone, wood, and metal, and what they didn't know before they came, he taught them himself, bishop though he was. Not only did they build the beautiful abbey church of Saint Michael's—a classic of its type—but at the same time founded a school that became famous all over the region for its religious art. Bernward's own bronze doors, cross, column and candlesticks are still in the church at Hildesheim, and if you ever go there, you can see for yourselves whether they show *you* the powerful combination of love of creating and love of the Creator that Saint Bernward brought to Hildesheim.

November: Week Four

CECILIA (died 170ish)
noblewoman, patron of music (November 22)
(See Map 4)

Saint Cecilia is the patron saint of music, and music is one of the most glorious things the Church does: choir singing, organ music and oratorios and all. Many people like to listen to poet John Dryden's "Ode to Saint Cecilia" at this time of year, with all its complicated rhythms and sounds imitating different instruments and types of music (see the back of this book for a copy). But Cecilia would have been pretty surprised to discover that music was her "job" as a saint! She did actually hum a hymn to herself while the organ music played at her wedding (yes, the Romans did actually play organs at weddings in those days), mostly because she was nervous. After all, she had vowed never to marry and had intended to live as a nun, just praying and doing good deeds all her life, as we read in Valerian's story, earlier.

Cecilia, or Caecilia as she would have been known back then, was the daughter of an important Roman family, last in a very long line of important Caecilias. Her ancestor, Caecilia Metella, had been one of the richest women in Rome, and certainly has one of the biggest tombs you'll ever see on the Via Appia. Caecilia's father expected her to marry an Important Young Roman man, and have several Important Young Roman children. But it didn't work out that way. Caecilia met an old holy man on the Via Appia, a Christian named Urbanus, and from him she learned all about Christianity, and decided to be a sort of bride of Christ. She told her young husband Valerian about all this, and then he became a Christian, too, and they lived together like brother and sister, not having any children of their own. Then Valerian's brother converted, too, and when all their parents found out, they were furious! They felt cheated of grandchildren, and it was horribly illegal to be Christian in those days.

Word got 'round to the Emperors Marcus Aurelius and Lucius Verus that some Important Young Roman citizens had the audacity to become Christians ("It is bad enough for slaves, but *really!*" the emperors said), and the young folks were all hauled into court. I have put Valerian's story in another part of this book: he and his brother were killed first. We actually have the transcripts of Cecilia's trial, and we know that she scoffed at the judge: "How can you worship a thing of stone with a bird's nest behind its ear? What foolishness!" She was a very stubborn Important Young Roman citizen, so finally, she had to be executed, but very quietly as befitted a lady. So the soldiers locked her in her bathroom and turned the steam way up: no luck! Cecilia just became a little pink in the face. So someone pulled out a rather dull sword and tried beheading (her second option as a lady), but it was very difficult, and he only managed three cuts before leaving her alone . . . maybe they were only allowed three tries; I'm not sure. Anyway, poor Cecilia slowly bled to death for the next three days, stubbornly explaining Christianity to her friends, especially the part about the Trinity that they never could understand (remember, Saint Patrick had trouble explaining this, too, so he always had a shamrock handy).

When they opened her tomb in 1599, about thirteen hundred years later, they found Cecilia still lying on one shoulder in all her nice clothes, with her face turned away toward the ground and three cuts on her neck, just as fresh as when she'd been buried. They saw that one hand had her pointer finger sticking out, and the other hand had her first three fingers out, still explaining about the Trinity, up to the last moment. An excellently stubborn Important Young Roman saint, that Cecilia!

december

December: Week One

FRANCIS XAVIER (1506–1552)
missionary to the Far East (December 3)
(See Map 15)

Everyone's life makes a difference in the world, and East Asia was the part of the world where Saint Francis Xavier made the biggest difference, even though he came from Pamplona, in Spain. He was one of the first seven young men to become what is called a Jesuit, that is, a member of the Society of Jesus, a group of priests determined to improve the Church and spread the word about Christianity far and wide. Francis volunteered to go to India to do this, in case nobody there had heard about Christ yet.

When people go to India even today, especially to the big cities, they are shocked to see that there are so many poor people living on the streets or in slums, and that the people in the villages are still sometimes living much the same way they did back in Francis Xavier's time. But four hundred years ago things were much worse. Francis was so shocked by seeing all the people dying of disease and living in such incredible poverty, he said that it "left a permanent mark on my heart." Especially sad were the people called untouchables, whose religion told them that they were as bad as dirt and that nobody in a higher caste should even touch them, and all they were fit to do was to sweep dirt and tan dead animal skins for leather.

Francis started with them, because he wanted them to know that in *his* religion, every person is important in God's eyes.

The people there on the southern coast of India really liked what Francis Xavier had to say, especially the poor people; most of the rich people weren't in a big hurry to change things! When he sailed on to the islands of Japan, the people there also liked what he had to say, and enthusiastically became Christians in large numbers. He seems to have had the gift of tongues, which means that he could speak in whatever language he needed to, just like the apostles at Pentecost. He could also heal people and was just afire with his faith.

It is a sad fact, though, that because the different groups of Christian missionaries kept fighting among themselves (the Dutch had different ideas about how to be a Christian than the Spanish did, and so forth), the ruler of Japan later decided that all Christians must leave or die. But Francis still did a good job, and if you visit the church in Goa, India, where he is buried, you can meet people there whose great-great-and-so-forth ancestors went to church with Francis Xavier, the first apostle to East Asia.

December: Week One

JOHN of DAMASCUS (675–749)
poet and priest (December 4) *(See Map 3)*

There seem to be a lot of poet-saints honored in December, but John is perhaps the most interesting one. Even though he was a Christian, John worked as an official in the court of the Muslim Khalif Abdul Malek in Damascus, at a time when no *Christian* court would have allowed a *Muslim* to be an official, or even to be alive, for that matter! Also, the eastern half of the Mediterranean was doing Christianity differently from the western half at this time, and so maybe John wouldn't have even been allowed in any western Christian court, either! Many Muslim rulers like the Khalif of Damascus allowed any "people of the Book," that is, Jews and Christians, to serve in their courts. And where is Damascus? It is the capital of Syria, nowadays, one of the oldest cities in the world and the place where Paul became a Christian, literally "seeing the light" in the "Street Called Straight."

John of Damascus started out as a monk in the famous monastery of Mar Saba in Palestine, and maybe being out in the wilderness there inspired him, because he wrote some of the most beautiful and famous poems in the Church, which were turned into all sorts of inspiring hymns. It most definitely wouldn't be Easter morning church without these two: *"Come, ye faithful, raise the strain of triumphant gladness: God hath brought forth Israel unto joy from sadness . . ."* (translated into English, of course, and sung to the great tune called "Saint Kevin," by Sir Arthur Sullivan) and *"The day of resurrection! Earth, tell it out abroad: the Passover of gladness, the Passover of God!"* (this is one generally sung to the tune called "Lancashire").

This last one was written for the eastern church's great Vigil of Easter, a service held in the dark of the night before Easter, and when midnight strikes, everyone lights their candles, shouts (in Greek, of course), "He is risen! Christ is risen indeed!" and sings John's hymn in all its many verses, and then everyone stays up even later for more church and then goes home and knocks Easter eggs together and has a big feast. John would approve, I suspect!

December: Week Two

COLEMAN (555–611)
deaf man and abbot (May 26)

and **HIPPARCHUS** (died 297)
bald man and martyr (December 9)

Saints are famous for making the best of a really terrible situation, as when Saint Lawrence asking to be turned over on the grill! Here are two little stories of saints who had some big problems and turned them into a little joke upon themselves, even when things looked awfully serious.

Losing your hearing is no joke, but Saint Coleman of Lann Elo saw in it a message for him when *he* became temporarily deaf. Coleman was an Irish abbot in charge of a large monastery long ago, and was very proud of himself for writing a little book called *The Alphabet of Devotions*. You can imagine how it worked—"A is for Always, we should *always* remember to pray . . ."—that sort of thing. Soon after he finished it and everyone had said nice things about it, Coleman caught a terrible sort of cold that left him unable to hear anything at all, and he blamed himself, saying, "This is what I get for being so puffed up about myself!" Maybe he learned his lesson, because soon afterward, he could hear again, and after that, he was careful to be humble about whatever he did; certainly a good, saintly way to deal with a bad situation.

Saint Hipparchus was in a much worse situation, as he and his deacon Philotheus weren't just going to lose their sight, they would lose their lives as illegal Christians back in the Bad Old Days of persecutions. The Roman magistrates were giving them one more chance to change their minds and give up their faith or die. Hipparchus, who was completely bald, thought he would make a definite point that even the magistrates couldn't miss, saying (as is solemnly recorded by the court stenographer): "No, I will not! Not until hair grows on my head!" And that showed them, I guess, that saints can make the best of a terrible situation.

December: Week Two

LUCY (died 304)
martyr (December 13)

Lucy is such a nice, light-sounding name, and in its original Italian it is even prettier: *Lucia* ("Loo-CHEE-a"). Lucy was just a little Christian girl from Syracuse in Sicily, who refused to stop being a Christian just to please the Roman magistrates, and so she was killed—just like that—with a sword. But all the local people loved her and had a festival in her honor every year, with a special song in her memory: "Santa Lucia."

When people living way up in Scandinavia became Christians, it so happened that Lucy's festival day came deep in the winter at the time of year when the people there traditionally had a big celebration in honor of light, to somehow invite the light to return to the earth at that darkest time of the year, when some parts of Sweden and Finland, Norway and Iceland have no sunlight at all for weeks at a time. So the church folk thought it made sense to celebrate that old festival on Saint Lucy's day, since her name sounded like "light," and instead of being pretty noisy and drunken the way it used to be, they made it the kind of party a girl like Lucy might like: they made it into a "breakfast-in-bed" party!

After everybody in Europe discovered coffee in the 1600s, the festival got even better, and here's how they do it nowadays: every year before dawn on Saint Lucy's Day in houses all over Sweden the eldest girl in the house gets up and puts on a long white gown with a red sash, and puts a crown of candles on her head (somehow or other, she lights them), then goes to the kitchen and makes coffee. She puts the coffee on a big tray with mugs and cream and sugar and special curled-up saffron-flavored buns called "Lucy Cats," and goes around from room to room singing the Santa Lucia song (only in Swedish, of course) and serving up breakfast in bed to everybody in the family. What could be a nicer way to remember little Saint Lucy?

It is Christmas time once again, and time for pageants and parties while this storybook rests a little while. And off we go to Christmas vacation!

january

ALMACHIUS or TELEMACHUS
(died about 400)
shepherd and martyr (January 1)

Here is a good "New Year's Resolution" story. This Almachius was a real "shepherd on the green" and he is one of my favorite saints, because he made people see, all at once, that what they had been doing for a long time without thinking about it was *wrong*, and so they stopped doing it. We all get in the habit of doing things that may be cruel or stupid, but the rest of the gang does them, so we do them, too. Maybe we buy chocolate bars made from cocoa harvested by hungry children who aren't paid fairly, or clothes made in inhuman sweatshops . . . or maybe we just make fun of the new kid in school because everyone else in the class does it.

Well, the thing that worried Saint Almachius (that was his real name; people got his name confused with Telemachus, a famous character from *The Odyssey*, because they sounded a little alike) was the bloody gladiator fighting in the arenas all over the Roman Empire, which were still going on even though the empire had been officially Christian since 313 A.D. The old games had not only started out as pagan celebrations, they were also cruel and horrible. People needed to be shown that watching killing for pleasure was wrong, and Almachius, as a holy man, was out to change things. Although he came from the eastern Mediterranean, he decided to go all the way to Rome, where the games had all started. If he could

---

stop them in Rome, he figured all the other places would stop, too. And he was right!

So one day, when two gladiators had just squared off in the sand of the Coliseum, Almachius got onto the floor of the arena and ran over to separate them, calling on them to stop, in the name of God! But they just turned on him and killed him, maybe egged on by the crowd, and when the people in the stands saw the holy old man lying there dead, it was as if they had just awakened from a bad dream and saw for the first time what they had been doing all these years. Many of them left in horror right then and never came back. The emperor finally had the courage to ban the gladiatorial games, after that, though bullfights continued in many countries down through the years, and give you a small taste of the horrible attraction of the original fights. But wasn't Saint Almachius brave!

January: Week One

BASIL the GREAT (330–379)
and GREGORY of NAZIANUS (329–389)
bishops and friends (January 2) *(See Map 3*

This is a story of two friends who had a quarrel they never quite made up, even though they still loved each other all their lives. Be warned! Be careful not to send angry messages to your friends, and even saints can stop being best friends if one of them is unfair, or if they stop trusting each other.

Basil was the "great" one; not only was his grandmother a saint and his sister a saint (both of them named Macrina) but also his brothers Gregory and Peter of Nyssa were both saints, and so were his parents, Basil and Emmelia. Basil also became a "big cheese" in the Church: he became bishop of Caesarea (Kayseri, in modern Turkey) in the region of Cappadocia today (hmm . . . sounds like some kind of coffee drink), in the middle of the Anatolian peninsula, and he controlled the churches and the priests of a large area, as we will see. Basil built a whole city of churches and hospitals called the *Basiliad,* and he wrote lots of important books suspect, that maybe Basil began to believe a little too much in his own wonderfulness.

His best friend from college, Gregory of Nazianus, was a priest, and because he was a good friend Basil knew he could trust Gregory to become bishop in a part of his diocese (that's the area controlled by a certain bishop) called Sasima (Haskoy in modern Turkey), which Basil wanted to keep a hold of, right on the edge of his "kingdom," as it were. Well, Basil had never visited that town, and when Gregory complained that Sasima was a horrible, unhealthy place, and the people there were amazingly nasty and they did not want him to be there, for some reason, Basil decided that Gregory was just being wimpy and lazy and then made the huge mistake of *telling* him so. What Basil should have done, if he hadn't been so busy being "great," was to have visited Sasima for himself before writing anything more. But he didn't, and Gregory's feelings were so badly hurt because Basil didn't trust his judgment that, as a result, the two friends never wrote another letter to each other, *as long as they lived!*

But when Basil died, Gregory wrote a beautiful *panegyric* (that's a poem in praise of someone) about him, how brave and hardworking Basil had been, and he remembered all the great times he and Basil had had as university students back in Athens together. Then Gregory surprised everyone by becoming very important in Church business back in Constantinople; some people said the spirit of his friend Basil stood beside him to make him stronger and braver than he ever had been before. So now the two friends share a saint's day because after all, friends are friends at all times (or they should be), right?

January: Week Two

ABO (died 786) perfumer (January 8) *(See Map 26)*

and **AURELIUS and NATALIA** (died 852)
martyrs (July 27) *(See Map 6)*

We know that in the Medieval Bad Old Days it was often safer to live in Muslim countries if you were a Christian with possibly unusual ideas, or if you were a Jew, than it was to live in Christian lands. However, there were exceptions to this rule, especially if you lived in a Muslim country with a slightly crazy Caliph, or if you *used* to be a Muslim and then you switched to being a Christian . . . as we'll see in these two stories.

The first story is particularly interesting because in this part of the book we are specially noticing all the different kinds of people who become saints, and Saint Abo had a rather unusual job: he was a *perfumer*. This very important servant made sure that his master, the prince of the beautiful country of Georgia deep in the Caucasus mountains of central Asia, smelt just as beautiful as his country at all times. Abo was an Arab, and a Muslim, but when he and his master were sent into exile in the eastern lands of Kazan, Abo became a Christian and was baptized. When he got back to Tbilisi, the capital city of Georgia (the country, remember, not the state; the capital of the state of Georgia is Atlanta, as you know), people found out he wasn't a Muslim any more. This made him what they called a "renegade from Islam," and the law required that he had to have his head chopped off. So he did, and even today, he is a big saint in Georgia, and patron saint of perfumers.

Unfortunately, I don't know what Aurelius and Natalia did for a living, but they had the same sort of difficulties that Abo did while they were living in Córdoba, Spain. In those days, Spain was still ruled by the Muslims, and Emir Abd ar-Rahman II had decided to clean up Córdoba: the behavior of the Christians shocked him, especially the way Christian women marched around without wearing any veils over their faces . . . so I guess he thought he would teach them a lesson. Aurelius and Natalia were secret Christians, and their cousin Felix had been a Muslim for awhile but then went back to being a Christian and married Liliosa, who had always been just a plain old Christian. Then there was a monk named George, who had been caught saying bad things about the Prophet Mohammed (on whom be peace) . . . so the emir rounded up the five of them and chopped their heads off, too. Which goes to show that even in the Better Old Days of Islam, sometimes (especially early on in their conquest) the Muslims were just as intolerant as medieval Christians were, and that's how Abo, Aurelius, Natalia and the rest of them all became saints.

January: Week Two

GUDULE (died 712) laywoman (January 9)
and **WAUDRU (Audrey)** (died 688)
patroness (April 9)

 The reason we celebrate these two saints together is that both of them have short stories and a couple of things in common: they both had at least one other saint in the family and they both were a great comfort to all those around them.

When you see pictures of saints in churches and museums, you can generally tell who's who even without nametags because of what art historians call their "attributes," that is, what they're carrying in their hands, whether there's a dog sitting next to them, that sort of thing. Gudule's "attribute" is a lit candle, because they say that every morning before dawn, Gudule would walk the two miles—and that's a good step!—from her father's castle (which was in Belgium, not far from Brussels, where the sprouts come from) to the little church where she liked to pray, and she got up soooo early that she had to carry a candle. She and her sister, Raineld, had pledged to each other to do holy things all their lives. Gudule decided she would stay in Belgium and be holy there, but Raineld thought she would go to the Holy Land, which she managed to do safely, but after she got back she was killed by some barbarian pirates in Antwerp, in Belgium, itself: those were the "Bad Old Days," all right!

Anyway, the very first morning Gudule tried walking to the church before dawn, at the part of the road where it was the darkest and she was the most scared, the candle in her little lantern suddenly blew out, *whoosh*, and Gudule thought she heard some mean laughter, so she suspected that the devil was having a little fun with her. She prayed really hard for a little light, her candle came back on again with a *pop*, and then she went on praying and doing her good work for people in need, for the rest of her life. When Gudule finally died, as an old, old lady, they buried her under the front steps of her little church, and declared her a saint, and made her "attribute" a lit candle.

Now, Waudru (or Waldetrudis for long, or Audrey for modern) was also from Belgium, from a place called Mons. She was married for a while, but her husband decided to become a monk, so Waudru became a nun, helping the poor and sick and later starting her very own convent near when Mons is today, and eventually became a saint. It was not too surprising because her whole family were saints, from her parents, Walbert and Bertilia, to her sister, Aldegund of Mauberge, to her husband, Madelgaire, and their four children, Landric, Dentelin, Aldetrude and Madelberte. Quite a family of interesting names *and* good saints.

January: Week Three

THORFINN (died 1285) bishop (January 8)

and **HALVARD** (died 1043)
patron of Oslo (May 15)

(See Map 16 for both)

Here we have two short stories about medieval Norwegians. When you are old enough to read the famous Kristin Lavransdattar books, you will learn all about what they are like. Maybe the first thing you need to know about Norwegians in the meantime is that not all of them were Vikings who sailed around the coasts of Europe during the Dark Ages killing off innocent monks and carrying off as many of the women-folk and as much of the plunder as their snaky little ships could stagger along under. Not all the Vikings were bad, anyhow, and they actually bathed once a week (unlike most other folks in those days) and their ships really were fabulously fast. No, some Norwegians stayed home and were fine farmers and had upright characters, a generous nature, a strong sense of honor, and a grim but well-developed sense of humor. They also believed in trolls and elves long after they became Christianized (and the ones who went to Iceland still do), so there you are: a *resolute* sort of people.

Our Saint Thorfinn is described as having "resolute goodness," the sort of goodness that is expressed with big bushy Norwegian eyebrows and a tight-set mouth. In fact, while he was bishop of Hamar, Thorfinn had to leave dear old Norway along with some other bishops because they were *so* resolute with King Eric II about their rights to have freely-elected bishops without the king's interference. King Eric II had some pretty strong objections to these bishops' notions, so Thorfinn resolved to visit Rome and then go settle down near Bruges, in Belgium, being "resolutely good" *there* for the rest of his life, and earning his sainthood.

Our Saint Halvard, on the other hand, didn't have to leave Norway to become a saint, and he also didn't have to wait around for years and years to become one, either. He became a saint in just a few minutes, because he, too, was "resolutely good." It all happened very quickly: Halvard, who was a wealthy landowner's son from Lier (called Lierbyen, today), was just getting into his trusty boat one day to cross the Drammen Fjörd (that's a big sea inlet, like a broad river), not far from the capital city of Oslo. He had most of his gear in the boat and was about to untie the painter (that's the rope) and shove off, when down the slope behind him this woman came running, just as fast as her legs would carry her, and maybe a little faster, sobbing and calling to him to take her into his boat and row her across the fjord: there were evil men behind her who were out to kill her!

Well, naturally, he took her into the boat, and they were out on the water when, sure enough, a band of furious men came pelting down the path on the slope, all armed with swords and bows, and quivers full of long, dark arrows. They yelled that the woman was a thieving slave, and that he must return her at once, but Halvard could easily see that they would not wait for any court of law but meant to kill her right then without a hearing—and she swore to him that she was innocent—so he refused to return to shore. One of the men, in a fury (he must have been a real, old-time Viking type), picked up his bow and arrows and shot them both dead, right there in the boat! Later, when it was all sorted out, even most of the "evil men" had to agree that Halvard had acted in good faith, and had died in defense of what he believed was innocence. The Norwegians admired his resolution so much that they voted him a saint (people could just decide like that about saints in those days) and made him patron of the capital city of Oslo, hoping that everyone (especially every judge) there would always assume that everyone was innocent until absolutely proved guilty, in honor of Saint Halvard.

January: Week Three

PETER ORSEOLO (928–987)
doge and hermit (January 10)
(See Maps 6 and 14)

One of my favorite stories by Rudyard Kipling is called "The Miracle of Purun Bhagat," about a man who rose to be prime minister of a whole province of India and then gave it all up when he retired, to become a holy man in the "hills" (that is, lower ranges of the great Himalaya Mountains). Our story is much like that one, but in a very different place. Saint Peter Orseolo was no less a person than the doge of Venice, one of the most important people in all Italy or even all Europe at the time. Venice was already a rich and beautiful city, beginning to be famous for its streets made of water and its one hundred islands all joined together with bridges and stairs.

Even back in the tenth century when Peter was alive Venice was an important place, trading with all the ports on the coast of the Adriatic, and all the way to Egypt and Turkey in the east of the Mediterranean. Three hundred years later, Marco Polo and his father would set off overland from Venice to China itself . . . trade came to Venice from absolutely everywhere! The ruler of Venice was called the doge ("DOEzh"), and he was always an older man, chosen from one of the ruling families of Venice by a sort of rotation. That way each family got a turn being in power and no one family was in power long, because the doges wouldn't live very long (already being old men, after all). It was a lot of hard work running the city, but the doge had a beautiful palace to live in, with the nicest food and the best parties in town. Peter Orseolo didn't mind the hard work, since he had been an able soldier and fine statesman for years, but in his heart he had wanted to spend his old age in quiet prayer someplace, and was never completely at his ease at those lavish parties.

So, one day without telling anyone—not even his wife or his son— and after putting all his business in order, Peter Orseolo left behind all that good food and all those grand rooms and vanished from Venice! He went all the way to a little place called St. Michel-de-Cuxa, in the foothills of the rugged Pyrenees, the mountains between France and Spain—far, far from Venice!—and lived there as a hermit. He was as good a holy man as he had been a soldier and a doge, and pretty soon the people who came to him for advice began calling him *Saint* Peter Orseolo, and that sounded much sweeter to his ears than *Doge* Peter Orseolo ever had.

January: Week Four

THEODORE the CENOBIARCH (423–529)
abbot (January 11)

and DENIS the CEPHALOPHORE (died 258)
bishop (October 9)

I just had to put these two saints side by side because their titles are both so grand and strange . . . don't you just love big words like that? Words like *carnivore*, and *cephalopod*, and *patriarch*? And I suppose you are going to want to know what they *mean*, too! A *cenobiarch* is a fancy way of saying "someone in charge of those dining together," sort of an abbot or den mother, and a *cephalophore* is "someone carrying his own head." Oh, and a *carnivore* is "a meat eater," a *cephalopod* is a "head-foot," for example an octopus, and a *patriarch* is "someone in charge who is (like) a father." But back to our saints!

Theodore the Cenobiarch was one of those early saints who helped to get everything started and organized. After all, in this book you are always hearing about monks and nuns and abbots and abbesses, but somebody must have gotten all that business started and organized, setting up monasteries and all that. Actually, as you may have read earlier in this book, a lot of people contributed to the whole business, and one of those people was Saint Theodore. He headed up a small community in Bethlehem, one of the earliest places people did that sort of thing, made up of men from all over, who spoke all sorts of languages, all of whom liked to work together to help the sick, the elderly, and people who were mentally ill. They also liked to worship together and eat together and camp out together, too. All this being and praying together made them strong enough to do the hard work they needed to do to help people every-day. It was a new thing, and they decided to call themselves *cenobites* from the Greek everybody around there spoke, meaning "people who eat together," and so, naturally, Theodore became the *cenobiarch*, their chief (just as an *arch*angel is a chief angel), and he did it so well he became a saint.

Now Denis (you may pronounce that French style, if you like: "Den-EE") the Cephalophore was rather different, even if his title was also Greek: for one thing, he was around when it was still illegal to be a Christian in the Roman Empire, and though he was the person in charge of all the Christians living in Paris at that time (when it was still called Lutetia), it was more likely that he would end up as a *cephalophore* carrying his own head than being a nice, peaceful *cenobiarch* like Theodore. As the leader of his people, he would naturally be found by the authorities sooner or later and executed as a "dangerous Christian," because that's what happened to Christians in those days if they didn't stop being Christians after they'd been caught. What is really amazing and *almost* impossible to believe is that, after Denis was properly be-headed, he apparently didn't think much of the location beside the Seine River where he'd been killed, so he picked up his head, tucked it under his arm and walked off to a spot about five miles away before he finally flopped over. If you go to Paris and see the great church of Notre Dame de Paris, you can see a statue of him there, head on hip! Not every saint gets to be a *cephalophore*!

January: Week Four

FELIX of NOLA (died 260)
priest (January 14) *(See Map 25)*

Nola was an important town even before Felix came along: it is a town on what has always been the great central north-south trade route of Italy, and is situated right in the middle of the "boot," just left of Mount Vesuvius as you go south from Rome. Nola had been around when Vesuvius blew its top in 79 A.D., but it didn't get covered up with ash like Pompeii; people there just brushed off and kept going. Now Saint Felix would make it important for another reason: as a place to visit *him* when he became a famous saint, especially after his biggest fan, Saint Paulinus, moved there and started making up poems and hymns about him. So what really was so great about Saint Felix? Well for one thing, he managed—just barely—not to die for his faith, but to *live* instead, and keep serving his congregation in the middle of the terrible persecutions of the late Empire. How he did so is a nice adventure story.

It all began when Felix was a priest at Nola, doing the best he could to preach and take care of folks when any minute he could be arrested for being one of those "horrible Christians" that the emperor was so worried about, who wouldn't worship his Divine Spirit, and so forth. Felix didn't hide or anything, so eventually the authorities caught him being a Christian, and they dragged him off to prison and beat him up something terrible. Now, before they caught him, Felix had a feeling this was going to happen, so he hid away his boss, old Bishop Maximus of Nola, so that *he* wouldn't get beaten up something terrible, because poor Maximus was already ill and weak.

Well, in prison the guards were pretty rough, as I said, because they were trying to get Felix to tell him where all the other Christians were, and what their names were, who his boss was, and all that sort of thing. Felix knew he had to escape before they made him tell anything, and he was worried about Maximus, who was all alone in an old deserted house with no one else to take care of him or even know where he was. Felix prayed very hard, and somehow the prison opened up that night the way it had for Saint Peter, and by that miracle, he escaped. He rushed off to Maximus, who by now could hardly move, and carried the old man on his shoulders to someone who could hide him and care for him.

But now the hunt was on for Felix! The furious guards were out after him, and this time they meant business, so Felix hurried back to the old deserted house and hid in a corner, breathing just as quietly as he could. The guards finally came rushing up when it was almost dawn, but when they came to the old ruined door, the only way in through the high walls, they saw that there was a great big spider web woven all across the entrance, which they figured must have taken days at least for the spider to make, and so they moved on. "He can't be here," they said to each other, and that was a second miracle for Felix. After that, he was a little sneakier helping his people, because he wanted to live long enough to help them and didn't ever want to worry about betraying them again. When old Maximus died, Felix could have been bishop and could have made all sorts of important decisions, but he left that to someone else; he just wanted to be a priest to his people at Nola, and so that's what he did for the rest of his fairly long life, thanks to a helpful spider!

January: Week Four

*Once again, we have a third choice for this week's saint.
January is just loaded with good stories!*

JOHN (GIOVANNI) BOSCO (1815–1888)
priest and teacher (January 31) *(See Map 14)*

School may not be fun all the time, but imagine growing up without being able to read anything or write to anyone or even add up your pennies, all because you've never been able to go to school: wouldn't that be frustrating? In Torino (or Turin, as we call it in English for some reason), the town in Italy where our saint grew up and worked as a priest, it seemed as though there were all these boys and young men who didn't care much about anything, partly because nobody seemed to care much about *them* and partly because they had never been able to go to school, so they couldn't get decent jobs because they couldn't read or write or anything you learn at school. John (or Giovanni as they called him at home in Italy) Bosco had noticed this, and was wondering what was the best way to help these young fellows, since they also didn't seem to care much about going to church, where he was most of the time. So he began to imagine how he could give them some other reasons to come to church.

The first thing John Bosco did was to study the situation. He noticed that a lot of boys worked as apprentices all day, to learn how to become shoemakers, or silversmiths, or tailors, or whatever, and didn't have time during the day to go to school. So John decided to start an *evening* school in the church classrooms, starting things off with a chapel service. Next, since most of the apprentices had terrible places to sleep and almost nothing to eat, he started a boarding house for them, run by his own mother and paid for by donations. It turned out that—as you probably already suspected—there were also girls, apprentice dressmakers, mostly, who needed school and food and lodging, and John's friend and future fellow-saint Maria Mazzarello took care of *them*.

Somehow, by doing all this, John Bosco made Christianity something even young men could be interested in, something that not only made them feel better inside, spiritually, but also that God actually seemed to take pity on them and to help them live better lives, too. It made them want to help other people, and they became John Bosco's best helpers of other kids who needed help. John always seemed to have faith that things would work out like this: "God will help us," he said, every time they really needed something for the boarding house or the school, and God always did manage to make the food supply come out just right, or find help for the jobs that needed doing, whenever Saint John Bosco asked: a sure-fire sign of a saint!

february

February: Week One

JOAN of FRANCE (1464–1505)
ugly queen (February 4)

We've noticed that you don't have to be beautiful to be a saint, but today's saint demonstrates that it helps to be a saint if you are born an ugly princess! Princesses really do have to be beautiful, sad to say, because most of the time, even nowadays, the big thing is to have them marry just the right prince or king, and have lots of beautiful baby princes and princesses so they can marry and so on and on and on. The whole point is making alliances through marriages so that all the kings are related to each other and so they don't fight as much. So, if you are the rightful daughter of King Louis XI of France, and you have a hunchback, smallpox scars all over you, and are generally not easy on the eyes, you will probably have your feelings hurt constantly.

Joan was the sweetest girl in the castle, always helpful and kind, and gave the most thoughtful gifts at Christmas, and was witty and funny, but even her own father didn't like her, and her own husband, who was bullied into marrying her, was very cruel to her and eventually went off to marry someone else. Poor Joan really did put up with it all with the patience of a saint! When her husband, another Louis who also became king, found a prettier queen twenty years after he had married Joan, he sent Joan back home to the duchy of Berry, where she spent the rest of her life. Joan used her time and money helping all the people of Berry, and they loved her very much and they didn't care what she looked like; they knew her heart was beautiful, and that was all they cared about.

February: Week One

SCHOLASTICA (480–543)
abbess (February 10) *(See Map 18)*

Scholastica and Benedict were twins born in the Umbrian hill town of Norcia, Italy (also famous for its hams and sausages), and like most twins, they played together all the time. One of their favorite games growing up must have been "make-believe saints," because both of them grew up just burning to do holy things. When Benedict was old enough, he went off into the hills to live in a cave, as we have seen elsewhere in this book, but he refused to take Scholastica with him; he said that all the monks he had heard of didn't allow girls in their monasteries! You can imagine how sad and angry Scholastica was: Benedict always got to do things first that she had always wanted to do. But she made Benedict promise that at least she could visit him once a year, on their birthday, no matter what. "Oh, all right," he finally said, "but only outside the monastery: inside, it's *no girls allowed*!"

Scholastica meanwhile kept working to become just as holy as she could possibly be. Since girls weren't allowed out of the house much, she had a little sort of cave in her backyard like Benedict's, and every year on their birthday she would visit Benedict and they would share ideas about monasteries. Finally, she organized her own big convent of holy women, and they did all sorts of good works and became especially good at praying: if you needed something and they prayed for you, you could be pretty sure your needs would be taken care of.

One year when Scholastica came to Benedict's big new monastery of Monte Cassino for their birthday chat, she had a feeling this would be their last time together in this world, so when he came to dinner at her little guest house down the hill with a few of his monk-buddies, she had a big favor to ask. Could he stay and talk and pray with her *all night long* this time, instead of their usual short little dinner visit? There were so many religious questions she wanted to discuss. But Benedict got that stubborn look on his face; he was the one who had written the rule that said, "No Monks Allowed Outside Their Cells Overnight," after all, so he couldn't very well break it, could he?

But then Scholastica got that look upon *her* face, and she put her hands together, put her head down on her hands, and set to praying, and praying hard. And pretty soon they all heard thunder, and soon after that, the rain came pouring down out of the sky and then, if they had tried to go home to the monastery, they all would have been washed down into the river Liri! Benedict was shocked, but he stayed and they talked and prayed and talked some more about what heaven was like and everything. And don't you know, a couple of days later, just before she was supposed to go home, Scholastica died, and Benedict thought he saw a little dove fly out of her window and go straight up to heaven. So for once Scholastica got to do *something* before Benedict did, namely become a saint.

February: Week Two

VALENTINE (died 268)
priest and martyr (February 14)

Everyone knows when Saint Valentine's Day is, but that's about all we do know about him for sure. We know he died for his faith in Rome, and that there was a very old church built in his honor near the Milvian Bridge, north of Rome, and that the gate into the city from there was called the Porta Valentina in his honor for a long time. We *think* he may been a doctor, and that he may have died along with his two friends, Marius and Martha, and there is a beautiful legend that he cured his jailer's blind daughter, just before they all went off to the lions, one February 14 long ago.

We know for sure that there was an old Roman festival on the day after his "lion day," a festival in honor of the goddess of marriage, because this was the day when birds were supposed to choose their mates and start building their nests. Now, the early Christians were clever about turning popular pagan festivals into church festivals—remember Gregory the Wonderworker?—so instead of pulling a girlfriend's or boyfriend's name out of a jar, as the pagans did, they pulled the names of their favorite saints, or wrote nice things about each other, and had their own party in honor of Valentine, not of What's-Her-Name the goddess.

Love is a big part of being a saint, after all: "Love your neighbor as you love yourself" is right next to "Love God with all your soul and strength and mind," as the Two Commandments taught by Jesus. "Love your enemies," he said, "and bless those who curse you." So let's celebrate by singing that good old hymn, "Love Divine, All Loves Excelling," and by making Valentines and decorating our Valentine's boxes, exchanging fond wishes, and eating lots of sweet things, all in honor of good old Saint Valentine and all the other good old saints!

February: Week Two

CYRIL and METHODIUS (827–869 and 815–885)
translators (February 14) *(See Map 3)*

These saints were brothers—Methodius being twelve years older than Cyril—and they came from the Greek town of Salonika (or Thessaloniki, as it's also known), at the north end of the Aegean Sea. Salonika is close to all those interesting countries where they speak all those Slavic-type languages, so the brothers grew up hearing all sorts of interesting ways of speaking, and meeting all sorts of interesting people. Methodius became governor of the province, and Cyril was a distinguished professor at Constantinople Imperial University, both of them serious, hard-working men.

Now, let's consider for a moment how important language is if you want someone to understand you. Let's say you go into a shop in a foreign country—you can probably point at something and buy it, but if you had to do something complicated, like tell a doctor where it hurts and exactly how you feel, you would be in big trouble. Imagine trying to explain your innermost feelings, or discuss the meaning of life, or try to preach the Gospel or something: you'd need to know the language pretty well to do all that. Then what if the language you were trying to learn had never even been written down—in fact it didn't even have an *alphabet*—how would you be able to get a dictionary to help you learn it? These are all problems that missionaries have had for hundreds of years, and missionaries have invented a lot of alphabets.

Cyril was one of the first missionaries, at least in Europe, to do something about this. He and Methodius had decided to quit their jobs and become priests, because they thought it would be a better use of their talents. When they were sent off to preach to the Khazar people, first they had to learn the Khazaric language, which they did so well that when they later were sent off to preach to the Slavic Moravians, they knew exactly what to do. Cyril worked out an alphabet that worked for Slavonic (it was a lot like the Greek alphabet), and then he and Methodius translated the Gospels into Slavonic. It was such a success that all the languages in the area started to use the alphabet and people there began to learn to read and write. Cyril wanted to call the alphabet Slavoretic or Methodiic or something like that, but everyone else called it *Cyrillic*, and it's still called that today. So if you are a big alphabet fan and are ever in San Clemente Church in Rome, go down into the basement where they're buried and pay your respects.

February: Week Three

ETHELBERT of KENT (560–616)
king (February 25) *(See Map 1)*

I don't know about you, but every time I hear about Kent, I think of Sir Thomas Tom of Appledore from A.A. Milne's poetry book *Now We Are Six.* You know: "For years they'd called him down in Kent, The Knight Whose Armour Didn't Squeak"? But this story isn't about Sir Thomas Tom, it is about Ethelbert, and about Canterbury, that great pilgrimage town of Kent.

This King Ethelbert, with his wonderful Saxon name, was one of many pagan Saxon kings who married a Christian wife and made her very happy by inviting a bishop into his kingdom, bringing with him as many monks as he could. Ethelbert's wife, Bertha, certainly was very happy when he asked Pope Gregory the Great down in Rome to send him along Saint Augustine to be archbishop of Canterbury and begin de-paganizing Britain. The pope had hoped to put the chief church of England in London, but Ethelbert was so generous with land and promises of protection that Canterbury it was! Naturally, seeing Bertha so happy made Ethelbert happy, and he built a cathedral for Augustine, and all the other necessary buildings, and wound up becoming a Christian himself—which is often the way these things work out.

The really pleasant thing about King Ethelbert was that he didn't immediately force all of his subjects to become Christian, too, "or else"; he thoughtfully left it up to their personal consciences, which shows he had really become Christian, don't you think? Another good thing about Ethelbert was that he was great at settling disputes, writing down laws so that there wouldn't be so many disagreements among his people—something people in the ancient Middle East had done a zillion years earlier, but Ethelbert's were the first written laws "in a Germanic language." So, what with being a peacemaker (who as we know are called "Children of God") and inviting Saint Augustine into England, and by making his wife so happy, it's really no wonder King Ethelbert was made a saint.

February: Week Three

NICETIAS of REMESIANA (died 414)
missionary and poet (June 22) *(See Map 24)*

Since February has a dearth of really thrilling saints, I've moved in Nicetas from June. What makes Nicetias of Remesiana so thrilling, or even gripping, you ask? Was he eaten by lions? Did he save the nation of France from destruction? Or has he written something really immortal? Yes! That's it, you guessed it! Nicetias wrote some truly immortal hymns, as did several of our other saints, but Nicetias' were some of the best hymns ever. In fact, there's a good possibility he wrote the words to the part of the old church service called the *Te Deum*, which manages to sum up pretty much anything you want to say in praise of God, and begins (in English), "We praise thee, O God, we acknowledge that thou art Lord. Everlasting Father, all the Earth doth worship thee. To Thee all the angels the heavens and all the powers, all the cherubim and seraphim, unceasingly proclaim, 'Holy, Holy, Holy, Lord God of Hosts!'" and so forth. One translation of his *Te Deum* is a hymn we sing all the time in chapel: "Holy God, We Praise Thy Name." It's stirring stuff, something you can really sing out, good and loud!

Anyhow, Nicetias learned a thing or two about writing and singing good hymns, and while he was a missionary over in Remesiana in the old Roman province of Pannonia (that's modern Bela Palanka in central Serbia)—the region where Saint Martin of Tours came from originally—he taught people there a thing or two about singing in church. His ideas were so good that people nowadays (one and a half thousand years later) still take his advice: *"Sing wisely,"* he said, *"that is, understandably, thinking about what you are singing . . . Tunes should be in keeping with the sacredness of religion . . . not savoring of the theater. . . . Sing together, and do not show off . . . everything in our worship must be done in God's sight, not to please man."* Amen! Immortal words from Saint Nicetias, but don't you wonder what "theater tunes" were like, back in 400 A.D.?

February: Week Four

Unlike January which has too many saints, February has too few. Feel free to go back and borrow a couple!

SIMEON SALUS (died 590)
eccentric (July 1) *(See Maps 3 & 11)*

Note: Might be good for April Fools!

In his book about C.S. Lewis, who wrote the Narnia books, Alan Jacobs says that when a country's people love their *eccentrics*— that is, people who are different from everyday people, who have unusual ideas or ways of doing things or unusual things they're interested in—it shows a basic goodness about the people of that country, an ability to laugh at themselves that is really a healthy thing. Like old Saint Aldhelm, and like the puppeteers who take today's saint as their patron, Saint Simeon Salus was certainly an eccentric who encouraged people like us to laugh at ourselves and the silly things we think are so important, so that we can see what the really important things in life are.

Simeon Salus really was eccentric, too. Just as the the Greek cynic philosopher Diogenes had, Simeon lived out in the open in the town of Emesa, in Palestine, like a stray dog (*cynic* means "dog" in Greek). Simeon started out living as a holy hermit in the wilderness of Sinai for twenty-nine years, doing miracles and having heavenly visions, and everybody believed he was a saintly man. It seemed to him that the city people weren't getting the message, however, so he came back into his hometown of Emesa and lived in the "wilderness" right there in the middle of town.

Simeon tried to show people that although they *thought* they were being good Christians, really they were usually hypocrites (in other words, they said one thing but did another). They said that they "loved their neighbors as themselves," but then they would be cruel to people they didn't approve of, like homeless people. Simeon would care for these street people when they were sick or hungry, and so people said he was *salus*, which is Syriac for "crazy," but the humblest of the humble folk in Emesa loved him for it.

Simeon thought that everybody else was crazy for making a big deal about following ritual—like making sure the candles were lit just right or not eating any meat on Fridays—instead of being good neighbors and forgiving each other. To prove his point, he would come into church and blow out the candles at the beginning of the service sometimes, and on Good Friday one year, he ate a big sausage, right there in front of everyone! Being a "fool for God" was a very brave thing, but the people of Simeon Salus' town seem to have been pretty good sports, too!

march

March: Week One

JOHN of GOD (1495–1550)
penitent and founder (March 8) *(See Map 4)*

 After people fight in wars—which are terrible anyway—and they experience something really amazingly terrible, sometimes they just can't get it off their minds (nowadays it's called "post-traumatic stress syndrome"); this is basically what happened to our John (or *Juan de Dios*, as he's called in Spain). John certainly did *not* start out as a saint, even though his first job was as a shepherd. Mostly he was a wild boy, and then a wild man, traveling all over Europe and North Africa as a *mercenary* (that's a soldier who fights for whoever will pay him enough) in the army of the rather unholy Holy Roman Emperor Charles V. One of the things this army did was sack the city of Rome in 1527, and there's no reason to think that John didn't do some of the burning, killing, and looting involved. Anyway, what he had done in that war seemed to eat away at him, and he started drinking too much liquor, to try to forget, and his drinking just about killed him and definitely drove him a little crazy.

Finally, when he had lost all his money and was selling religious books down in Gibraltar, on the coast of Spain, trying to make a living, John had a vision of Jesus as a little boy, talking to him and calling him "John of God." This seemed to clear his mind, so he quit the army for good and started working as a wood merchant in the city of

Granada in southern Spain, determined to use whatever money he earned to try to make up for how rotten he'd been, to try to help as many miserable people as he himself had made miserable in his life so far. So he rented a house and set it up as a hospital or shelter for anyone who needed it, no matter who they were or what they had done, because he felt that they couldn't be worse people than he himself had been. If people were too ill to come on their own, he carried them there himself, and if they were even too sick to beg for money on the street, he would beg for them.

The archbishop of Granada and other good people helped John out, and helped him organize a group of men that got the nickname—in Italy at least—of the *Fatebenefratelli* (the "Do-Good Brothers"), who did everything from nursing to firefighting. But our John always tended to push himself too hard, and one time, when he was getting older and was maybe a little sick already, he heard yelling from the river—the wild river Darro, which pours off the Sierra Nevada Mountains and runs through the center of the town of Granada—and he jumped into the chilly water to save a man from drowning. He saved the man, but caught a terrific cold that turned into the pneumonia that killed him. You can imagine how much he was missed; and everyone who knew him knew that they had been working with a real saint.

March: Week One

CAMILLUS (1550–1614)
penitent and founder (July 14)

In the Bad Old Days of war, when there weren't any hospitals or medics or nurses to patch soldiers up at the battlefront—or anywhere else, for the most part—you were on your own if you were wounded, unless you happened to have a buddy nearby, or if your wife had come along with you to war. Now our Camillus had been a mercenary soldier for years, fighting on the side of whoever would pay him, but finally he gambled so much that he lost all the money he had earned and then his foot had become infected so badly that he couldn't fight to earn any more. But he was still a big, strong man—he was six feet six inches tall—and he could work hard if he didn't have to march around much, so he started to work on a building that was being constructed for some monks, moving things around. As he worked, Camillus began to think about all the friends he'd lost in the wars, and he began to go to church, and one day he heard a cracker-jack sermon that made him want to become a Capuchin monk and start preaching all over the place.

The trouble was, of course, that with his bad foot Camillus couldn't go "all over the place," so the Capuchins wouldn't let him be a monk. Then his foot got *so* bad that they sent him off to a hospital in Rome, where he met the soon-to-be-saint Philip Neri, his priest. Camillus was so disgusted at the way the hospital was run that, when he was just the tiniest bit better, he started helping out by moving patients, cleaning up and organizing the stuffy, smelly rooms . . . and went to school for the first time in his life, sitting next to the little boys, to learn how to read and write! When he had learned enough, Camillus organized a group of priests and helpers called "the servants of the sick" (the Camillans) that started the first combat ambulance unit, built a whole series of new hospitals with plenty of light and fresh air, special diets, isolation wards for people with diseases that were catching . . . he even worked out a special fail-safe system for making sure that coma patients weren't buried alive by accident! In Naples, his workers went on board galleys and even took care of galley-slaves who had the plague. By the time Camillus died, there were fifteen new rest-houses, eight hospitals, and finally a way to care for soldiers on the battlefield . . . his fellow-soldiers must have been awfully grateful to him.

March: Week Two

FRANCES OF ROME (1384–1440)
foundress (March 9)

In her native Italian, Frances is called *Santa Francesca Romana* and in any language she is recognized as a saint who had a great deal of spunk. Frances was from a wealthy family of Roman nobles who taught their children that you don't just have wealth, you have the responsibilities that go along with it, what people call *noblesse oblige*. Frances was a tremendously good housekeeper, organizer and a really capable woman, with a good big measure of religious faith to go along with all that—which was all just as well, because she had a very busy, difficult life.

Frances was married to another noble-person when she was just thirteen, and soon they had five children: her first big job. Then, since she had a big house, a big budget, many servants and a very large sense of duty—and since there were some plagues and wars going on—she did a huge amount of work taking care of whoever in Rome needed help. Next, her husband Lorenzo lost a battle and had to hide out far away for five years. When he finally came back, his health was completely broken down, and Frances had to be his nurse on top of everything else that she had going on.

Frances had some good friends who were also noble ladies with big houses, large budgets and a strong sense of duty, and they joined together to help each other out, forming an organization called the Oblates (after the word *oblation*, which means "an offering," because they were offering their time and talents to help people) that would go on helping people long after the ladies had "gone to their reward," as they say. So, because of Frances and her spunk and her faith and money, that organization is still going today: the clear mark of a saint at work!

March: Week Two

NICHOLAS VON FLUE (1417–1487)
hermit and patriot (March 21)

You may know the story of William Tell (I'm sure you have heard Rossini's overture), the great Swiss patriot, and how one of the cruel foreigners ruling Switzerland thought it would be funny to make him shoot an apple off his son's head, just to show how great he was with a crossbow—and how William Tell had a spare arrow tucked away to shoot at the cruel foreigner if his son had been hurt at all! You may also know that Switzerland is a confederation of many states that has been united and at peace since the 1400s. Well, today's Swiss saint is as much of a hero as William Tell and had something to do with making Switzerland united and peaceful, as we'll see.

Nicholas von Flue was a farmer and a soldier, to start with. He was married, and he and his wife, Dorothy, had ten children. Ever since he was a little boy, Nicholas had been a member of a Christian youth group called the *Gottesfreunde* ("God's Friends"), meeting and praying together and vowing to be saints, if they possibly could, so that the idea of serving God was always in the back of Nicholas' mind. Like many men of his time, he could not read or write, but he knew the law by heart, and was so wise that people from all over the region knew him and respected his opinions. So, when a court unfairly ruled against him one time, he gave up his regular life in disgust at the ways of the world and became a monk, with his wife's permission. He lived in a little cottage in the woods, contemplating God and eating nearly nothing.

"Bruder Klaus," as they called him now, lived there for twenty years, and people came to him more than ever for advice and inspiration, and to see for themselves whether he really ate nothing at all except the Eucharist. Then, when the Swiss Confederation threatened to collapse into civil war, the leaders of the different sides went down into the woods to ask his advice, and the compromise he suggested basically created Switzerland as it is today. At the end of his long life his wife and children and grandchildren and all gathered around him as he died, a real saint and the *real* hero of Switzerland!

March: Week Four

(Spring Break took out Week Three.)

VLADIMIR (955–1015)
prince and penitent (July 13) *(See Map 2)*

Prince Vladimir, grand duke of Kiev and all Russia, who lived back in the days even before Alexander Nevsky, back when most Russians were still worshipping trees, had, as the great poet A. A. Milne said of Bad King John, "his little ways." By that I mean he was the sort of prince who might grow up to be called "Vladimir the Terrible," or who might never live to grow up at all! He was a good-looking fellow, but he drank too much vodka, beat his horses and his servants, and even kicked his dogs! Vladimir loved to watch gory sports like bear-baiting (basically poking a bear with a stick until it was furious and hurt someone) and to go hunting whatever he could get a spear into. And no one wanted to marry him, whatever he looked like!

All this caused his good old grandmother, Saint Olga, great distress and even despair. But she *was* a saint, and her prayers were powerful, and Vladimir did love his grandmother and even listened to her sometimes. She told him *many* times that everything would go better for him if he would stop drinking, go to church, and try to learn how to rule his people properly. He thought and thought about this, and finally said he would give it a try, maybe also thinking about the beautiful Princess Ann, sister to the Byzantine emperor, whom he wanted to marry but who just now couldn't stand the sight of him, handsome though he was.

The first thing Vladimir did was to start going to church and actually listen to what they said there. The next thing he did was stop drinking, and then he discovered that he felt better in the mornings, and so it was easy to do the next thing, which was to stop beating his horses and servants and kicking his dog. Amazingly, he found that now they all actually behaved better, because they wanted to be helpful, and his dog actually wagged his tail at him now. Finally, he discovered that all this made him a better ruler for his people because he felt happier and could think straight and when he started doing all that ruling, he was soon too busy for bear-baiting, anyway.

But the best part was that the beautiful Princess Ann, when she discovered the handsome-but-nasty Vladimir was now a sweet, Christian sort of guy, was perfectly willing to marry him, so Vladimir could now be happy *and* have the emperor for a brother and ally. It was great to live in the days of Prince Vladimir: he was merciful to criminals, generous to the poor, and *most* of the time, he didn't force people to become good Christians like himself. Truly saintly!

april

April: Week One

BENEDICT of PALERMO (1526–1589)
abbot (April 4) *(See Map 23)*

In most parts of the United States, you can look around you and see people with all different colors of hair and eyes, and all sorts of shades of skin; we're used to it, and we like it. In some parts of the world people may be more of one sort or the other, and other kinds of people might look strange to them. We know that one of the things that makes a saint a saint is the way that they face difficulties; Benedict of Palermo looked different from most of the people around him, and it was one of the challenges he had to face.

In the great port of Palermo in Sicily you can see many more different sorts of people than in some parts of Italy, because people have come to the beautiful island of Sicily down the centuries from all over the Mediterranean Sea: there are small, slim, biscuit-colored people with jet-black hair and big brown eyes who came over as Phoenicians or Saracens; and also big, pink-faced, red-haired blue-eyed types who came from Germany in the days of the Crusades and—from the Bad Old Days of slavery—there are people the color of precious ebony wood whose ancestors were brought over from the Gold Coast of Africa. Benedict was of this last type of Palermitan, because his parents had worked as slaves on a plantation outside of Palermo, but he himself had been freed as a little boy. On the day that changed his life, he was a grown man, walking down a street—maybe a different street than he usually took—in Palermo.

Some rude folk—and maybe they were drunk—made some horrible comment about what they thought of his nice dark skin, as foolish, drunk, rude people sometimes do. But Benedict had made it a personal rule never to lower himself to be rude back at people; he just put up his chin and walked away.

It so happened that a group of Franciscan hermits had seen the whole thing, and came running after him. "What saintly patience!" they said. "Like Christ himself! Would you like to join us? *Please?*" Benedict was touched, and agreed—perhaps he had been already thinking of just such a move. He joined them in their little retreat in the mountains behind Palermo, studying and praying alone, and gathering with the others for simple meals and worship, and soon he was their leader. Then he came into town and joined a monastery *there*, and there, too, he was asked to be the abbot. He refused at first, saying he wasn't worthy, but they insisted and after that he took firm control, reorganizing them to live closer to the original way of Saint Francis of Assisi. Everyone in Palermo began to hear what a good healer he was, and a counselor for people in trouble, too . . . and no-one said rude things about Saint Benedict of Palermo again!

April: Week One

ZENO of VERONA (died 372) bishop (April 12)

If you ever go to the fine town of Lucca in the part of Italy called Tuscany, you should first take a walk on the walls that go around the city. The walls are very wide, and are actually planted on top with trees, and give a lovely view of the city and surrounding hills. Then, after you climb the strange Guinigi ("Gwee-NEE-jee") tower with the tree on top, you can visit the Duomo, that is the main church in town, to see the carvings and tombs and maybe go to a worship service. There you will see, while you are resting your legs and looking around, an old statue of a bishop in a *mitre* (the special, flame-shaped bishop hat), with a *crosier* (a staff like a fancy shepherd's crook) in his hand, only the crosier has a fish hanging from it like a fish from a fishing pole! You will also notice that the old statue is smiling. Rather odd, don't you think? Not if you know that it's Saint Zeno! Of course, if you go to Verona itself, you can see where Zeno was actually buried—*and* you can visit Juliet's balcony where she talked to Romeo . . . but that's another story.

Saint Zeno came from North Africa in the days when it was *the* place for saints to come from, when Augustine was bishop of Hippo Regius there. Zeno's family moved up to northern Italy where they had some family connections and Zeno became a priest and later the bishop of Verona. People called Arians, up in northern Italy, had become pretty confused about their Christian doctrine, apparently, and people like Zeno needed to straighten them out, so he spent a long time preaching and writing that Jesus really was both human and divine at the same time, not just human . . . and this was a big deal for the Arians. Well, Zeno straightened things out *so* successfully that more and more people came and wanted to be baptized so he had to build more and more churches of various sizes.

People liked Zeno because he was always cheerful and smiling, no matter how bad things seemed to be. Nobody knows for sure any more, but it seems that one of the things that made Zeno happy was going down to the Adige River, which runs through Verona—maybe standing on the famous bridge there—and just *angling*, which is fishing like Saint Peter only with a pole and a hook instead of a net. Maybe it was his quiet time for thinking about his sermon, or maybe people came and chatted with him while he fished, or maybe it was his informal time away from being a bishop, or maybe it is all just symbolic of how many people he baptized. In any case, you always see pictures or statues of Zeno smiling and fishing, so there is *some* kind of connection, and it made him happy. Good old Zeno the Angler!

April: Week Two

BENEDICT JOSEPH LABRÉ (1748–1783)
holy beggar (April 16) *(See Map 4)*

Just about my favorite city anywhere is Rome, Italy, and not just because it is so old and has so many beautiful and ancient buildings and things to see, or because it has a pretty nice climate (except for January, which is too cold) or because the food there is great. The people there are part of what makes it a great city: they are proud of their city but they welcome you to share it with them. For the most part they are kind and helpful and cheerful, and patient with all the strange people who come to visit. It is a city with a big heart, as today's saint found out.

Benedict Joseph Labre (I am going to call him "B.J." for short) was from the city of Boulogne in northeastern France, and he was the oldest son of a shopkeeper there, a wealthy man. But B.J. was not at all interested in becoming a shopkeeper. He was a dreamer, and not a very strong boy, physically. The other boys were always picking on him, but he never complained or fought back. He wanted to be a monk, but no monastery would take him; they said he was too weak, too young, and he didn't pay attention. B. J. took it all patiently, and when his family finally gave up on his ever "amounting to anything," he decided to leave home and visit all the holy places in Europe he could think of, taking hardly anything with him, walking everywhere, and begging for his food and shelter. People didn't go on pilgrimages much any more in the seventeen-hundreds, but B.J. went from one famous shrine to another, to Echternach, to Lourdes, to Compostela, and finally to Rome.

When he got to Rome, B.J. was ragged and muddy, smelly and dirty and covered with fleas, but he had a sweet face, big blue eyes, and a little tricorne hat that he held out for alms. It was his habit to give away any extra money or food people gave him to people even poorer than he was, to spend his days praying in churches and his nights sleeping out in the open somewhere, and begging a little in between. He found a neighborhood in Rome that loved him, in the old part called the Subura near the Forum, and found a favorite church there, Santa Maria dei Monti, right on the corner of Via dei Serpenti just one block north of Via Cavour, and the people there did their best to help him out, to keep him from getting beaten up by bullies or from giving away all his food and money. The butcher and the grocer generally had some leftovers for him. But one day, all that hard living and giving away food finally caught up with him and he collapsed in the church and died a little later in the butcher's arms. They still remember Saint "B.J" Labre there in the Subura of Rome, and anywhere there are people living on the streets, he is their saint.

April: Week Two

ANSELM (1033–1109)
bishop (April 21) *(See Maps 1, 14 & 21)*

By now you've met tons of saints who could think all of us into the ground yet who had faith as large as cathedrals . . . and here's another one. Saint Anselm was utterly solid, theologically; popes used to ask for his "take" on some particularly delicate question of Christian doctrine, and he also could—and did, in his big fancy book known as the *Prologion*—give "ontological proof of God's existence," in other words prove through logical argument that God exists. But that doesn't mean his big brain ran his life. It was his brain that asked his heart interesting questions, or as they used to say about him, "his mind wanted to understand the Truth his heart already knew."

Truth was something very important to Anselm, because he knew what Jesus said, which used to be printed on the outside of the Science Building at my old public high school: "You Shall Know The Truth, And The Truth Will Set You Free." Even when he was a little boy in Aosta, up in northern Italy, surrounded by the great Alps, Anselm wanted to know the Truth about things. And when he became bishop of Canterbury, England—that favorite haunt of saints, where the most important bishop of England was—Truth was still his watchword. Saint Anselm was the sort of wise man that every king used to wish he had for an advisor, and several lucky British kings did have him to advise them, both before and after the Norman Conquest. Once or twice he told them a Truth they really didn't want to hear, and they threw him out of England for awhile, but they always needed him back again for more advice, for more hard Truths. Anselm knew that the Truth isn't always easy to say or even to explain—but it is always the Truth. I expect you all know it too, even if you may not all be able to give "ontological proof" of it like Saint Anselm.

April: Week Three

MARCELLA (325–410) matron (January 31)

and **EUPHRASIA PELLETIER** (1796–1868)
foundress (April 24)

We have two saints today, with short stories but a single theme: *telling people what they don't want to hear can be unpopular and sometimes very dangerous.* Sometimes even if we are good people we can slowly get into bad habits of doing things, little by little, and a brave friend who really loves us—or loves the institution we work for—has to come along and show us where we went wrong and to help us, to paraphrase the song by Lennon and McCartney, "get back to where we once belonged." We may crab and complain and drag our feet, but we *know* that changing our ways is the right thing to do in the end.

Our first saint, Marcella, found out that her friend Jerome, even though he was doing a great thing—translating the Bible into the language of western Europe of the time, Latin—he was *not* always a great person. Marcella was a brave woman, an old-timey type Roman matron who wouldn't put up with his grumpy attitude; told him he was being positively un-Christian, and eventually Jerome had to agree with her and tried to behave better. Marcella had a big house on the Aventine Hill in Rome, where all the wealthy folks lived, and in her house lived a bunch of woman friends who helped the poor and sick and worshiped together, the way the apostles did in Jerusalem. Her husband had died, and she had no family, so her friends and the people they took care of were her family, and she happily spent her wealth on them. But in 410, when the terrible Visigoths came to Rome and sacked it for the first time in eight hundred years, she had to tell the Visigoths something they surely didn't want to hear: no, she had no treasure hidden in her house; she had *given it all away.* They didn't believe her, of course, because they couldn't imagine anyone doing that, and they kept slapping her around to make her tell them . . . but she was an old lady now, and a few days later she died because they had been so rough with her. But she had told the Truth, no matter how unpopular it was.

Our second saint, Euphrasia (her name when she was a little girl was Rose Virginia, but she changed it when she became a nun—much more impressive) came to the convent of the Good Shepherd Sisters in France and found that they *weren't* being very good shepherds, and when she told them so, they were not very sisterly about it. The funny thing is, even when you may be working for a church, which is supposed to be God's work, you can get pretty human in how you go about it! The sisters complained that Euphrasia was just changing things there so that she could become the person in charge of some other more famous convent somewhere else, and that the way she wanted to do things was wrong and they had never done them like that before, and that she was going to be in big trouble with the people back in Rome if she kept on trying to do things her way . . . *blah, blah, blah,* even though she had been told by "the people in Rome" themselves that the changes needed to happen! Maybe facing angry Visigoths would have been easier, she thought. They say that Euphrasia "could have ruled a kingdom if she'd wanted to," and sure enough, change finally came after much prayer and patience and hard work.

So remember: sometimes the most saintly thing you can do is to tell someone (gently, if you can manage it) the truth that they don't want to hear, but that they need to hear anyway.

April: Week Three

MESROP (345–439) teacher (February 19)

STEPHEN of PERM (1345–1396)
bishop and missionary (April 26)

(See Map 26 for both)

Here are two more saints with a similar story, namely *talk to people in their own language and they will take you to their hearts*. You have probably met people who don't speak the same language you do, and you can still communicate with them by smiling and pointing for simple things, but if you try to explain anything too complicated or if you try to read something in another language, you know it is almost impossible. Being able to bridge the reading gap is about as powerful as establishing an electrical connection to a lightbulb: *flash!* Once you have an alphabet, it is like putting a plug in a wall socket. As we've seen, Cyril and Methodius worked out an alphabet for the Slavic-type languages, and today's two saints took on two more languages: Mesrop in Armenian was the earliest, and Stephen of Perm in the language of the Zyrians of Komi, way up in the Ural mountains, a thousand years later.

People have lived in the beautiful mountain country of Armenia since Noah and his ark floated by there some nine thousand years ago, and they have been Christians for 1700 years, ever since Mesrop made them an alphabet and they could read the scriptures for themselves. The Armenians had always been wise, but once they could read and put the books of other wise people like the Greeks into Armenian with the help of Mesrop, they became real intellectuals, learning how to be doctors and lawyers and priests.

And up to Komi, far north of Armenia, came a Russian priest named Stephen who had grown up with Zyrian folks and could speak the language, and he brought with him a Bible in Zyrian for them, just as Mesrop had done for the Armenians. The Zyrians weren't too sure about Stephen at first, but when their old pagan priest challenged Stephen to a kind of a "wizard's duel," he accepted, and offered to hold the old man's hand while they went together through a burning hut and a freezing lake. But the evil old man was just trying to kill Stephen and when he refused to go with him, the people knew he was a fake and decided to become Christians after all! In fact, they decided to help Stephen burn down their old temple and the statue that they had been worshipping all those years. Then they were happy to read all about their new God in their own language, once Stephen showed them in the sign language of courage how much he faith *he* had in that God.

Mesrop and Stephen: saints who were rather like electrical conduits for bringing people the wisdom and power of God!

April: Week Four

ZITA of LUCCA (1218–1278)
servant (April 27) *(See Map 14)*

Y ou have probably heard me talk about the city of Lucca already, and how there is a statue of Saint Zeno of Verona there, but this story is about someone who actually came from Lucca itself. In the middle of Lucca is a tall church with a big stone angel on top, Saint Michael, and he is certainly very popular there, but the saint everyone in Lucca probably loves the best is Zita, who was *not* an archangel but just a little servant girl. Now, we've seen that sometimes the greatest trials saints have are not lions or swords but the people who call themselves our friends, and Zita certainly found that out, too.

Back in Italy in the thirteenth century (and even today in some parts of the world), a lot of poor farm-girls went to work as maids in the great houses of the wealthy nobility. (Saint Notburga started this way too, as you may have heard.) When Zita was twelve years old she left her family's farm and went to work in the house of the Fatinelli family of Lucca, and stayed there the rest of her life. Zita was a model servant, doing everything quickly and carefully, always being cheerful and honest. But did her fellow servants appreciate all that? They did not! For years, they thought she was just showing off, and they also made fun of her for going to church every day. They made up stories about her to the Fatinellis which always turned out to be lies, but Zita never lost her temper or stopped being a good worker, so after a while the Fatinellis stopped listening, and the other servants began to think that Zita *really was* as good as she seemed to be.

Finally, rather like Joseph in the Bible, Zita was put in charge of the whole household and the family trusted her with everything they owned, even though they knew that she liked to give away her own dinner and blankets to anyone who needed them . . . they didn't mind if she gave away some of their own things, if she really thought the person was in trouble. But there is a story that one Christmas Eve, when Zita was off to church but had no coat (she'd given it away again), Mr. Fatinelli let her borrow his warm fur cloak, as long as she took good care of it.

Well of course when Zita got to church for the Christmas Eve service, there was a poor beggar in rags, outside the door, and she let *him* borrow the cloak, at least while she was inside. You guessed it: when she came out, the beggar was gone, and she was very sad that she had let Mr. Fatinelli down, and sure enough he was quite angry with her. But on Christmas morning a stranger came to the door to give back the cloak, and then everyone thought it was a miracle, that maybe that had been a holy angel at the church door (and it was called the Holy Door after that)!

All her life, Zita kept doing that kind of thing, just impulsively helping people whenever she could, all over Lucca, and after she died, people prayed to her for help—especially maids who had lost their house keys, or other ordinary people—hoping that she would keep on impulsively helping them, too, and apparently she often did.

April: Week Four

JOSEPH COTTOLENGO (1786–1842)
founder (April 30)

In a big city, there are always plenty of people who run into trouble once they get there. Maybe they came there because they had a promise of a job, but once they had sold all their things and come to the city there was nothing for them there, after all . . . or maybe they came with their parents and their parents died, and there was no one to take care of them. The big Italian city of Turin (or Torino, as it's known there, remember) was as full of trouble, about two hundred years ago, as most big cities are today. Joseph Cottolengo was just a regular parish priest there in those days, doing his job but not much more, when he helped out a poor homeless woman who died having a baby and then the baby died . . . and it all made him so sad and angry that he wanted to do something to really help the poor people of Torino, not just to be with them when they died. So Joseph started a shelter for the sick and homeless in the poorest part of Torino called *Valdocco*.

One thing that made Joseph successful in the good things he did was that he never, never, *never* lost hope, but always just assumed that God would provide all he needed for his house at Valdocco; in other words, he had complete faith in Providence. When people would give him money, he never kept track of how much money he had, he just went out and spent it on the things he knew the people in his house needed right then—like medicine or blankets or food—and when there wasn't money, he did other things that needed doing and didn't worry.

He called his house "The Little House (*Piccola Casa*) of Divine Providence," and it helped hundreds of poor Torinese folk. Joseph himself died there of typhus, in the Bad Old Days of disease before booster shots were invented. But nowadays people can get free inoculations against typhus at the *Piccola Casa*, thanks to Saint Joseph Cottolengo's faith in Providence.

may

ISIDORE the FARM SERVANT (1070–1130)
patron of Madrid (May 10) *(See Map 6)*

We've read by now about queens, doctors, shepherdesses—all of them saints—and here comes the great story of Isidore, patron of the Spanish capital city of Madrid. He was just a tenant farmer along with his wife, Maria de la Cabeza, working for a landowner near Torrelaguna, outside Madrid. Both Isidore and Maria were devout Christians as well as hard workers, going to church as often as they could, going on pilgrimages to holy places for holidays, and praying as they worked, and they were good neighbors to everyone around them. But it is hard to be generous when your time and all you own belong (apparently) to someone else.

One morning, his employer heard a rumor that Isidore (*Ysidro* in Spanish) was going to be a little late getting to the fields because he had been doing some charitable thing or other, and his employer hurried angrily over to the field where he was supposed to be working that day to scold "that Ysidro" for not getting the plowing done. But they say that when he got there, not only was Isidore hard at work behind his oxen, there was another pair of oxen, white ones, and another plow, and behind this plow was an angel, helping Isidore catch up!

Another time, when Isidore was carrying a big sack of grain to the mill to be ground into flour—and it was a bitterly cold winter's day—he saw a whole flock of sad-looking hungry birds huddled all together on a branch, and he just *had* to pour out half of the grain for them to eat. They flew down happily and pecked away until it was all gone (and I'm sure it saved their lives), but at the mill, the other half-sack miraculously yielded just as much flour as a full one would have, so Isidore didn't get into trouble!

Isidore is one of those saints who manage—miraculously—to balance hard work and generosity, and make every single thing they do somehow holy, something we can all try to do, even without angels helping with our homework.

May: Week One

FRANCIS di GIROLAMO (1642–1716)
missionary (May 11) *(See Map 25)*

 **B**ack when Naples, Italy was a romantic and chaotic port city, full of life, poverty and fishwives, madonnas, street theater, color and music—well, maybe as it is today—and life there was dangerous and exciting, there was a Jesuit priest who, instead of going off to China or India or the New World to do mission work, came instead to "far-away" Naples, just north and west of his hometown of Taranto.

Francis di Girolamo really was the man for the job: he was the kindest and most patient and hard-working visitor ever to help out the needy people in the little back streets of all the city's different neighborhoods, whether up on the hills or down by the water, on the streets or in the back lanes, all the "worst" places. He went fearlessly into prisons and onto galleys and into brothels and sickrooms. He saved orphans and rescued abused children, set up a charitable pawnshop, and started a working-man's volunteer club to help him get it all done.

But Francis was also a terrific preacher. They said that he was "like a lamb when he talks, and a lion when he preaches." His sermons were short, full of pep, and to the point, and he converted to Christianity great numbers of folk, even Muslim prisoners and a woman who had been serving in the army disguised as a man, after she killed her father. Pretty dangerous and exciting all right; *un vero uomo*, a real man, that Saint Francis di Girolamo!

May: Week Two

ANDREW FOURNET (1752–1834) priest (May 13)

and JULIE (MARY MARGARET) POSTEL (1765–1846)
teacher (July 16)

The French Revolution was a time when the farmers and other regular folk of France went a little crazy due to being treated so badly for so long by the landowners and other upper-class folk, and killed bunches of them with the guillotine or in various other unpleasant ways. These common folk were also angry at the Church, because too often it seemed as though church folk didn't care about anything but getting to be bishop and didn't take care of the sick and hungry people in their care. So the people in charge of the Revolution said go ahead and arrest priests and nuns and smash up churches and toss out the bones of the saints! And it was a mess, as you can imagine.

There was one young priest named Andrew Fournet who learned a lot about himself and his faith during this crazy time. He had been bored with life when his uncle talked him into becoming a *curé* (priest) at Maillé where he was born. But when the French Revolution came, Andrew's life became much more interesting. He refused to take the oath that would have made him an employee of the French government instead of the Church; he secretly held church services, and when he was arrested, he insisted on *walking* to jail, as Christ had done, instead of going in the prison wagon. That time he wasn't killed, though, and another time, he escaped from the police by changing places with a dead body at a funeral—*most* dramatic and not at all boring!

When things calmed down, Andrew went to work as a priest at a convent and school, where he became famous for multiplying food in hard times and generally doing interesting and even exciting things with the rest of his life.

Another hero of those times was Julie Postel, a teacher at a French girls' school who also ran an underground Eucharist service during the Revolution. She later started an order of teaching nuns, changing her name from Julie to the much more dramatic Mary Margaret, and also worked and prayed hard, like Andrew. Andrew and Julie: two saints who liked a challenge!

May: Week Two

DUNSTAN (909–988)
bishop and reformer (May 19) *(See Map 1)*

Have you ever wondered what to be when you grow up? Maybe it's something nobody can pronounce, like a *paleontologist,* or maybe you're pretty sure you would make a great fire-fighter, but what happens later on when you've done that for awhile and now you're interested in being something else? Well, you could be like good old Saint Dunstan, and be *many* things during a long, interesting lifetime!

After going to school at the monastery at Glastonbury, England, Dunstan was happy at the royal court, listening to stories of long ago, to the old pagan sagas, even dabbling in a little magic, and he was *almost* thrown out of court for being a magician. But when he caught a skin disease he was afraid that God was punishing him for being so frivolous, and vowed that he would give it all up and become a holy hermit. He wound up joining one of those well-designed monasteries where you learn a craft and really perfect it. Dunstan now tried to become the best painter of sacred pictures and the best embroiderer of sacred vestments in the land—and England was famous all over Europe for its painting and embroidery in those days.

Then Dunstan tried his hand at blacksmithing—an ancient, mystical craft—and they say that once the devil tried to distract him from his work, and was grabbed by the nose with Dunstan's hot tongs until he promised to leave him alone! Dunstan became especially good at bell-founding, maybe because he also loved music, and could also sing and even play the harp. They must have missed him at court! But he couldn't stay a monk forever; his family wanted him to become a priest at the royal court of King Edmund, and then Edmund made him abbot of Glastonbury Abbey, where he had gone to school and where they say King Arthur was buried. Dunstan ran the abbey as creatively as he did everything else, but he was also as tough on those who misbehaved as he had been on the devil that time! He straightened out the way things were run there, making them follow old Saint Benedict's Rule more closely than they had been. He also encouraged the founding of new monasteries near and far.

Dunstan was next made archbishop of Canterbury, and acted as an advisor to *six* Kings of England over his long lifetime. He was especially fond of King Edgar, and wrote for him a special coronation service that is still used in crowning rulers of England today. And when he was an old man, Saint Dunstan just taught school in Canterbury, as Saint Adrian had done before him, and although he was gentle with the boys, they minded their manners, perhaps remembering the devil and the tongs!

May: Week Three

GODRIC (1065–1170)
penitent pirate, hermit and poet (May 21)
(See Maps 1 & 12)

When John the Baptist wanted to tell a group of people to repent, he called them "a brood of vipers." Well, someone must have slung that epithet at today's saint, because he certainly needed to repent, and he had a fondness for vipers. A pirate with a heart of gold—who could ask for a better beginning to a story than that?

Even when Godric, who came from that northeastern coast of England called Northumbria, was a smuggler and a pirate, he always loved his mother: an encouraging sign! You could hire him for just about any job, legal or not, that involved a boat, but he also went on religious pilgrimages to Scotland, Spain and the Holy Land, and once he and his dear old Ma walked to Rome together to visit the tombs of the apostles. They say he was a big, strong, blue-eyed man with long hair and a wild outlook on life, but also, as we've seen, a religious streak.

After a dangerous adventure during which King Baldwin of Jerusalem hired his boat to escape from the Battle of Ramlegh in the Holy Land, and probably after his dear old Ma had died, Godric began to think of retiring and reforming his life. So he came back to Northumbria, wandered up the Wear River away from the sea and, somewhere in the wilderness near Durham and Finchale, where Finchale Priory is today, settled down to become a hermit. Godric wanted to do *penance* (that is, to make life hard on himself to somehow make amends for all the bad things he had done to everyone else for years and years) so he ate very little and prayed all he could. Like most hermits who try to be by themselves all the time, he attracted a fair number of people asking for his advice, especially because they said he could foretell the future. Also like most hermits in the wild, Godric became good friends with the animals all around him and seemed to have some kind of power over them, especially over some vipers that he kept as pets, maybe because they reminded him of his old self. But when he found himself thinking more about his pet vipers than about his prayers, he sadly sent them away.

After that, he got some book-learning and was inspired to compose lyrics and music for some little hymns: one for the Virgin Mary that would bring him her help whenever he sang it, and another one, this in English rather than Latin, in praise of Saint Nicholas, patron saint not only of children but also of his old sort of life: sailing and stealing. Godric had never written any music before, and he claimed that the music came from visions he had had of the Virgin Mary and his own dead sister, singing together. Who would ever have thought an old pirate would write a hymn? And who for that matter would ever have thought a hungry old pirate would *live* so long, because—goodness!—good old Saint Godric lived to be one hundred and five years old!

Godric's song for Saint Nicholas, among the earliest recorded songs in Anglo-Saxon

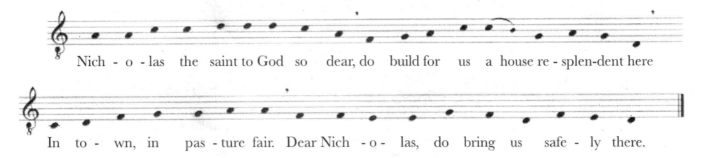

Nich - o - las the saint to God so dear, do build for us a house re - splen-dent here

In to - wn, in pas - ture fair. Dear Nich - o - las, do bring us safe - ly there.

source: Helen Deeming, *The Songs of St. Godric: A Neglected Context*, Music and Letters -- Volume 86, Number 2, 2005, pp. 169-185. Translated by Michaela White, versified by Kathryn Lucchese.

May: Week Three

RITA of CASCIA (1377–1447) wife and nun (May 22)

Some people might complain that there are not enough women saints in the canon (that is, the saint list). Maybe part of the reason is that until very recently the more traditional types of churches didn't allow women to be bishops or priests—which is how a lot of men saints got their starts, after all—and another part may be that the girls' families wouldn't even let them go to school: they expected their daughters to hurry up, get married and raise a family. It is hard to find time for a rich spiritual life when you are wrestling with dirty diapers and housecleaning . . . but not impossible, as today's saint proves.

Certainly our Saint Rita would have liked to have spent her life contemplating God and helping the poor, but her parents insisted she marry . . . and what a man they picked for her! He was certainly wealthy, but apparently a real brute: always drunk and slapping her around. But Rita decided that maybe this was her big test of character, something like facing the lions in the Coliseum in the olden days, and she tried to be a good wife, and a good mother, even though her two little boys looked like becoming as bad as their father. It was an awfully hard life, and not even her own parents liked her to go to church; they made fun of her for going so much. Finally, her husband seemed to get the message and decided to repent and be a better man, but then he was murdered! The sons were all ready to take up the *vendetta* (that's a revenge killing type of fight) and kill the murderers, but they fell deathly ill, told Rita they were sorry for having been so rotten all their lives, and died.

After that, Rita devoted herself full-time to church business and began to spend long hours contemplating Christ on the cross—so long, in fact, that she got a sort of sympathetic wound on her forehead that wouldn't heal, a lot like a deep scratch from a thorn. Another miraculous thing was that, just before she died, her favorite rosebush bloomed for her, even though it was the wrong time of year for roses. All this happened so long ago, but the people in Cascia, Italy, remember Rita by being extra hospitable to visitors, by growing special roses, and by having lots of sister-cities all over Europe. And not surprisingly, Rita is the special saint for those who have really rough married lives or generally lots of problems.

May: Week Four

PHILIP NERI (1515–1595)
founder and reformer (May 26)

 You can be very sure that sometime around his special memorial day in May, some group in the city of Rome will be performing an oratorio in honor of Saint Philip Neri. And what is an *oratorio*, you ask? It's sort of like an opera, only the people in it don't dress up in costumes and act it out, and the story is always something from the Bible, like the story of Samson and Delilah, or the Passion of Christ, or the Creation. Probably the most famous oratorio is "The Messiah," written in a white heat of creativity by Georg Friderick Handel over a period of about a month. But the man who came up with the idea of an oratorio in the first place was our Philip Neri. He was full of great ideas, and Rome in those days needed all the good ideas it could get.

In 1527, when Philip was twelve years old, an incredibly terrible thing happened to his hometown of Rome, Italy: an angry army of Bavarian lansquenet soldiers, who hated the city and the pope and everything connected with them both, descended on Rome, took it over, then plundered and destroyed and behaved horribly there for months and months. Boys like Philip managed to hide out and get by, but they say that for years afterward you couldn't find any old men in the whole city, because they had all been caught and killed!

One of the things that most upset the Romans was that when the lansquenets attacked, all the priests and other clergymen locked themselves up in the Castel Sant' Angelo and wouldn't let any women or children in, especially women, as they might make the priests forget their vows not to marry! After the Bavarian barbarians finally left, the people of Rome were not just angry at *them*, but also angry with the pope and the clergy; it was enough to make them never want to go to church again as long as they lived!

Although our Philip knew that the pope and the clergy were just human beings, and also that God did not deserve to be blamed for what had happened to the Romans, he just as certainly knew that people needed their faith strengthened and their hurts healed. He knew that they wouldn't trust priests yet; he himself wasn't a priest (though he became one much later). He was still just a schoolteacher and a philosopher, but his idea was have lay-people—that is, regular people who were not priests—get together to worship and pray and plan out what they could do to help the community. They started by building hostels for pilgrims visiting Rome, then set up rest houses for people who were just getting over illnesses, and they even built a new hospital called Holy Trinity. Later, when Philip did become a priest, he got permission to build a new church for his congregation, and there they could hold what they called *oratories* ("prayer sessions"), which were meetings for worship and planning. Part of every service featured Bible stories put to music, those *oratorios* I was talking about, and soon everyone was composing them. Well, I could go on and on, but probably the only last important thing you need to know about Philip Neri is that he was very fond of cats, which makes sense, since Rome is as famous for its cats as it is for its saints.

May: Week Four

BONA of PISA (1156–1207)
nun and pilgrim (May 29) *(See Maps 6 & 14)*

Whenever I lead a group of students or grown-ups on a trip abroad, I always try to avoid making the same mistakes I made on the last trip; this sometimes means that I make *new* mistakes, of course! It is comforting for me to know that there is actually a patron saint for this kind of activity, and that she, too, learned from her mistakes and tried to help others to have a great trip, every time.

Back when Bona was growing up in the great Italian west-coast port city of Pisa, people went on *long* trips to make up for some bad thing they had done. This making up for doing bad things was called "doing penance," and it was supposed to be punishment. This kind of long religious trip was known as a *pilgrimage,* a sort of offering of your time and risking of your life to go visit a holy place, thus making it more likely—so the belief went—that you got into heaven. In Bona's day, one of the best places you could go for a pilgrimage was Santiago de Compostela, in northern Spain, a place sacred to Saint James the Apostle. When Bona was a little girl, she dreamed that Saint James had specially blessed her, but her own first journey was not to Spain but all the way to Jerusalem in the Holy Land, where her father was on a Crusade. She got there all right, but on the way back, she was captured by pirates, got wounded, and was kept in prison until some fellow Pisans rescued her: definitely a travel mistake to learn from!

Now Bona knew what *not* to do, and from then on she went to Spain instead of to Jerusalem, under the protection of the Knights of Saint James, her personal patron saint. All told, she went to Compostela *nine* times, leading other pilgrims. Bona was always full of energy, cheering up anyone who got sick along the way, always ready to help them out however she could. In fact, she was about to set out on a *tenth* trip, but didn't feel too well and died before she could leave Pisa. As you may have guessed, she is the official patron saint of flight attendants, couriers and tour guides and—along with Saint Christopher—of travelers. Like other saints, she risked her own life to help other people in their faith . . . by taking them on pilgrimages.

JUNE

JUSTIN (100–165) and **BLANDINA** (died 177)
martyrs (June 1 & 2)

In Roman history—now, don't fall asleep before I've even started—people like to talk about the time of the Five Good Emperors. Unlike Nero or Caligula, these "Good" Emperors weren't crazy, and they didn't go around killing members of their own family, they didn't burn down Rome to beautify their neighborhood and make room for a nice big palace and they never made a horse into a senator. But they weren't good for *everyone*. For example, the merciful and beloved Emperor Titus also helped his benevolent father Vespasian completely flatten Jerusalem and its Temple, and then took the Temple's famous menorah—the very same one that had miraculously burned for eight nights on the oil for one night—off to Rome as a trophy, along with the people of Jerusalem as slaves!

The wise "good-emperor" philosopher-king Marcus Aurelius couldn't stand Christians and launched the next big "kill-Christians" spree since Nero blamed the Christians for the Great Fire! The word from Marcus Aurelius was that, not only were Christians (or Nazarenes, as Christians were often called in those days, after the town where Jesus grew up) bloody traitors to Rome since they refused to worship either Father Jove or the emperor as gods, but also Christians were cannibals, which was strictly illegal then (as it still is now). After all, Christians were supposedly always going around "eating the flesh and drinking the blood" (the bread and wine of communion, or Eucharist) of their leader, Christ! Then there was the disgusting notion that Christian brothers and sisters married each other (that's called incest, also illegal then as now), because the Romans didn't understand that, among Christians, "brother" and "sister" were just how people addressed one another. So, in the time of Marcus Aurelius, a lot of Christians died for their faith.

Justin and Blandina were two of those: Justin died in Rome, and Blandina died in the big fancy new Roman city of Lyons, in France. Justin had begun his grown-up life as a Platonic philosopher like the emperor himself, but questions about ultimate Good, ideal forms, and the dialectic quest for Truth naturally led Justin to become a Christian. He even spoke to the emperor about his ideas, but in vain. He was so certain that all his big questions had finally been answered that when the prefect Rusticus urged Justin to sacrifice to the chief gods of Rome and so save his life, Saint Justin turned mildly to Rusticus and explained: "No right-minded man forsakes Truth for falsehood," and had his head chopped off.

In Lyons, the people were absolutely furious with the Christians, convinced that they were horrible incestuous cannibals, and poor Blandina was treated pretty roughly, but she absolutely refused to lie and say that there was any nastiness going on at church services. She tried to explain that her people certainly didn't *eat* people, even though by faith the bread and wine did become the flesh and blood of Christ. Finally Blandina tried to make it simple for them, by declaring, *"I am a Christian, and we do nothing vile!"* But they didn't believe her, and fed her to the lions of Lyons. So I hope you are all very careful to think for yourselves when people say terrible things about other people—even if the person telling you those terrible things is, say, the emperor of Rome—and stop to find out the Truth for yourselves.

June: Week One

COLUMBA (521–597)
missionary and abbot (June 9)
(See Maps 1 & 17)

Columba, they say, was related by direct descent to Niall (pronounced "Neal") of the Nine Hostages. No, I don't know what that means exactly, but I *think* it means that he was of royal Celtic blood, and could have been a king, himself, even High King of Ireland, if he had wanted to. What he wanted instead was to be a monk and serve God, the High King of High Kings. But back in those Strange Old Days, disagreements between groups of Irish monks were settled the same way the Irish clans in the hills used to settle things between each other, that is, really violently. On one occasion, when Columba copied from another monk's Psaltery (that's a book of Psalms) without asking the monk's permission first, there was an actual *battle* between Columba's monks and the others, and some monks were killed!

To make up for his sins, Columba set out to convert as many pagan souls to Christianity as he had gotten killed through his careless copying, so he set off for the wilds of Scotland, where the Painted People lived: the Picts, who covered themselves with a blue dye called *woad* in order to terrify their many enemies. So Columba set up a monastery on the little Isle—the holy isle—of Iona, off the southwestern coast of the Scottish Isle of Mull, and he went up and down the coast, an "island soldier," but for God, not for the clans, preaching the Good News, always cheerful and friendly, doing the kinds of miracles in Scotland that Saint Patrick did in Ireland. Columba didn't scare any snakes out of Scotland, but he did make the Loch Ness monster leave the vicinity by making the sign of the cross over it! Iona is still a holy isle today, and a very popular place for church retreats. If you are ever lucky enough to visit, remember that the place was made sacred by good old Saint Columba, the "island soldier!"

June: Week Two

GERMAINE of PIBRAC (1579–1601)
shepherdess (June 15)

Here, at last, is another "shepherdess on the green," which the hymn about saints promised us (the last one was Joan of Arc), and her story is a lot like something from a fairy tale, only unfortunately the "wicked stepmother" really existed.

Germaine came from a little place in the countryside of France near Toulouse, and when her own mother died, her father married again, and neither her father nor her stepmother liked Germaine very much, I'm sorry to say. This was not because, like Cinderella, Germaine was more beautiful than her step-sisters; it was because Germaine was not more beautiful than anyone. She was unhealthy, her hand was all shriveled, and she had some sort of ugly skin disease. Her stepmother did not want Germaine anywhere near her own children, and poor Germaine had to sleep in a cupboard under the stairs like Harry Potter, or out in the stable with the donkey. Really, they didn't seem to realize that she was not a beast, but just a girl; they fed her the scraps from the table as if she were a little dog, and from the time she was eight years old, they sent her out all day, every day, to take care of the sheep, whatever the weather was like.

Now, you might think that all this mean treatment would have made Germaine as grumpy as it sometimes made Harry Potter, or have made her as mean as her family was, but no, Germaine had a strong belief in a God who loved her as much as her dead mother used to love her, and her faith in God and the memory of her mother's love kept her sweet and cheerful, no matter how rottenly she was treated. She liked being with the sheep, for another thing, and the countryside was much more beautiful than her house. She liked to watch the seasons change in the trees and see the little lambs born in the springtime. But she also liked to go to church every day, and for that her family called her "the little bigot." She liked especially to help poor people the best she could, even giving them the little leftovers she got from the table, or even extra food, as her stepmother suspected, and for that she always got into trouble.

One cold winter's morning, when Germaine was twenty-two years old, she did take an extra loaf of bread out with her to the fields for a poor person—maybe for a sick woman who was out staying with the sheep to keep warm—and her stepmother was furious and ran after her full of evil glee: she would catch her stealing this time, and give her a good whipping, she thought! So she caught up with Germaine, fetched her a smack on the cheek, and told her to open her apron at once, and there she saw, in the middle of winter, an apron full of spring flowers—a miracle of God to try to keep Germaine safe. But a few days later, Germaine was found dead in her little cupboard. After she was buried all sorts of miracles seemed to spring up around her tomb until everyone knew she had been a saint, and maybe even her family was sorry, and maybe even became better people. Let's hope so!

June: Week Two

PAULINUS of NOLA (353–431)
bishop and hagiographer (June 22)
(See Map 25)

We finish this two-year celebration of saints with a saint who was a big fan of other saints (often the way it happens, actually), especially his personal favorite, Saint Felix of Nola. Pontius Meropius Paulinus (we'll just call him Paulinus, if that's okay) was a well-to-do, kind, easy-going man who loved his beautiful Spanish wife, Therasia, and liked to write poetry. He had the makings of a great poet according to his teacher, Ausonius, as well as a good *rhetorician* (public speaker), which is what most wealthy Romans hoped for, so they could be senators and do great things for Rome. In fact, Paulinus did become a politician, and he and Therasia enjoyed traveling around Italy, Spain and France, between their many estates.

On visiting their land in central Italy, they came for the first time to the busy city of Nola, behind the sinister double peak of Mount Vesuvius, and visited the church of Saint Felix. He and Therasia were so impressed by Felix's story and the faith of the Christians in Nola that they both became Christians, and started a little monastery there, and Therasia volunteered to take care of them all, a bit like Wendy and the Lost Boys, with Paulinus as Peter Pan.

For awhile, they had to move to Barcelona in Spain, and there the church asked Paulinus to be their bishop, even though he was just a new Christian, and still married and all. But he agreed, and officially studied to be a priest. After a time in Spain, he and Therasia sold all their estates except the ones near Nola, moved back there and used the money to build a great big new church there, all decorated with Bible stories in mosaic ("to keep the visitors respectful," so the stories go, but it was definitely an idea that caught on in other churches all over), and he even provided the church with a nice aqueduct to bring water to the church so pilgrims to Nola could wash and drink whenever they needed to, and they built a comfortable guest house for pilgrims to stay in: he and his monks stayed upstairs, and Therasia went back to running the whole thing! Paulinus became bishop of Nola, and he used his poetical skills to write hymns, especially a series of poems for Saint Felix's Day, one poem each year. At this time, he also wrote a poem to Ausonius, his old poetry teacher from pagan days, entitled: "I Am Not He, Whom You Knew Then."

Paulinus wrote an especially good poem in honor of Saint Felix in 401, the year that Alaric the Goth was beginning to raid the north of

Italy, the beginning of the terrible barbarian raids that would bring down the western Roman empire. This poem has been translated and used as the popular hymn, "Another Year Completed":

> *Another year completed, the day comes 'round once more,*
> *Which with our patron's radiance is bright as heretofore.*
> *Now, strong in hope, united, his festival we greet;*
> *He will present our troubles before the mercy-seat.*

Which can apply to Christ, or Felix, or Paulinus, or any other of the brave souls seen as intercessors for mere mortals here on earth, the saints who also were once just "folk like me."

The end for now . . .

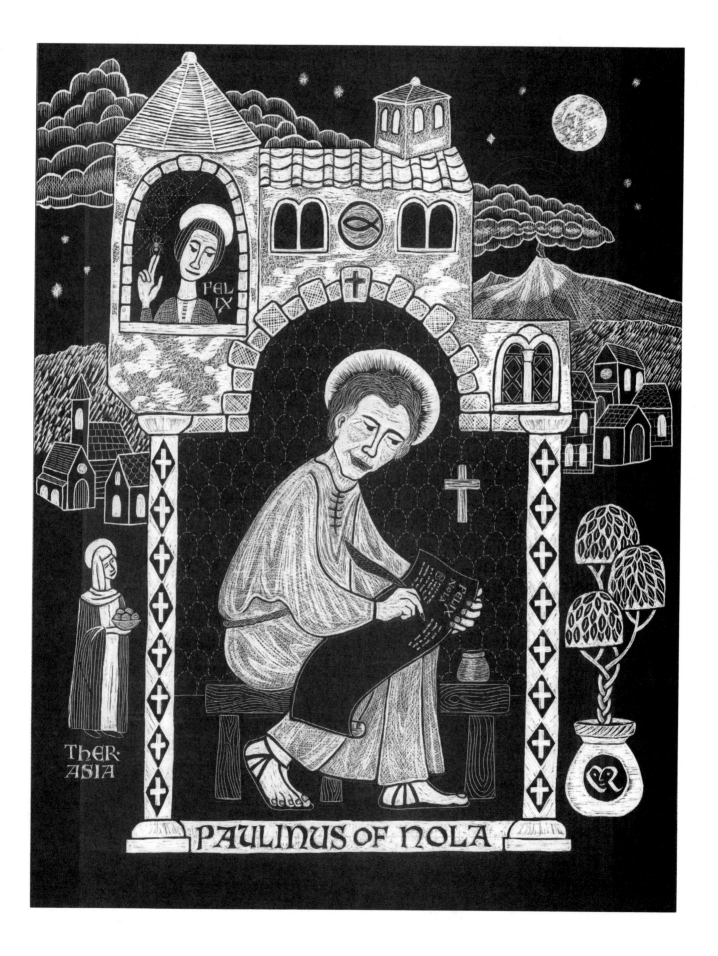

ᗰaps

Locations in this style are old regions or kingdoms

MERCIA

Map 1: Locations in Great Britain associated with:

Saints Adrian of Canterbury, Aldhelm, Anselm, Columba, Cuthbert, Dunstan, Ethelbert, Godric, Guthlac & Pega, Hugh of Lincoln, John of Beverley, Maughold, Michael, Mildred, Oswald, Sigfrid & Venerable Bede

See also detailed maps for saints from Wessex, Northumbria, and East Anglia.

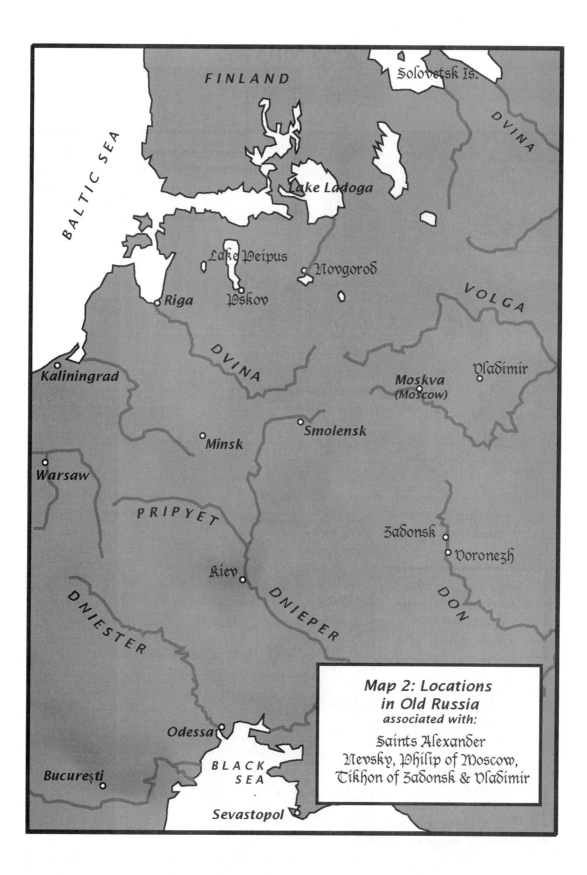

FINLAND

Solovetsk Is.

BALTIC SEA

DVINA

Lake Ladoga

Lake Peipus

Novgorod

VOLGA

Riga

Pskov

DVINA

Vladimir

Kaliningrad

Moskva
(Moscow)

Smolensk

Minsk

Warsaw

PRIPYET

Zadonsk

Voronezh

Kiev

DNIEPER

DON

DNIESTER

Odessa

BLACK
SEA

București

Sevastopol

**Map 2: Locations
in Old Russia**
associated with:

Saints Alexander
Nevsky, Philip of Moscow,
Tikhon of Zadonsk & Vladimir

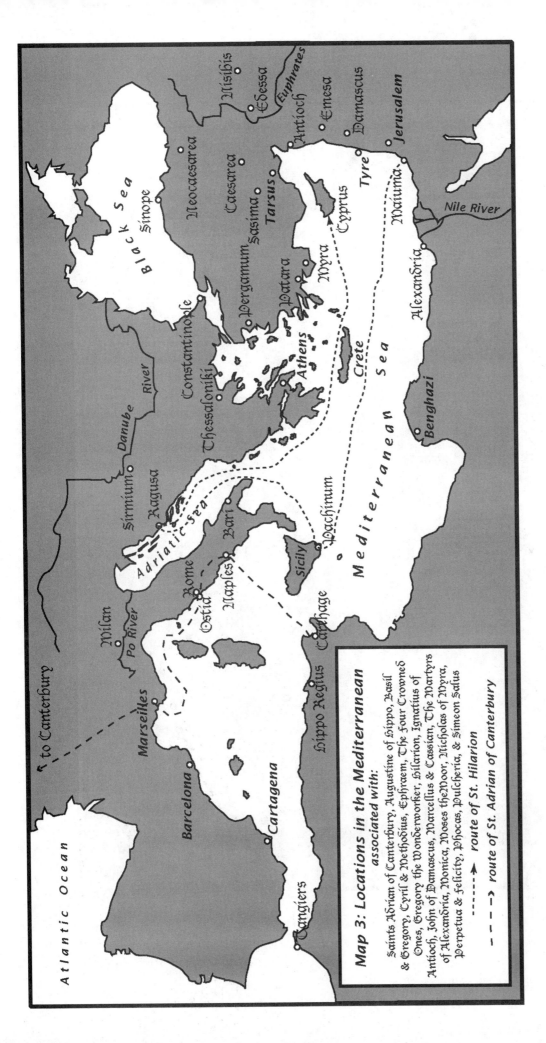

Atlantic Ocean

to Canterbury

Barcelona

Cartagena

Tangiers

Marseilles

Milan

Po River

Danube

River

Sirmium

Ragusa

Adriatic Sea

Rome

Ostia

Naples

Bari

Sicily

Carthage

Hippo Regius

Dachimum

Black Sea

Sinope

Neocaesarea

Caesarea

Sasima

Pergamum

Patara

Constantinople

Thessaloniki

Athens

Myra

Crete

Cyprus

Tarsus

Antioch

Nisibis

Edessa

Euphrates

Emesa

Damascus

Tyre

Jerusalem

Maiuma

Nile River

Alexandria

Benghazi

Mediterranean Sea

Map 3: Locations in the Mediterranean
associated with:

Saints Adrian of Canterbury, Augustine of Hippo, Basil & Gregory, Cyril & Methodius, Ephraem, The Four Crowned Ones, Gregory the Wonderworker, Hilarion, Ignatius of Antioch, John of Damascus, Marcellus & Cassian, The Martyrs of Alexandria, Monica, Moses the Moor, Nicholas of Myra, Perpetua & Felicity, Phocas, Pulcheria, & Simeon Salus

——→ route of St. Hilarion

– – –→ route of St. Adrian of Canterbury

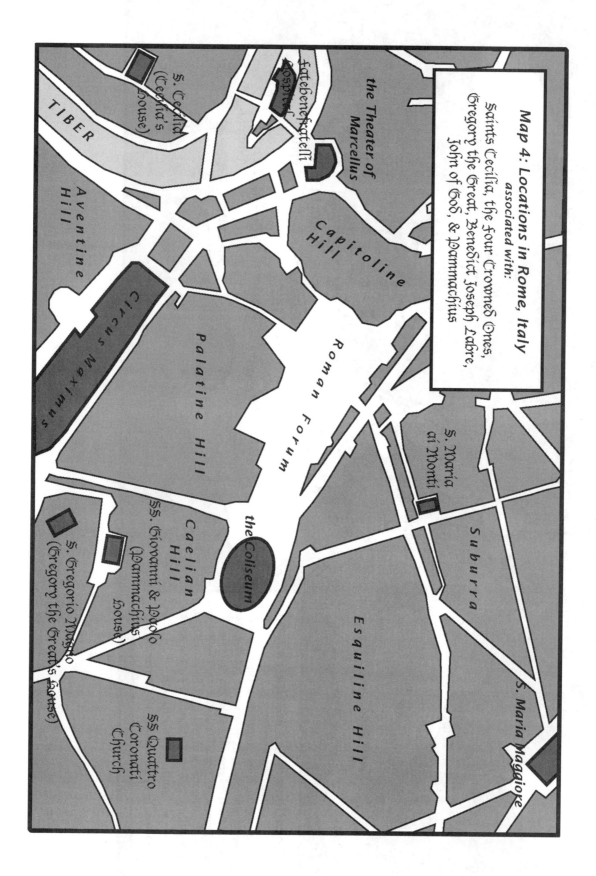

Map 4: Locations in Rome, Italy
associated with:
Saints Cecilia, the Four Crowned Ones,
Gregory the Great, Benedict Joseph Labre,
John of God, & Pammachius

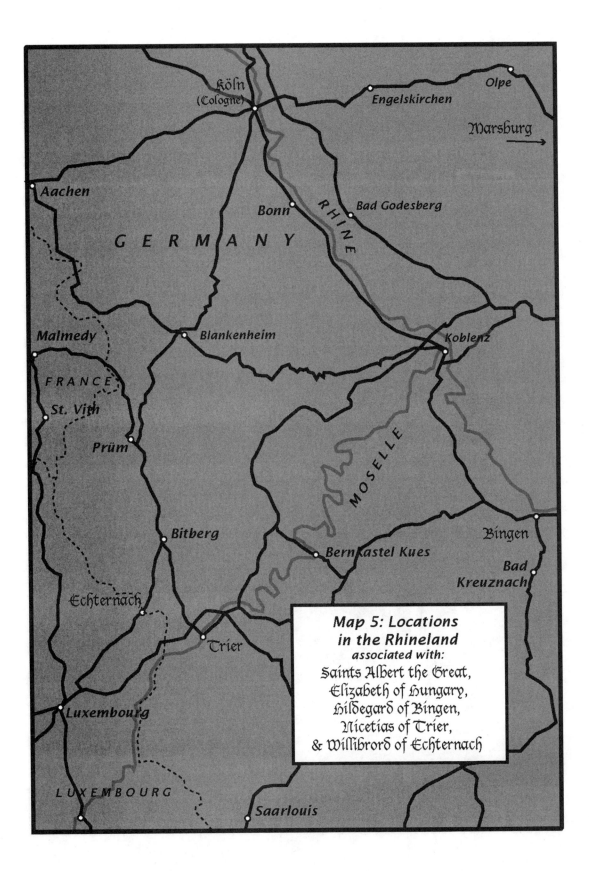

Map 5: Locations
in the Rhineland
associated with:
Saints Albert the Great,
Elizabeth of Hungary,
Hildegard of Bingen,
Nicetias of Trier,
& Willibrord of Echternach

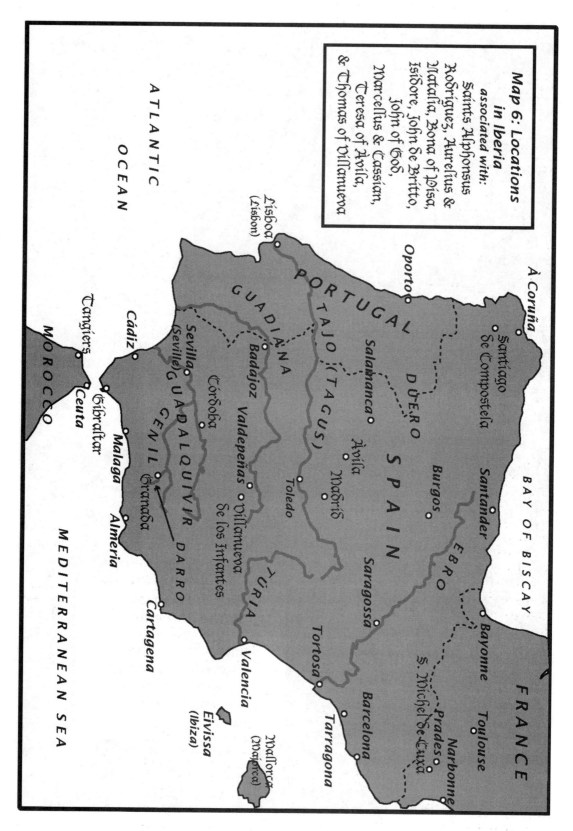

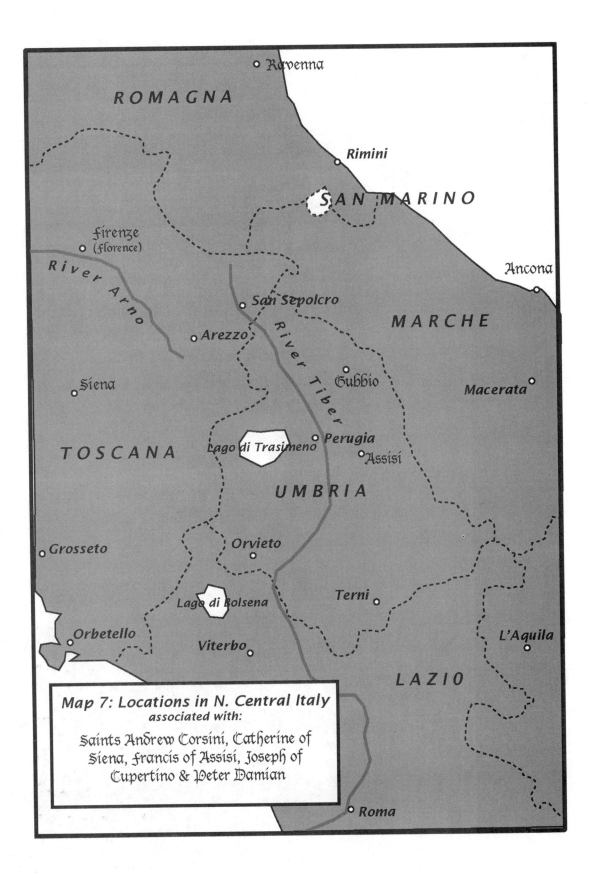

Map 7: Locations in N. Central Italy
associated with:

Saints Andrew Corsini, Catherine of Siena, Francis of Assisi, Joseph of Cupertino & Peter Damian

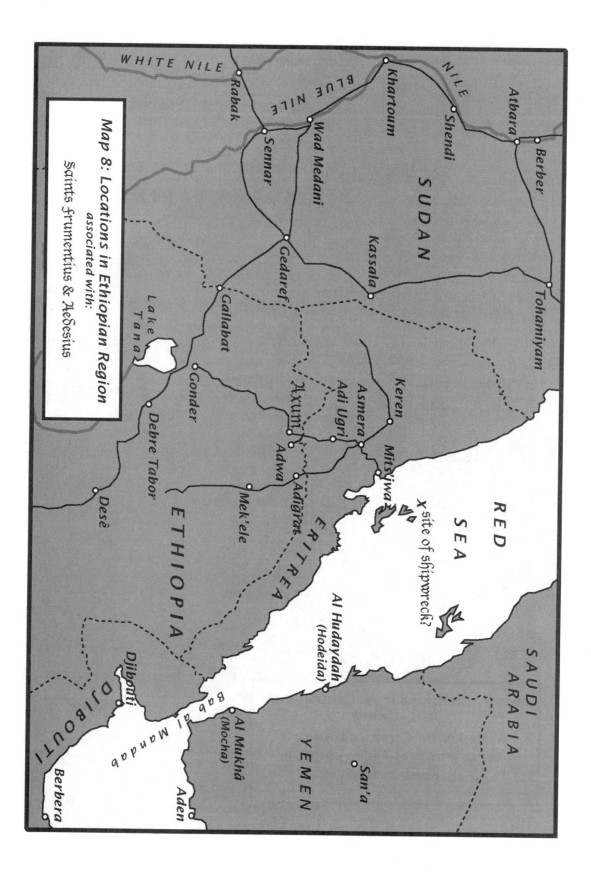

Map 8: Locations in Ethiopian Region
associated with:
Saints Frumentius & Aedesius

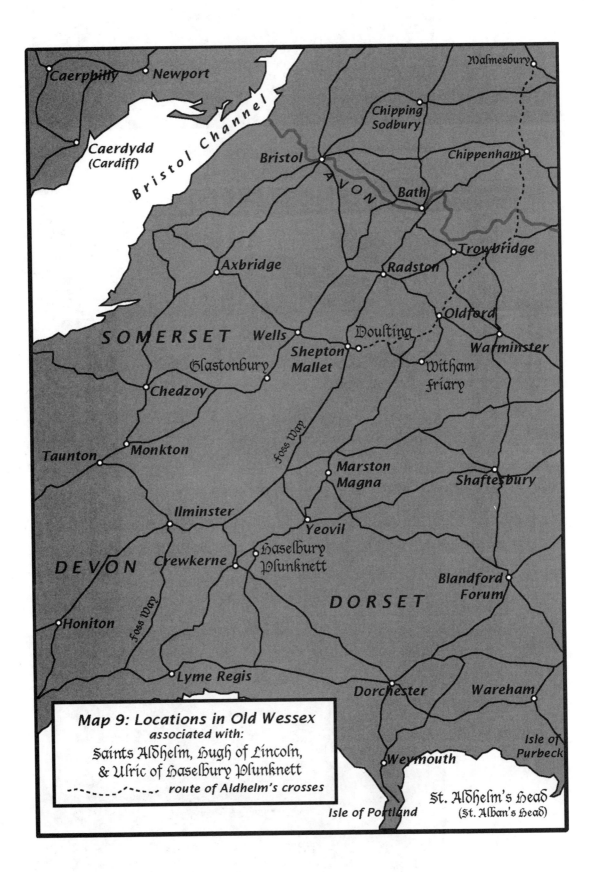

Map 9: Locations in Old Wessex
associated with:
Saints Aldhelm, Hugh of Lincoln,
& Ulric of Haselbury Plunknett
-------·------- route of Aldhelm's crosses

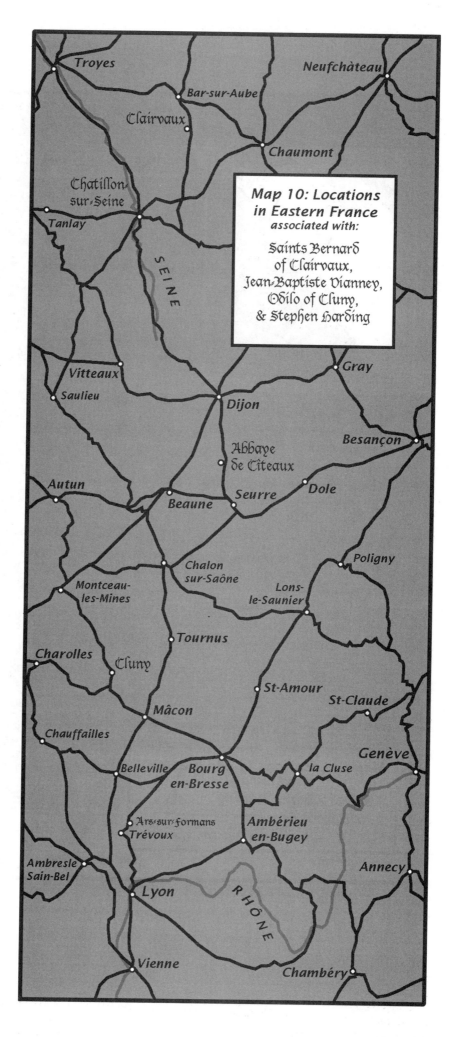

**Map 10: Locations
in Eastern France**
associated with:

Saints Bernard
of Clairvaux,
Jean-Baptiste Vianney,
Odilo of Cluny,
& Stephen Harding

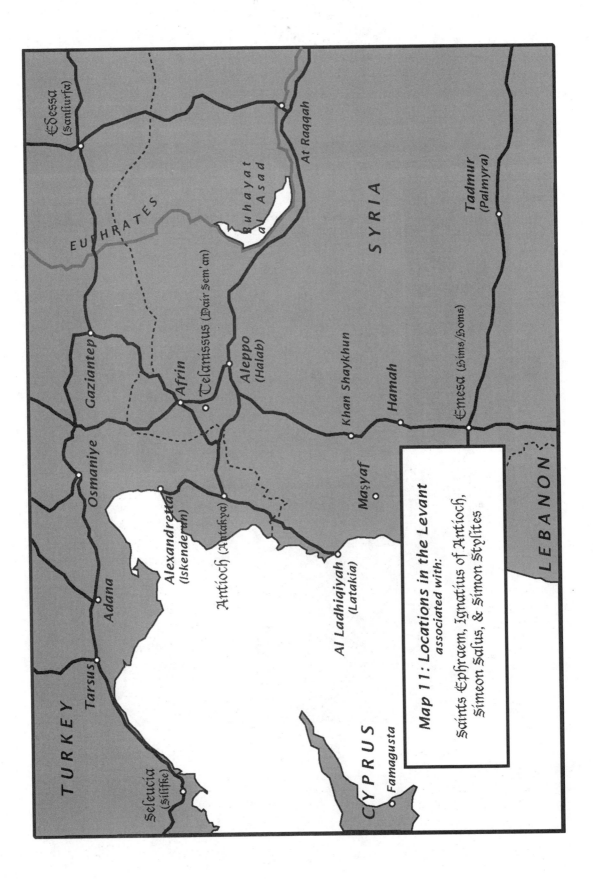

Map 11: Locations in the Levant *associated with:*

Saints Ephraem, Ignatius of Antioch, Simeon Salus, & Simon Stylites

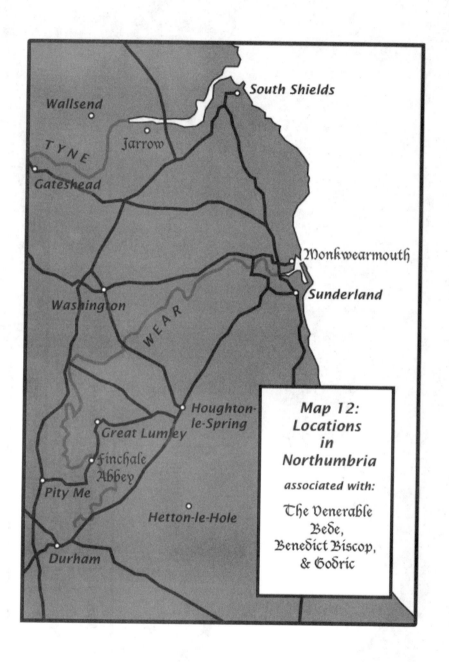

Map 12:
Locations
in
Northumbria

associated with:

The Venerable
Bede,
Benedict Biscop,
& Godric

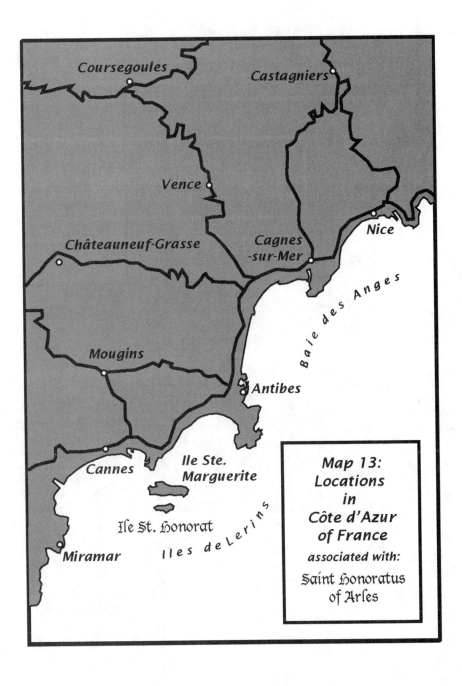

Coursegoules

Castagniers

Vence

Châteauneuf-Grasse

Cagnes
-sur-Mer

Nice

Baie des Anges

Mougins

Antibes

Cannes

Ile Ste.
Marguerite

Ile St. Honorat

Iles de Lerins

Miramar

Map 13:
Locations
in
Côte d'Azur
of France
associated with:
Saint Honoratus
of Arles

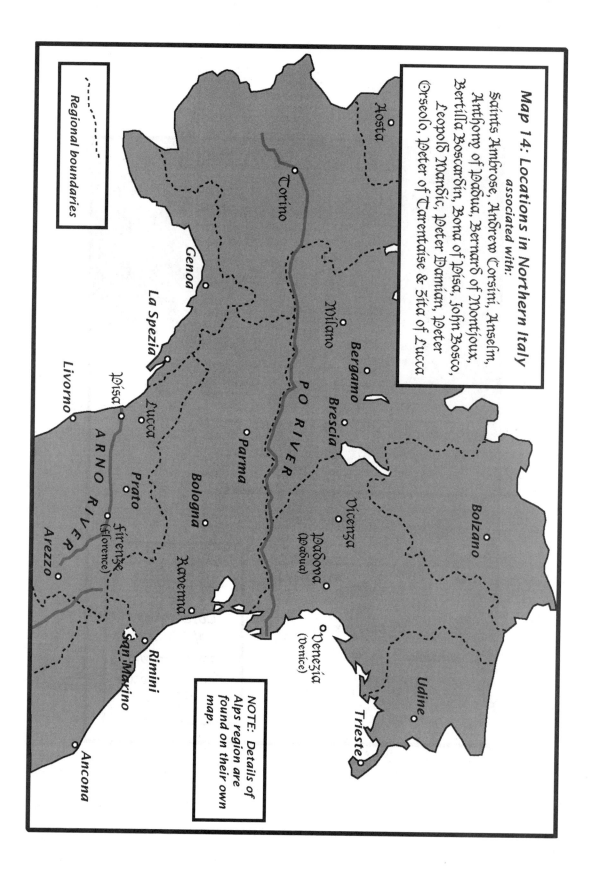

Map 14: Locations in Northern Italy
associated with:

Saints Ambrose, Andrew Corsini, Anselm, Anthony of Padua, Bernard of Montjoux, Bertilla Boscardin, Bona of Pisa, John Bosco, Leopold Mandic, Peter Damian, Peter Orseolo, Peter of Tarentaise & Zita of Lucca

Regional boundaries

NOTE: Details of Alps region are found on their own map.

Aosta

Torino

Genoa

La Spezia

Livorno

Pisa

Lucca

ARNO RIVER

Prato

Firenze (Florence)

Arezzo

San Marino

Rimini

Ancona

Parma

Bologna

Ravenna

Milano

Bergamo

Brescia

PO RIVER

Vicenza

Padova (Padua)

Venezia (Venice)

Bolzano

Udine

Trieste

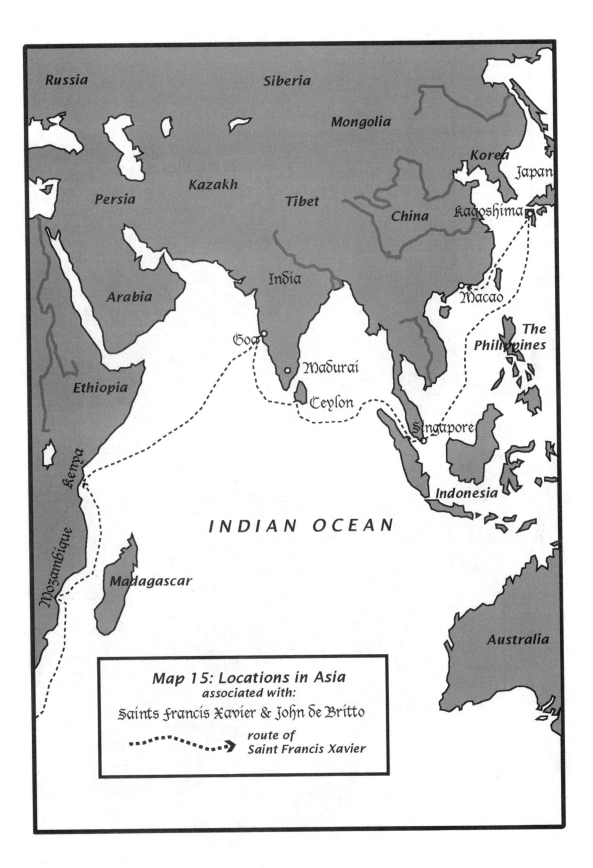

Map 15: Locations in Asia
associated with:
Saints Francis Xavier & John de Britto

route of
Saint Francis Xavier

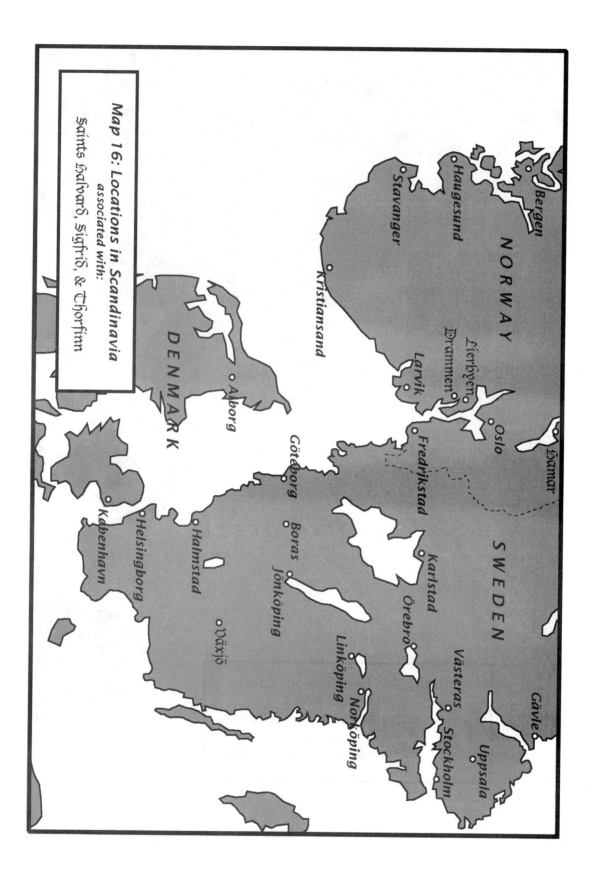

Map 16: Locations in Scandinavia
associated with:
Saints Hallvarð, Sigfrið, & Thorfinn

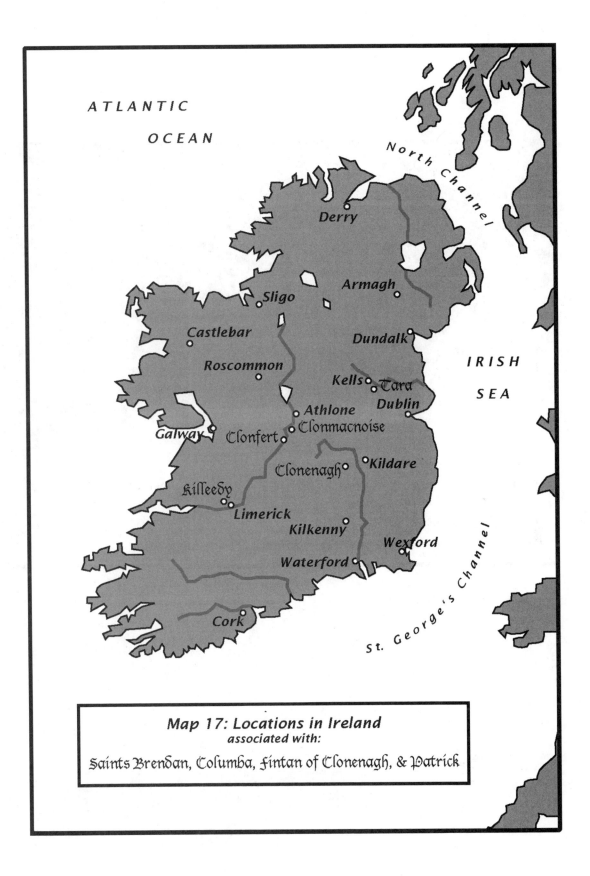

ATLANTIC

OCEAN

North Channel

IRISH

SEA

Derry

Armagh

Sligo

Dundalk

Castlebar

Roscommon

Kells Tara

Dublin

Athlone Clonmacnoise

Galway Clonfert

Kildare

Clonenagh

Killeedy

Limerick

Kilkenny

Wexford

Waterford

St. George's Channel

Cork

Map 17: Locations in Ireland
associated with:
Saints Brendan, Columba, Fintan of Clonenagh, & Patrick

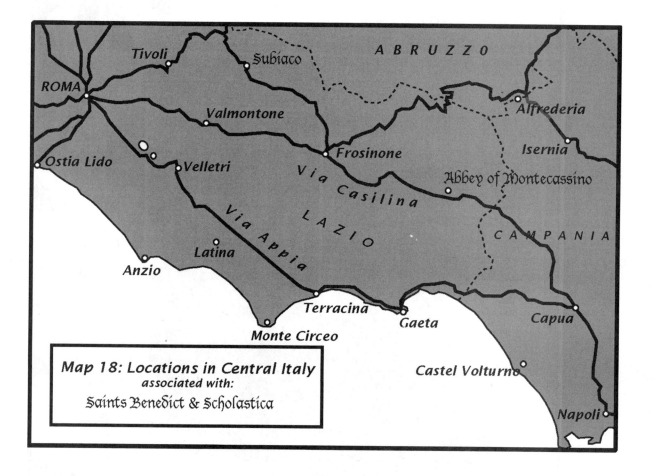

Map 18: Locations in Central Italy
associated with:
Saints Benedict & Scholastica

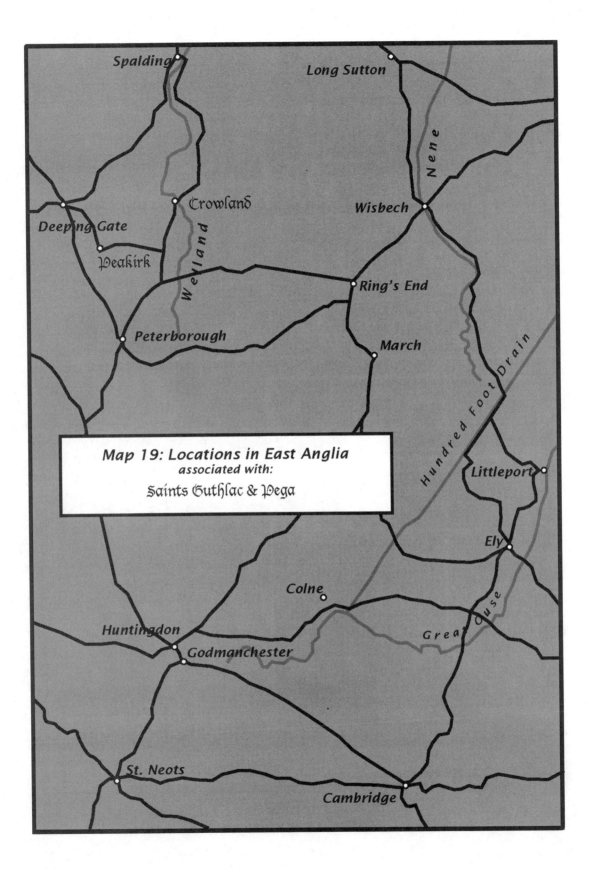

Map 19: Locations in East Anglia
associated with:
Saints Guthlac & Pega

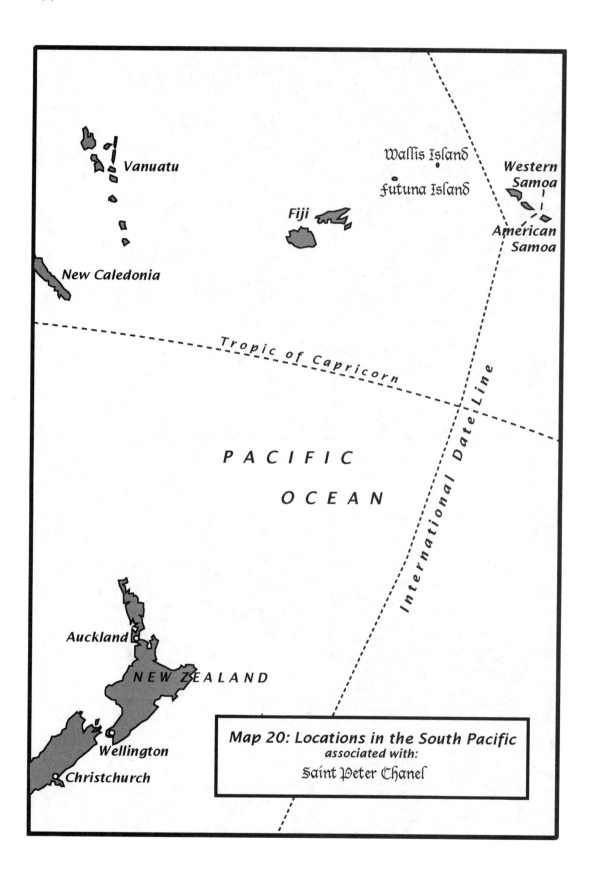

Vanuatu

Wallis Island

Western Samoa

Futuna Island

Fiji

American Samoa

New Caledonia

Tropic of Capricorn

International Date Line

PACIFIC

OCEAN

Auckland

NEW ZEALAND

Wellington

Christchurch

Map 20: Locations in the South Pacific
associated with:
𝔖aint 𝔓eter 𝔠hanel

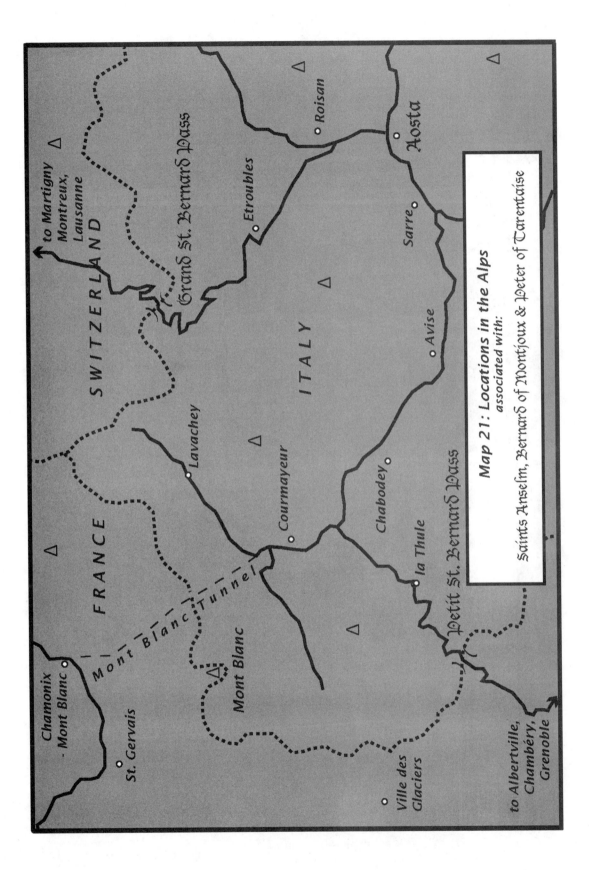

Map 21: Locations in the Alps
associated with:
Saints Anselm, Bernard of Montjoux & Peter of Tarentaise

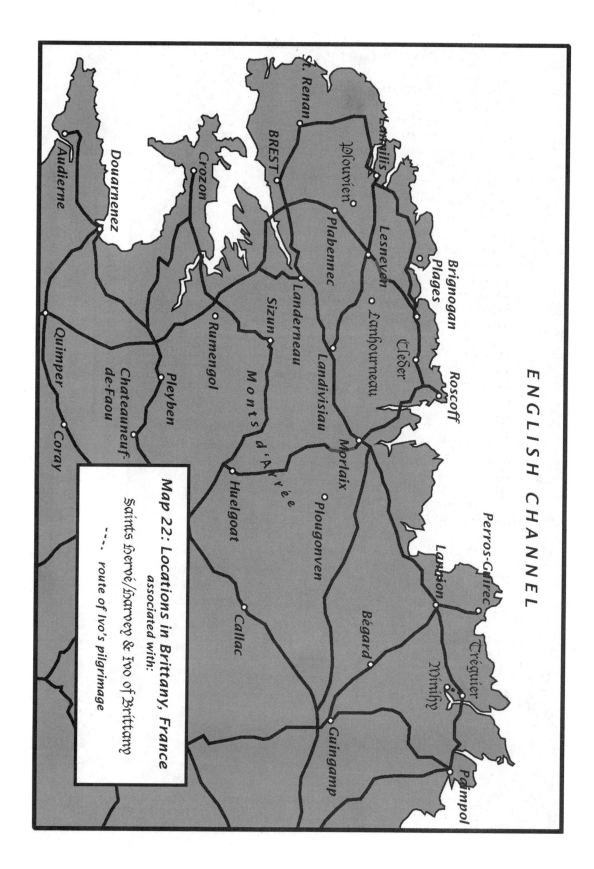

Map 22: Locations in Brittany, France
associated with:
Saints Hervé/Harvey & Ivo of Brittany
---- route of Ivo's pilgrimage

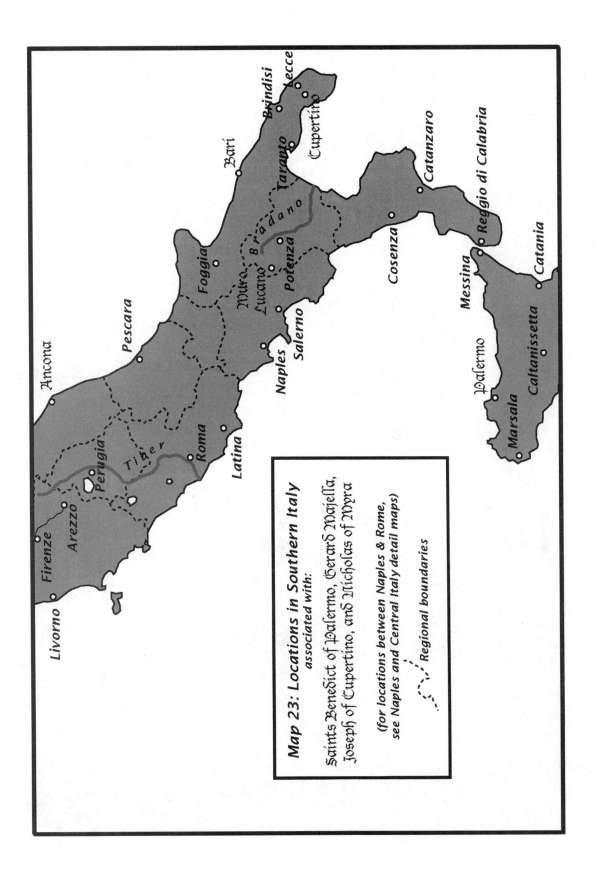

Map 23: Locations in Southern Italy
associated with:
Saints Benedict of Palermo, Gerard Majella,
Joseph of Cupertino, and Nicholas of Myra

(for locations between Naples & Rome,
see Naples and Central Italy detail maps)

- - - - Regional boundaries

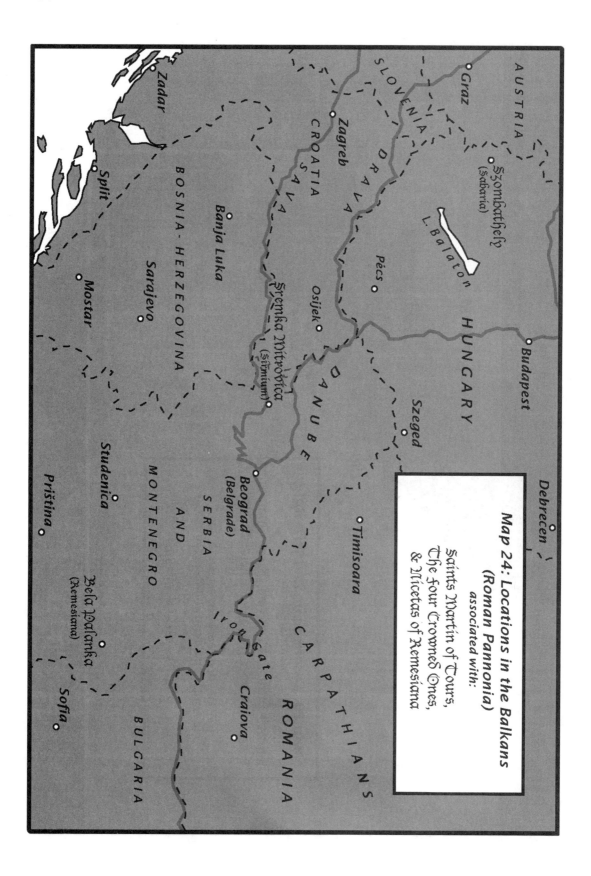

Map 24: Locations in the Balkans (Roman Pannonia)
associated with:
Saints Martin of Tours,
The Four Crowned Ones,
& Nicetas of Remesiana

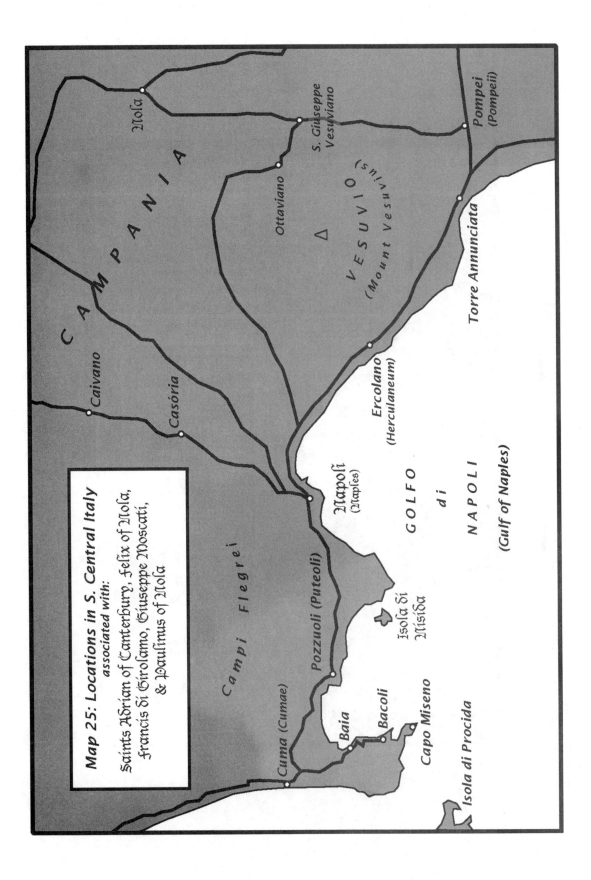

Map 25: Locations in S. Central Italy
associated with:
Saints Adrian of Canterbury, Felix of Nola,
Francis di Girolamo, Giuseppe Moscati,
& Paulinus of Nola

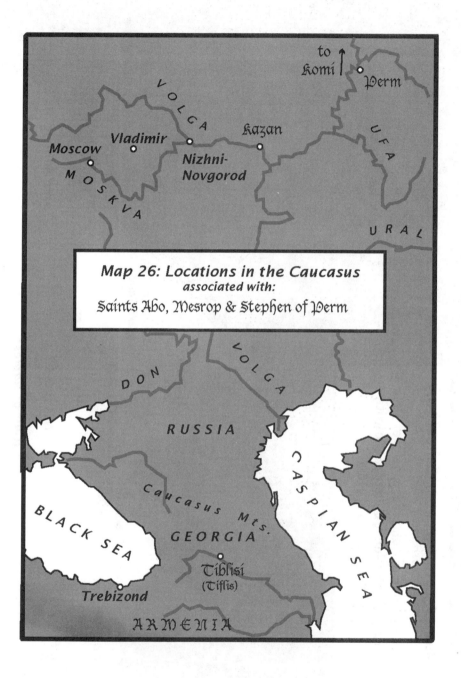

Map 26: Locations in the Caucasus
associated with:
Saints Abo, Mesrop & Stephen of Perm

εxτrα resources

Tres Filiae ("Three Daughters"):
A Miracle Play of St. Nicholas

by K. M. Lucchese

Works well performed at parties or in chapel, by students alone, students and teachers, or (for a special treat) by teachers alone.

Dramatis Personae (as performed December 2006)

Narrator (and Rooster)

Nobilis Pauper, *a formerly wealthy nobleman*

Prima, *filia pauperi ("daughter of the Pauper")*

Secunda, *filia pauperi (yup, the second daughter . . .)*

Tertullia, *filia pauperi (you got it: the third)*

Sanctus Nicholas, *episcopus Myrae ("bishop of Myra")*

Venalicia Foeda *("Horrible Female Slavedealer"—*
    change to Venalicius Foedus *for a male)*

* Ianua, *the door*

* Fenestra, *the window*

* Primus Saccus Aurei *("First Sack of Gold")*

* Secundus Saccus Aurei *("Second . . .")*

* Tertius Saccus Aurei *("Third . . .")*

(* added in 2007 to make enough roles for twelve students; may be removed as desired.)

[There is a simple stage-set: upstage, a human window frame, a human door, and downstage a kneeling rail or row of chairs, representing a fireplace, plus a wide pallet with an old quilt midstage, a chair near the window, to the left and upstage of the fire, and a bench directly to the right of the fire.

[For costuming, simply put over regular clothes: a dressing gown, night-cap and slippers for N.P., flannel nighties for the Filiae, a bishop's mitre for S.N., a flashy cape for V.F., a cardboard window frame for Fenestra, a cardboard door for Ianua, and a broad gold ribbon for the neck of each Saccus (or a simple label: "Sack of Gold #1" etc). Each daughter needs a large knit stocking (or a pair) to hang on the "fireplace." If you don't use human sacks, three foil balls of pennies, sprayed gold, should be easy to slip into and out of the stockings.

[NOBILIS PAUPER sits a little apart on the chair by the window, smoking a long pipe or stroking his sneaky old chin. The FILIAE sit on the bench to the other side of the FIREPLACE and pretend to be darning their stockings with imaginary needle-and-thread.]

NARRATOR:
> This is a story of Nicholas the great
> > who raised three girls out of their lowly state
> and saved them from a life of shame
> > and brought upon himself undying fame.
> We open in a wretched hovel, chill and bare,
> > on a narrow street in Myra Town the Fair.
> Here is a door has seen good fortune come and go,
> > and window shutterless and open to the snow,
> And fire itself so starved of food for heat
> > it scarcely keeps the chilblains off their feet.

NOBILIS PAUPER:

[*to the audience*]

Pity me, Nobilis Pauper, once a man of means,

Now fallen on hard times, and hatching endless schemes

To keep myself well fed, and my daughters shod,

And them demanding dowries, for the love of God!

PRIMA:

[*a little haughty*]

I, Prima, the eldest, wedded first should be,

But linger on in spinster poverty!

SECUNDA:

[*a little whiney*]

And I, though Secunda, still deserve some hope,

But what is there to do but sit, and mend, and mope?

TERTULLIA:

[*indignant*]

And I, Tertullia, though fairest, am abandoned, too.

I ask you, Sisters: what are we to do?

In Myra, it is not allowed

to marry maidens unendowed!

PRIMA:

Bishop Nicholas has said that, if we pray,

Then better luck will surely come our way.

SECUNDA:

Good Bishop Nicholas has served the church since he was eight!

What in the world would *he* know of our state?

TERTULLIA:

Nicholas is a kind and sensible man

Who will help us, I know, if anyone can!

* FENESTRA:

[*to the audience*]

And here is Bishop Nicholas, in his silks and furs!

Will he mark the plight of his parishioners?

SAINT NICHOLAS

[*Looking in at the FENESTRA, speaks to himself.*]

I think I heard my name, spoke out quite clear!

I fancy I should stop awhile to hear:

If it be slander, then it were well to know,

But if be praise, then quickly will I go.

[*Listens.*]

NOBILIS:

Daughters, up now, off you go to bed!

Your father must think up some way to earn our bread.

PRIMA:

We will, as soon as evening prayers are said,

Hang up our stockings here to dry, and then lay down each
weary head.

DAUGHTERS:

[*Together, kneeling.*]

Dear Lord, please bless the poor, for so are we,

And send us husbands wealthy as can be,

For Father will not work a single stitch,

And acts for all the world as if he still were rich.

Please send us dowries so that we may leave this place!

[*Crossing themselves fervently*]

Praise Father, Son, and Holy Ghost of Grace.

[*They go to sleep on the pallet, close together*]

SAINT NICHOLAS

[*To FENESTRA*]

What I have heard has given pause to think;

'Til I learn more, I shall not sleep a wink!

* [*FENESTRA nods wisely. S. N. peeks in.*]

NOBILIS PAUPER

[*Toward his sleeping daughters*]

If you would leave this place, indeed you will,

But sold as slaves, my pockets for to fill!

And here is my partner, Foeda Venalicia,

for buying slaves, there's no-one sneakier!

VENALICIA FOEDA:

[*Pops in at the door, gloating*]

We have a plan, as neat as it can be:

He'll tell them they are to travel on the sea,

But really, I shall take them to a house of shame!

NOBILIS PAUPER:

They shouldn't have been born girls! I am not to blame!

[*The slave dealer rubs her hands in glee, and leaves*]

* IANUA:

What evil have I let in? Oh, keep her out!

I wish my panels once again were stout

And iron-bound, as once they were, I think,

Until this miser had the metal sold for drink!

SAINT NICHOLAS

[*To the audience, through the window.*]

So that is the old sinner's plan?

Hunger has made him a desperate man!

I will see what my family fortune can do

To make these maidens' dreams come true.

[*Leaves. NOBILIS falls asleep. SAINT NICHOLAS returns, and the IANUA silently lets him into the house with three BAGS OF GOLD, which he slips next to the (imaginary) stockings or (if small enough), into them.*]

* Primus Saccus Aurei

Clang, clink! I'll bring happiness, I think!

* Secundus Saccus Aurei

Pling, plong! Food, good fires and song!

* Tertius Saccus Aurei

Ting, ding! Wealth is a comfortable thing!

SAINT NICHOLAS

Thus will the girls their true lovers wed!

(Now I am off to home and into bed!)

[*A ROOSTER crows. The DAUGHTERS wake and go to the fireplace. But as they take down their stockings . . . surprise!*]

PRIMA

Why, what is it that fills my stocking so?

SECUNDA

They were empty when we to bed did go!

TERTULLIA

[*Emptying out gold.*]

Praise Heaven, Sisters, let us call our sweethearts here!

With all this gold we will be merry many a year!

DAUGHTERS

[*Shaking their father awake.*]

Father, Look! We can all marry and be gone!

You'll have to feed three fewer from now on!

NOBILIS PAUPER

A miracle! We're saved! My work is done!

I'll visit at your houses one by one:

Your husbands will take care of me, I know . . .

[*Looking around, and at the gold.*]

But who has done this deed? Where did he go?

[*They all look around, then "freeze," theatrically speaking.*]

SAINT NICHOLAS

[*Peeking through the window, to the audience.*]

It is a joy of mine my people to deliver;

My motto is: "God loves a secret giver."

So do not ever think that I'll be found

When Christmas morning present time comes 'round,

Or any other time my work is done . . .

NARRATOR:

Our play is finished. Thank you, everyone!

[*All rise and take a bow!*]

(* indicates optional parts)

The Boy Who Laughed at Santa Claus

By Ogden Nash[1]

In Baltimore there lived a boy.
He wasn't anybody's joy.
Although his name was Jabez Dawes,
His character was full of flaws.
In school he never led his classes,
He hid old ladies' reading glasses,
His mouth was open when he chewed,
And elbows to the table glued.

He stole the milk of hungry kittens,
And walked through doors marked NO ADMITTANCE.
He said he acted thus because
There wasn't any Santa Claus.
Another trick that tickled Jabez
Was crying "Boo!" at little babies.
He brushed his teeth, they said in town,
Sideways, instead of up and down.

Yet people pardoned every sin,
And viewed his antics with a grin,
Till they are told by Jabez Dawes,
"There isn't any Santa Claus!"
Deploring how he did behave,
His parents swiftly sought their grave.
They hurried through the portals pearly,
And Jabez left the funeral early.

1. In Ogden Nash, *Good Intentions* (Boston: Little, Brown, and Company, 1937, 1939, 1940, 1941, 1942). Used by permission.

Like whooping cough, from child to child,
He sped to spread the rumor wild:
"Sure as my name is Jabez Dawes
There isn't any Santa Claus!"
Slunk like a weasel or a marten
Through nursery and kindergarten,
Whispering low to every tot,
"There isn't any, no there's not!"

The children wept all Christmas Eve
And Jabez chortled up his sleeve.
No infant dared hang up his stocking
For fear of Jabez' ribald mocking.
He sprawled on his untidy bed,
Fresh malice dancing in his head,
When presently, with scalp a-tingling,
Jabez heard a distant jingling;
He heard the crunch of sleigh and hoof,
Crisply alighting on the roof.

What good to rise and bar the door?
A shower of soot was on the floor.
What was beheld by Jabez Dawes?
The fireplace full of Santa Claus!
Then Jabez fell upon his knees
With cries of "Don't," and "Pretty please."
He howled, "I don't know where you read it,
But anyhow, I never said it!"

"Jabez," replied the angry saint,
"It isn't I, it's you that ain't.
Although there is a Santa Claus,
There isn't any Jabez Dawes!"

Said Jabez then with impudent vim,
"Oh yes there is; and I am him!
Your magic don't scare me, it doesn't" -
And suddenly he found he wasn't!

From grimy feet to unkempt locks
Jabez became a jack-in-the-box,
An ugly, vastly ghastly jack
In Santa Claus' bulging pack.
The neighbors heard his mournful squeal;
They searched for him, but not with zeal.
No trace was found of Jabez Dawes,
Which led to thunderous applause,
And people drank a loving cup
And went and hung their stockings up.

All you who sneer at Santa Claus,
Beware the fate of Jabez Dawes,
The saucy boy who mocked the saint.
Donder and Blitzen licked off his paint.

A Song for St. Cecilia's Day, 1687

By John Dryden (1631–1700)

From harmony, from Heav'nly harmony
    This universal frame began.
When Nature underneath a heap
    Of jarring atoms lay,
    And could not heave her head,
The tuneful voice was heard from high,
    Arise ye more than dead.
Then cold, and hot, and moist, and dry,
    In order to their stations leap,
    And music's pow'r obey.
From harmony, from Heav'nly harmony
    This universal frame began:
    From harmony to harmony
Through all the compass of the notes it ran,
    The diapason closing full in man.

What passion cannot music raise and quell!
    When Jubal struck the corded shell,
His list'ning brethren stood around
    And wond'ring, on their faces fell
    To worship that celestial sound:
Less than a god they thought there could not dwell
    Within the hollow of that shell
    That spoke so sweetly and so well.
What passion cannot music raise and quell!

The trumpet's loud clangor
    Excites us to arms

With shrill notes of anger
    And mortal alarms.
The double double double beat
    Of the thund'ring drum
Cries, hark the foes come;
Charge, charge, 'tis too late to retreat.

The soft complaining flute
    In dying notes discovers
    The woes of hopeless lovers,
Whose dirge is whisper'd by the warbling lute.

Sharp violins proclaim
    Their jealous pangs, and desperation,
    Fury, frantic indignation,
Depth of pains and height of passion,
For the fair, disdainful dame.

But oh! what art can teach
    What human voice can reach
    The sacred organ's praise?
Notes inspiring holy love,
Notes that wing their Heav'nly ways
    To mend the choirs above.

Orpheus could lead the savage race;
And trees unrooted left their place;
    Sequacious of the lyre:
But bright Cecilia rais'd the wonder high'r;
    When to her organ, vocal breath was giv'n,
An angel heard, and straight appear'd
    Mistaking earth for Heav'n.

As from the pow'r of sacred lays
    The spheres began to move,
And sung the great Creator's praise
    To all the bless'd above;
So when the last and dreadful hour
    This crumbling pageant shall devour,
The trumpet shall be heard on high,
    The dead shall live, the living die,
    And music shall untune the sky.

Bibliography

Attwater, Donald and Catherine Rachel John. *The Penguin Dictionary of Saints, Third Edition.* London: Penguin Book, 1995.

Automobile Association, *AA Big Road Atlas Britain.* Basingstoke: Automobile Association, 1981.

Automobile Association, *AA 2007 Driver's Atlas Britain*. 5th ed. Basingstoke: Automobile Association, 2007.

Bosio, Antonio. *Historia Passionis B. Caeciliae Virginis, Valeriani, Tiburtii, et Maximi Martyrum necnon Urbani et Lucii Pontificum et Mart. Vitae atque Paschalis Papae I Literae de eorundem sanctorum corporum inventione et in urbem translatione*... Rome: Stephanus Paulinus, 1600.

Butler, Alban. *Butler's Lives of the Saints.* New Full Edition. Tunbridge Wells, UK: Burns & Oates, 1997.

deBlij, H.J. and Peter O. Muller. *Concepts and Regions in Geography.* 2nd ed. Hoboken: John Wiley & Sons, 2005.

Deeming, Helen. *The Songs of Saint Godric: A Neglected Context,* Music and Letters, Vol. 86, No. 2, 2005, 169–85.

Farmer, David Hugh. *The Oxford Dictionary of Saints.* 4th ed. Oxford: Oxford University Press, 1997.

Lactantius, Lucius Caecilius Firmianus. *De Mortibus Persecutorum Liber; Accesserunt Passiones SS. Perpetuae & Felicitatis, S. Maximilianus, S. Felicis.* Oxford: from the Sheldonian Theatre, 1680.

Mappe Iter. *Campania: Carta touristica e automobilisitica.* 1:250,000. Rome: Edizione Iter, 1989.

Michelin et Cie. *Michelin Europe: Tourist and Motoring Atlas.* 7th ed. Clermont-Ferrand: Michelin et Cie, 2004.

Michelin et Cie. *Michelin France: Tourist and Motoring Atlas*. 2nd ed. Clermont-Ferrand: Michelin et Cie, 2004.

Michelin et Cie. *Michelin Italy: Tourist and Motoring Atlas*. 7th ed. Clermont-Ferrand: Michelin et Cie, 2001.

Readers Digest Press. *The Reader's Digest Complete Atlas of the British Isles*. London: Readers Digest Press, 1965.

Shepherd, William R. *Historical Atlas*. 8th ed. New York: Barnes & Noble, 1956.

Times Books. *The Times Atlas of the World*. 9th ed. London: Times Books, 1992.

Touring Club Italiano. *Europe: atlante stradale e turistico*, 1:900,000. Milan: Touring Club Italiano, 2003.

Touring Club Italiano. *Guida d'Italia: Roma e Dintorni*. 7th ed. Milan: Touring Club Italiano, 1977.

www.catholic-forum.com (used to find locational details of saints)

www.cyberhymnal.org (for texts of hymns)

www.newadvent.com (detailed corroborative or additional saint information)

saints organized by week

I = Year One, "Song of the Saints"
II = Year Two, "Patient and Brave and True"

Note that if saints have been moved from their traditional days, the location reference is given as either the saints to whose dates they have been moved or the week upon which they can now be found.

Abo—January 8 (II)

Adamnan—see September Week Three (I)

Adrian of Canterbury—January 9 (I)

Aedesius—October 27 (I)

Albert the Great—see November Week Two (I)

Aldhelm—May 25 (I)

Alexander Nevsky—November 23 (I)

Alipius—August 18 (II)

Allowin/Bavo—October 1 (II)

Almachius/Telemachus—January 1 (II)

Alphonsus Rodriguez—see Gerard Majella

Ambrose—see December Week Two (I)

Andrew Corsini—February 4 (I)

Andrew Fournet—May 13 (II)

Anselm—see April Week Two (II)

Anthony of Padua—see June Week One (I)

Antony Mary Claret—see October Week Three (I)

Augustine of Hippo—August 28 (I)

Aurelius and Natalia—see January Week Two (II)

Basil the Great/Gregory of Nazianus—January 2 (II)

Bavo/Allowin—October 1 (II)

Bede, the Venerable—see May Week Three (I)

Benedict—see February Week Three (I)

Benedict Biscop—see January Week Three (I)

Benedict Joseph Labré—see April Week Two (II)

Benedict of Palermo—April 4 (II)

Bernard of Clairveaux—see Stephen Harding

Bernard of Montjoux—see May Week One (I)

Bernward—see November Week Four (II)

Bertilla Boscardin—see October Week Two (II)

Blandina and Justin—June 2 (II)

Bona of Pisa—May 29 (II)

Bonaventure—see March Week Four (I)

Brendan the Voyager—May 16 (I)

Caesarius of Arles—see August Week Three (I)

Camillus—see March Week One (II)

Cassian of Tangiers—see Marcellus the Centurion

Catherine of Siena—April 29 (I)

Cecilia—November 22 (II)

Ciaran of Clonmacnois—see September Week One (II)

Clare of Assisi—August 11 (II)

Coleman—see Hipparchus

Columba—see June Week One (II)

Crispin and Crispinian—October 25 (II)

Cuthbert—see March Week Four (I)

Cuthman of Steyning—see Ciaran of Clonmacnois

Cyprian—September 16 (I)

Cyril and Methodius—February 14 (II)

David—see Margaret of Scotland

Denis the Cephalophore—see January Week Four (II)

Dunstan—see May Week Two (II)

Edwin—see October Week One (II)

Elizabeth of Hungary—November 17 (II)

Ephraem—see June Week One (I)

Ethelbert of Kent—see February Week Three (II)

Euphrasia Pelletier—see April Week Three (II)

Fabiola—see Pammachius

Felicity—see March Week Two (I)

Felix of Nola—January 14 (II)

Felix of Thibiuca—see October Week Three (II)

Fintan of Clonenagh—see February Week Two (I)

Four Crownéd Ones—see November Week One (II)

Frances Cabrini—November 13 (II)

Frances of Rome—March 9 (II)

Francis di Girolamo—see May Week One (II)

Francis of Assisi—October 4 (I)

Francis Solano—March Week One (I)

Francis Xavier—December 3 (II)

Frumentius—October 27 (I)

Genesius of Arles—see August Week Three (II)

Geneviéve—January 3 (I)

George—see April Week Three (I)

Gerard Majella—see October Week Four (II)

Gerasimus—March 5 (I)

Germaine of Pibrac—see June Week Two (II)

Germanus of Paris—see Nicetas

Giles Aegidius—September 1 (II)

Giovanni Bosco—January 31 (II)

Giuseppe Moscati—November 16 (II)

Godric—May 21 (II)

Gregory of Nazianus/Basil the Great—January 2 (II)

Gregory the Great—September 3 (I)

Gregory the Wonderworker—November 17 (I)

Guardian Angels—see Michael (I)

Gudule—January 9 (II)

Guthlac—see April Week One (I)

Halvard—see January Week Three (II)

Harvey/Hervé—see June Week Two (I)

Hilarion—see October Week Two (I)

Hilary of Poitiers—see January Week Three (I)

Hildegard of Bingen—see September Week Two (I)

Hipparchus—December 9 (II)

Honoratus of Arles—see January Week Four (I)

Hubert—November 1 (I)

Hugh of Lincoln—see November Week Four (I)

Ide—see Brendan the Voyager

Ignatius of Antioch—see October Week Two (I)

Irenaeus—see June Week Two (I)

Isidore the Farm Servant—see May Week One (II)

Ivo of Brittany—May 19 (I)

Jean-Baptiste de la Salle—April 7 (I)

Jean-Baptiste Marie Vianney—August Week One (II)

Jeanne la Pucelle—May 30 (I)

Joan of Arc —May 30 (I)

Joan of France—February 4 (II)

John Bosco—January 31 (II)

John de Britto—February 4 (I)

John of Beverly—see October Week Three (I)

John of Damascus—December 4 (II)

John of God—see March Week One (II)

John the Almsgiver—January 23 (I)

Joseph Cottolengo—April 30 (II)

Joseph of Cupertino—September 18 (II)

Julie Postel—see May Week Two (II)

Justin and Blandina—June 1 & 2 (II)

Lawrence—see August Week One (I)

Leo the Great—November 10 (I)

Leopold Mandic—see May Week One (I)

Lioba—September 28 (II)

Louis of France—see August Week Three (I)

Lucy—December 13 (II)

Marcella—see April Week Three (II)

Marcellus the Centurion—October 30 (I)

Margaret of Scotland—November 16 (I)

Marguerite d'Youville—see October Week Two (II)

Martin de Porres—November 3 (II)

Martin of Tours—November 11 (II)

Maughold—see April Week Three (I)

Maximilian Kolbe—August 14 (I)

Maximus—see Valerian

Mesrop—see April Week Three (II)

Michael and All Angels—September 29 (I)

Mildred—see Elizabeth of Hungary

Monica—see August Week Three (II)

Moses the Moor—August 28 (II)

Nicetas of Trier—December 5 (I)

Nicetias of Remesiana—see February Week Three (II)

Nicholas of Myra—December 6 (I)

Nicholas Von Flue—see March Week Two (II)

Notburga—September 13 (II)

Odilo of Cluny—January 1 (I)

Oswald—see August Week One (I)

Pachomius—May 14 (I)

Pammachius—August 30 (I)

Patrick—see March Week Two (I)

Paulinus of Nola—see June Week Two (II)

Pega—see April Week One (I)

Perpetua— see March Week Two (I)

Peter Chanel—April 28 (I)

Peter Claver—see September Week One (I)

Peter Damian—February 21 (I)

Peter of Tarentaise—May 8 (I)

Peter Orseolo—see January Week Three (II)

Petroc—see Giles Aegidius

Philip Neri—May 26 (II)

Philip of Moscow—January 9 (I)

Phocas—September 22 (II)

Plague of Alexandria, Martyrs of— February 28 (I)

Polycarp—January 26 (I)

Pulcheria—September 10 (II)

Rita of Cascia—see May Week Three (I)

Roch/Rocco—see August Week Two (II)

Scholastica—see February Week One (II)

Scillitan Martyrs—see Felix of Thibiuca

Sergius of Radonezh—September 25 (II)

Severinus Boethius—see October Week Three (II)

Sigfrid—see February Week Two (I)

Simeon Salus—see February Week Four (II)

Simon Stylites—January 5 (I)

Stephen Harding—April 17 (I)

Stephen of Perm—see April Week Three (II)

Telemachus/Almachius—January 1 (II)

Teresa of Ávila—see October Week One (I)

Theodore the Cenobiarch—see January Week Four (II)

Thomas Becket—see December Week Two (I)

Thomas of Villanueva—September 21 (I)

Thorfinn—see January Week Three (II)

Tiburtius— see Valerian

Tikhon of Zadonsk—August 13 (I)

Ulric of Haselbury Plunknett— see Hubert

Valentine—February 14 (II)

Valerian—April 14 (I)

Venantius Fortunatus—see Ambrose

Vincent de Paul—September 27 (I)

Vladimir—see March Week Four (II)

Waudru—January Week Two (II)

Willibald—see August Week Four (II)

Willibrord of Echternach—November 7 (I)

Zeno of Verona—see April Week One (II)

Zita of Lucca—April 27 (II)

saints organized by characteristics

Hopefully helpful in finding which saints are connected with your favorite stories, good teaching themes, and such.

Addictions, a saint who could teach
    a thing or two about—Alipius
African saints, some:
  Alipius
  Augustine of Hippo
  Cassian of Tangiers (see Marcellus)
  Cyprian
  Felix of Thibiuca
  Frumentius
  Marcellus the Centurion
  Monica
  Moses the Moor
  Scillitan Martyrs, the
  Zeno of Verona
Agincourt, the battle and the song—
    Crispin and Crispinian
Aidan—see Oswald
Alexandria, Patriarch of—John
    the Almsgiver
All Soul's Day, originator of—Odilo
    of Cluny
Alphabet, invented an:
  Cyril and Methodius
  Mesrop
  Stephen of Perm

Alphabet of Devotions, The, wrote—
    Coleman
Angel helps plow a field—Isidore the
    Farm Servant
Angel told him to "pick it up and read it"
    —Augustine of Hippo
Angel with a big sword—Michael
Angel who guarded Tobias—Raphael
Angel who told Zacharias to name his
    son John—Gabriel
Angler, always depicted as an—Zeno
    of Verona
Angles = Angels—Gregory the Great
Animals, Patron of—Francis of Assisi
Anno Domini, first historian to use—
    Bede, the Venerable
"Another year completed"—Paulinus
    of Nola
Apprentices, opened night schools for—
    John Bosco
Apron full of spring flowers—Germaine
    of Pibrac
Archcantor of Saint Peter's Basilica,
    brought to Northumbria—
    Benedict Biscop
Armenian translator—Mesrop
Artists/Artisans:
  Bernwald
  Dunstan
  Hildegard of Bingen

Attila the Hun, turned away from
Paris—Geneviéve
Attila the Hun, turned away from
Rome—Leo the Great
Axum—see Ethiopia
Babies, Patron of—Harvey/Hervé
Bag of scriptures, got caught holding
the—Speratus, one of the Scillitan
Martyrs
Bald—Hipparchus
Bandit, started out as a—Moses the Moor
Bath-house, they tried to steam her in
her own—Cecilia
Beam of light, saw the world in a—
Benedict
Bedouins, converted lots of—Simon
Stylites
Bees, dreamed of—Stephen Harding
Beggar, was himself one—Benedict
Joseph Labré
Beggar, saw Jesus in the guise of a—
Martin of Tours
Belgium, some saints from there
or nearby:
  Gudule
  Waudru
  Willibrord of Echternach
Belt, threw down his—Marcellus the
Centurion
"Bigot, the little"—Germaine of Pibrac
Birds, fed grain to starving—Isidore the
Farm Servant
Bishop, chosen when only eight years
old—Nicholas of Myra
Bishops, was exiled for insisting on
independent election of—Thorfinn
Blind daughter, cured the jailer's—
Valentine
Blind, was:
  Coleman (temporarily)
  Harvey/Hervé
Bocca Aperta—Joseph of Cupertino
"Bodies are not made of brass, our"—
Clare of Assisi

Bowed toward Jerusalem 1000 times a
day—Simon Stylites
Boys, started a school for little—Ide
(see Brendan the Voyager)
Bread in the oven, looked like—
Polycarp
Bridge, a sort of human—John
of Beverley
British saints, some:
  Adamnan
  Adrian of Canterbury
  Aldhelm
  Anselm
  Augustine of Canterbury
    (see Gregory the Great)
  Bede, the Venerable
  Benedict Biscop (Benet)
  Brendan the Voyager
  Ciaran of Clonmacnois
  Columba
  Cuthbert
  Cuthman of Steyning
  Dunstan
  Edwin
  Ethelbert of Kent
  Fintan of Clonenagh
  Godric
  Guthlac
  Hugh of Lincoln
  Ide (see Brendan the Voyager)
  John of Beverly
  Lioba
  Margaret of Scotland
    (actually a Saxon)
  Maughold
  Mildred
  Oswald
  Patrick
  Thomas Becket
  Sigfrid
  Stephen Harding
  Ulric of Haselbury Plunknett
    (see Hubert)
  Willibald (and his "W" siblings)

Brittany, some saints of:
 Herve/Harvey
 Ivo of Brittany
Brother founded a monastery with him—
 Sergius of Radonezh
Brother founded a monastery without
 her—Scholastica
Brother rescued him from his other
 brother—Peter Damian
"Brother Sun," wrote the "Canticle of"—
 Francis of Assisi
"Brüder Klaus"—Nicholas Von Flue
Bubonic Plague, born the first year of
 the—Catherine of Siena
Buddhism, studied to be a better
 missionary—Maximilian Kolbe
Buried an excommunicate—Hildegard
 of Bingen
Butcher, died in the arms of his friend
 the—Benedict Joseph Labré
Candle, had hers blown out by the
 devil—Gudule
Cannibal Islands, King of—see Peter
 Chanel
Cannibals, Christians thought to be—
 Justin and Blandina
Cappella, origin of the word—Martin
 of Tours
Carried his bishop to safety—Felix of Nola
Cathedral, killed in his own—Thomas
 Becket
Cats, was fond of—Philip Neri
Cistercian—Stephen Harding
"Chain-reaction" saints—Valerian,
 Tiburtius, and Maximus
"Childhood, the things we learn in, are
 part of our souls"—Irenaeus
Children, Patron of—Nicholas of Myra
Chivalry, Patron of—George
Christmas, really loved—Leo the Great
 (and most other saints!)
Classics teacher—Adrian of Canterbury
Cloak, lent her master's fur—Zita
 of Lucca

Cobblers—Crispin and Crispinian
Coliseum, basically stopped games in—
 Almachius/Telemachus
Coliseum, obsessed with the games at—
 Alipius
College buddies:
 Alipius and Augustine of Hippo
 Basil the Great/Gregory of Nazianus
Column, lived on top of one for thirty-six
 years—Simon Stylites
Compostela, led nine trips to—Bona
 of Pisa
Concentration camp, died in a—
 Maximilian Kolbe
Confessors (especially famous):
 Antony Mary Claret
 Jean-Baptiste Vianney
 Leopold Mandic
Convent, founded first one in Gaul—
 Caesarius of Arles
Cow, drove a, to keep him in milk and
 butter—Ciaran of Clonmacnois
Cows of Frey, killed the sacred—
 Willibrord
Craftsmen:
 Bernward
 Dunstan
Crazy, maybe a little, for a while:
 John of God
 Simeon Salus
Croatian, originally—Leopold Mandic
Crowlands, lived in a hermitage at—
 Guthlac
Crown of Thorns, made a chapel for—
 Louis of France
Crows (or ravens) guarded his body—
 King Oswald
Crows rescued him from poisoning—
 Benedict
Crusade, died on—Louis of France
Cupboard under the stairs, slept in a—
 Germaine of Pibrac
"Curé d'Ars, the"—Jean-Baptiste
 Vianney

"Dang me if I don't believe in your God!"—Maximus, see Valerian

Darro, jumped into the River—John of God

Day of the Dead, originator of—Odilo of Cluny

Dead body, disguised himself as a—Andrew Fournet

Deer, had pet:
  Giles Aegidius
  Petroc

"Deranged"—Jean-Baptiste Vianney

Desert Father, one of the original—Gerasimus

Devil, grabbed the, by the nose—Dunstan

Diogenes, lived very much like—Simeon Salus

Disciple of John the Evangelist—Polycarp

Doctor—Giuseppe Moscati

Dog, has one named after him—Bernard of Montjoux

Dog named "Reste" nursed him back to health—Roch/Rocco

Doge of Venice—Peter Orseolo

Donation of things to the poor and imprisoned—Vincent de Paul

Double Monastery at Repton—Guthlac

"Dove and Eagle, the"—Teresa of Ávila

Dragon, converted a—Petroc

Dragon, slew a—George

"Dragony"—Hildegard of Bingen

Drainage and hydrology, fascinated by—Philip of Moscow

Dreamed of travel and adventure—Leopold Mandic

Drinking problem, had a little bit of a—Monica

Druid, Coifi the—see Edwin

Dug his own grave—Phocas

"Eagle and Dove, the"—Teresa of Ávila

"Eccentrics:"
  Aldhelm
  Simeon Salus

Embarrassed by his sketchy education—Patrick

Emperor Charlemagne's wife's friend—Lioba

Empress of Byzantium—Pulcheria

England, Patron of Merry—George

English, Apostle to the —Gregory the Great

English, Apostle to the, wrote a poem in praise of—Peter Damian

"Escape artist"—Hilarion

Ethiopia, Apostle to —Frumentius

Evil stepmother, really had an—Germaine of Pibrac

Eustace, roasted in a metal bull, becomes patron saint of coffee roasters—see Hubert

Fairs, invented the idea of saint's, to increase church attendance—Gregory the Wonderworker

Farm girls—Notburga, Zita

Father died in Lucca—Willibald

"Father of Charity"—Martin de Porres

Family of saints, from a:
  Basil the Great
  Waudru
  Willibald

Fatebenefratelli, founded—John of God

Fires, had to light all the—Notburga

Fish, preached to the—Anthony of Padua

Fjord, was about to cross a—Halvard

Floated in the air—Claire of Assisi, Joseph of Cupertino

Florence a rowdy, dangerous place—Andrew Corsini

Flowers, the bread in her apron turned into—Germaine of Pibrac

Force his subjects to convert, didn't:
  Edwin
  Ethelbert of Kent

Fourteen Angels: see Saint Michael and all Angels

Fourteen Holy Helpers: not covered in my book, but really interesting, and associated with the gorgeous baroque *Vierzehnheiligen* church in Bavaria and are traditionally the following saints: Achatius, Barbara, Blaise, Catherine of Alexandria, Christopher, Cyriacus, Denis, Elmo, Eustace, George, Aegidius, Margaret of Antioch, Pantaleon, and Vitus

Franks, helped to civilize:
  Geneviève
  Germanus
  Nicetas of Trier
  Odilo of Cluny
French Revolution, difficulties during the:
  Andrew Fournet
  Julie Postel
French saints, some:
  Andrew Fournet
  Benedict Joseph Labré
  Bernard of Clairveaux
  Bernard of Montjoux
  Bonaventure
  Caesarius of Arles
  Denis the Cephalophore
  Euphrasia Pelletier
  Geneviéve
  Genesius of Arles
  Germaine of Pibrac
  Germanus of Paris (see Nicetas)
  Giles Aegidius
  Harvey/Hervé
  Hilary of Poitiers
  Honoratus of Arles
  Hubert
  Ivo of Brittany
  Jean-Baptiste de la Salle
  Joan of Arc
  Jean-Baptiste Vianney
  Louis of France
  Odilo of Cluny
  Peter Chanel
  Peter of Tarentaise
  Petroc

  Roch/Rocco
  Vincent de Paul (a Gascon)
Frey, killed the sacred cows of—Willibrord
Friends who argued but loved each other—Basil the Great & Gregory of Nazianus
Frogs, told to be silent—Harvey/Hervé
Frugally, lived very, without using farm animals—Fintan of Clonenagh
Galley-slaves, helped—Vincent de Paul
"Gaper, the"—Joseph of Cupertino
Gardener—Phocas
Generous (especially) saints:
  Ciaran of Clonmacnois
  John the Almsgiver
  Nicholas of Myra
  Notburga
  Thomas of Villanueva
  Vincent de Paul
German saints, some:
  Albert the Great
  Bernward
  Elizabeth of Hungary
  Hildegard of Bingen
  Nicetas of Trier
  Notburga
  Venantius Fortunatus (sort of)
Gladiators, killed by when he tried to separate them—Almachius
Gnostics, refuted the—Irenaeus
"God will help us"—John Bosco
Gottesfreunde, member of—Nicholas Von Flue
Grandmother, listened to his—Vladimir
Greats:
  Albert
  Basil
  Gregory
  Leo
Gridiron: "I'm done on this side"—Lawrence
"Halfbreed dog"—Martin de Porres
Hansel and Gretel song—see Michael

Harlots, helped out—Simeon Salus

Harry Potter, coins minted—Maughold

Harry Potter, treated worse than—
Germaine of Pibrac

Head not quite chopped off—Cecilia

Head, walked five miles holding—Denis
the Cephalophore

Heads, buried in his churchyard—Fintan
of Clonenagh

Heads, shown carrying three—Sigfrid

Henry V, the inspiring speech of—Crispin
and Crispinian

Hid in a deserted building—Felix
of Nola

Hid in the Pyrenees—Peter Orseolo

Hid the scriptures—Felix of Thibiuca

Hid to avoid his fans—Hilarion of
Antioch

Hid to avoid serving in Napoleon's
army—Jean-Baptiste Vianney

Hildesheim, build a beautiful church
in—Bernward

Historian—Bede, the Venerable

Holland, Patron of—Willibrord
of Echternach

Holy and healthy-looking—Fintan
of Clonenagh

Holy Spirit, chock full of—Gregory
the Wonderworker

"Holy Spirit, Harp of the"—Ephraem

Homeless, friends of the:
Benedict Joseph Labré
Simeon Salus

"Honey-sweet preacher"—Bernard
of Clairveaux

Hospitable city—Cascia, Italy (Rita
of Cascia)

Hospitals or Hospices, founded
(many saints, but especially):
Basil the Great
Camillus
Frances of Rome
John of God
Joseph Cottolengo

Marguerite d'Youville
Pammachius & Fabiola
Philip Neri
Theodore the Cenobiarch

Hospitals, worked in:
Bertilla Boscardin
Camillus
John of God
Peter Claver

"House of Divine Providence" run by—
Joseph Cottolengo

"Hulks," visited prisoners in—Vincent
de Paul

Hunters, former:
Bavo/Allowin
Hubert
Ulric of Haselbury Plunknett

Husaby, came from—Halvard

Hydrology and drainage, fascinated by—
Philip of Moscow

Hymns, encouraged use of or wrote:
Ambrose
Bede, the Venerable
Hilary of Poitiers (first in the West)
John of Damascus
Nicetias of Remesiana
Patrick
Venantius Fortunatus

Hymns, gave detailed instructions on
how to sing—
Nicetias of Remesiana

"I Am Not He, Whom You Knew Then"—
Paulinus of Nola

Iles de Lérins at Cannes, started a
monastery at—Honoratus of Arles

India, Apostles to:
Francis Xavier
John de Britto

Inn, died in an—Hugh of Lincoln

Innocent woman, died defending an—
Halvard

Irish, Apostle to the—Patrick

Island of Nisida, was Abbot on—Adrian
of Canterbury

Island sanctuaries, ran some:
    Cuthbert
    Honoratus
"Island soldier"—Columba
Italian saints, some:
    Ambrose (sort of)
    Andrew Corsini
    Anthony of Padua
    Benedict
    Benedict of Palermo
    Bertilla Boscardin
    Bona of Pisa
    Bonaventure
    Catherine of Siena
    Clare of Assisi
    Frances Cabrini (see also N. America)
    Frances of Rome
    Francis of Assisi
    Gerard Majella
    Giuseppe Moscati
    John (Giovanni) Bosco
    Joseph Cottolengo
    Joseph of Cupertino
    Leopold Mandic (by way of Croatia)
    Lucy
    Peter Damian
    Peter Orseolo
    Philip Neri
    Rita of Cascia
    Roch/Rocco (sort of)
    Scholastica
    Zita of Lucca
Italians, ministered to overseas—
    Frances Cabrini
Italy, Patrons of—Francis of Assisi,
    Catherine of Siena
Ivan the Terrible, murdered by—Philip
    of Moscow
Jack of all trades—Martin de Porres
Japan, Apostle to—Francis Xavier
Jerome, friend of grumpy Saint—
    Marcella
Jesus put him in the midst of them—
    Ignatius of Antioch

Jewish man, died in place of a—
    Maximilian Kolbe
Jews, saved, from an angry mob—
    Hugh of Lincoln
Jordan the Lion was a pet of—
    Gerasimus
Judges (excellent):
    Louis of France
    Nicholas Von Flue
    Pulcheria
Kent, for years they called him down in—
    see Ethelbert of Kent
Keys, will help you find your lost—Zita
    of Lucca
Khazars, Apostles to the—Cyril and
    Methodius
Kicked dogs in his unrepentant days—
    Vladimir
Kings, advised several English:
    Dunstan
    Hugh of Lincoln
King asked his thanes for input on
    conversion—Edwin
King Childeric, King Clovis, convinced
    not to be so barbaric—Geneviéve
King chopped up into small pieces, hung
    on tree—Oswald
Kingdom, could have ruled one if she'd
    wanted—Euphrasia Pelletier
King interpreting God's word—Oswald
King Oswy of Northumbria—see
    Benedict Biscop
King, the ideal—Louis of France
King's head guarded by pet wolf—Edwin
King who invited Augustine to England—
    Ethelbert of Kent
Komi, Zyrians of, converted—Stephen
    of Perm
Lake, fought a battle on a frozen—
    Alexander Nevsky
Languages, had a natural gift for—
    Francis Solano
Lavra, founded one on the Jordan
    River—Gerasimus

Lawyers:
 Cyprian
 Ivo of Brittany
 Severinus Boethius
Led about on a rope by a former
 servant—Bavo/Allowin
Lent, ate nothing at all during—Simon
 Stylites
Leopards, called his guards the ten—
 Ignatius of Antioch
Library-builder—Benedict Biscop
Lima, Peru, people of, told them to shape
 up—Francis Solano
Light, face radiated a dazzling—Sergius
 of Radonezh
Lindisfarne, founded monastery on—
 Cuthbert
Lion, had a pet one named Jordan—
 Gerasimus
"Lion, like a, when he preaches"—
 Anthony of Padua
Lions of Lyons, fed to the—Blandina
Loaf, looked like one in a fire—
 Polycarp
Loch Ness Monster, scared away—
 Columba
Love, saint in charge of—Valentine
Lullaby for Baby Jesus, wrote a—Ide,
 see Brendan the Voyager
Lullaby with guardian angels—Michael
 and All Angels
Madrid, Patron of—Isidore the Farm
 Servant
Madurai, India, ended up there—John
 de Britto
Magician, almost thrown out of court
 for being a—Dunstan
Maids:
 Notburga
 Zita of Lucca
Man, Patron of the Isle of—Maughold
Manners, great believers in:
 Margaret of Scotland
 Nicetas of Trier

Marcus Aurelius not such a Good
 Emperor—Justin and Blandina
Married saints:
 Elizabeth of Hungary
 Frances of Rome
 Isidore the Farm Servant
 Marguerite d'Youville
 Monica
 Nicholas Von Flue
 Pammachius
 Paulinus of Nola
 Pulcheria
 Rita of Cascia
 Vladimir
 Waudru
Megalomartyros—George
"Middle Eastern" saints (roughly
 corresponding to the area of
 the Byzantine or later Ottoman
 Empire), some:
 Basil the Great/Gregory of Nazianus
 Gerasimus
 Gregory the Wonderworker
 Hilarion (Gaza)
 Ignatius of Antioch
 Irenaeus
 John the Almsgiver
 Nicholas of Myra
 Pachomius
 Plague of Alexandria, Martyrs of
 Phocas
 Polycarp
 Pulcheria
 Simeon Salus
 Simon Stylites
 Theodore the Cenobiarch
Missionaries, too successful for own
 good—
 John de Britto
 Peter Chanel
Monasteries, started—see Rule
Monks killing each other—Columba
"Monks? why do we have to act like"—
 Tikhon of Zadonsk

Monte Cassino, founded—Benedict

Montreal, founded the Grey Nuns of—
Marguerite d'Youville

Mother, dear old, carried around in
a wheelbarrow couch—Cuthman
of Steyning

Mother saints:
Felicity (see Perpetua)
Monica
Perpetua
Waudru

Mother, went on pilgrimage with his—
Godric

Mother worried about him a lot, his—
Augustine of Hippo

Mountain passes, made them safe—
Bernard of Montjoux

Movie, has a great one made about
him (as do other saints)—Alexander
Nevsky

Mule bowed before Host—Anthony
of Padua

Music, loved—Peter Claver

Music, Patron of—Cecilia

Music, wrote:
Godric (the first written down in
English language)
Hildegard of Bingen

Muslim apostates, killed because
they were:
Abo
Aurelius and Natalia
Felix, Liliosa and George (see Abo et al.)

Muslim ruler, worked for a:
Abo
John of Damascus

Naples, did mission work in—Francis
di Girolamo

Naples, was doctor in—Giuseppe
Moscati

New World, first saint to the—Brendan
the Voyager

Night, wanted to spend it it all with her
brother, talking of God—Scholastica

Noble ladies with big houses,
organized—Frances of Rome

Non nobis, domine—Crispin and
Crispinian

Nonsense, won't put up with evil—
Marcellus & Cassian

Norman Invasion rears its ugly head—
Margaret of Scotland

North American saints:
Frances Cabrini
Marguerite d'Youville
Martin de Porres

Northumbria, brought library and cantor
to—Benedict Biscop

Nose, grabbed the devil by the—Dunstan

Nurses:
Bertilla Boscardin
Camillus

Oblates, founded order of—Frances
of Rome

"Ontological proof of God's existence"—
Anselm

Oratorio form, helped begin—Philip Neri

Organizer, terrific—Pachomius

Oslo, Patron of—Halvard

Ostia, died happy in—Monica

Padre de Caridad—Martin de Porres

Paradise, visited (aka the New World)—
Brendan the Voyager

Paradiso, the only Englishman in
Dante's—Bede, the Venerable

Pardon, started a Festival of—Ivo
of Brittany

Paris, lost his head in—Denis the
Cephalophore

Paris, Patron of—Geneviéve

Passes of the Alps, made safe—Bernard
of Montjoux

Patient, incredibly:
Germaine of Pibrac
Joan of France

Paulinus his biggest fan—Felix of Nola

Peacemaker, derided for being a—
Alexander Nevsky

Peacemaker between different groups—
    Andrew Corsini
"Peppery," called himself—Hugh
    of Lincoln
Pen, threw down his—Genesius of Arles
Perfumer—Abo
Philosophers:
    Anselm
    Severinus Boethius
Pilgrimages, folk longen to goon on—
    see Thomas Becket
Pigs, fed people instead of—Notburga
Pigs, took care of—Peter Damian
Pirate, a former:
    Godric
    Maughold
Pirates, nabbed by—Patrick
Plague, took care of victims of:
    Plague of Alexandria, Martyrs of
    Roch/Rocco
"Play-actors, Patron of"—Thomas Becket
Plow a field, angel helped—Isidore the
    Farm Servant
Plumbing, could fix your—Teresa of Ávila
Poets:
    Aldhelm
    Ambrose
    Ephraem
    Harvey/Hervé
    Hilary of Poitiers
    Hildegard of Bingen
    John of Damascus
    Nicetias of Remesiana
    Paulinus of Nola
    Peter Damian
    Teresa of Ávila
    Venantius Fortunatus
Popes:
    Gregory the Great
    Leo the Great
Popes, tried to reconcile—Catherine
    of Siena
Porters:
    Alphonsus Rodriguez
    Gerard Majella
    Martin de Porres
Prayed up a storm (literally)—Scholastica
Preached to birds—Francis of Assisi
Preached to fish—Anthony of Padua
Preachers, especially terrific:
    Anthony of Padua
    Francis di Girolamo
Predicted a chariot race victory—
    Hilarion
Pretended to be crazy to avoid being
    a bishop—Ephraem
Princes:
    Alexander Nevsky
    Vladimir
Princesses:
    Elizabeth of Hungary
    Mildred
Princess, married a beautiful, once
    he reformed—
    Vladimir
Professor at the Imperial University—Cyril
Protestants, made friends with:
    Frances Cabrini
    Peter Claver
    Vincent de Paul
Prison camp, monastery later turned into
    a—Philip of Moscow
Prisoners, visited—Peter Claver
Puppeteers, patron of—Simeon Salus
Pyrenees, hid out in the—Peter Orseolo
Queens:
    Joan of France
    Margaret of Scotland
Queen's confessor—Antony Mary Claret
Racist comments, ignored—Benedict
    of Palermo
Ravenna, came from—Peter Damian
Ravens as pet birds—Oswald
Read and write, nuns must be able to—
    Caesarius of Arles
Reformers (of . . .):
    Euphrasia Pelletier (Good Shepherd
    Sisters)

Teresa of Ávila (discalced Carmelites)
Reformer with a fierce sermon—Peter
    Damian
"Resolute goodness"—Halvard, Thorfinn
Retirement meant being *almost* as busy
    as before—Tikhon of Zadonsk
Retreat center, started—Columba
    (at Iona), Cuthbert (at Lindisfarne),
    Honoratus of Arles (at Cannes)
Riddles, loved writing—Aldhelm
River, dried up one with his prayers—
    Gregory the Wonderworker
Roman (or Roman-era Italian) saints,
    some:
  Almachius
  Benedict Joseph Labré
  Camillus
  Cecilia
  Crispin and Crispinian
  Felix of Nola
  Frances of Rome
  Justin and Blandina
  Lawrence
  Leo the Great
  Marcella
  Martin of Tours
  Maximus
  Pammachius
  Paulinus of Nola
  Philip Neri
  Gregory the Great
  Severinus Boethius
  Tibertius
  Valerian
Rome, Sack of in 1527, helped heal
    the wounds of—Philip Neri
Rome, Sack of in 1527, probably took
    part in—John of God
Rose bush, jumped into a—Benedict
Roses, associated with—Rita of Cascia
Rule, wrote an important one for
    monasteries:
  Basil the Great
  Benedict

  Cassian
  Pachomius
  Theodore the Cenobiarch
Russian saints, some:
  Alexander Nevsky
  Philip of Moscow
  Sergius of Radonezh
  Stephen of Perm
  Tikhon of Zadonsk
  Vladimir
Sack of Rome in 1527, helped heal the
    wounds of—Philip Neri
Sack of Rome in 1527, probably took
    part in—John of God
Sagum, the Roman military cape—
    Martin of Tours
Saint's days celebrated like big festivals—
    Gregory the Wonderworker
Santa Claus, *a.k.a.*—Nicholas of Myra
Sausages, ate some in church on Good
    Friday—Simeon Salus
Saxons, converted—Oswald
School terms named after them:
  Hilary of Poitiers
  Michael
  the Holy Trinity
Schoolboys, Patron of—Adrian
    of Canterbury
Schools, set up lots of:
  Frances Cabrini
  Jean-Baptiste de la Salle
Scientists:
  Albert the Great
  Antony Mary Claret
  Cuthbert (more of a naturalist)
  Hildegard of Bingen
Scottish saints, some:
  Margaret
  David (see Margaret)
Sculptors—The Four Crownéd Ones
Shepherd who stopped gladiators, sort
    of—Almachius
Shipwreck, saved slaves from a—Francis
    Solano

Shipwreck, stranded by a—Frumentius

Sickle, hers flew up into the air—
Notburga

Simple things, loved (most saints, but
especially)—
Bonaventure
Francis of Assisi

Sister taught him a tune from beyond
the grave—Godric

Sister started a convent:
Benedict (Scholastica)
Caesarius of Arles (Caesaria)

Shepherdess:
Joan of Arc

Slavs, Apostles to the—Cyril and
Methodius

Slave, former—Benedict of Palermo

Slaves, ministered to—Peter Claver,
Vincent de Paul

Smiling, always depicted as—Zeno
of Verona

Smyrna, martyred at—Polycarp

Snow, turned out into the—Elizabeth
of Hungary

Sold his servants to make money—
Bavo/Allowin

Soldiers:
Joan of Arc
Camillus
Guthlac
John of God
Marcellus the Centurion
Martin of Tours
Pachomius

Solovetsk Island, built a monastery on—
Philip of Moscow

Song, has a special one in her honor—
Lucy

Song, wrote one inspired by his sister—
Godric

South Pacific island converter—Peter
Chanel

Spanish saints, some:
Abo

Alphonsus Rodriguez
Antony Mary Claret
Aurelius and Natalia
Francis Solano
Francis Xavier
Isidore the Farm Servant
John of God
Peter Claver (actually a Catalan)
Teresa of Ávila
Thomas of Villanueva

Spare the unarmed in war—Adamnan

Sparrow flying through a lighted hall—
Edwin

Spiderweb saved his life—Felix
of Nola

Spy, arrested by the Franks as a—
Adrian of Canterbury

Stake, burned at the:
Agathonice
Joan of Arc
Polycarp (after death)

Stag, had a vision of a cross on the head
of a—Hubert (and Eustace)

Stenographers:
Cassian of Tangiers (see Marcellus)
Genesius of Arles

Stonemasons—The Four Crownéd Ones

Stubborn, very:
Cecilia
The Four Crownéd Ones (and
all martyrs)
Peter Claver
Vincent de Paul

Swan, had a pet—Hugh of Lincoln

Sweden, Apostle to—Sigfrid

Swedish coffee and pastry feast—Lucy

Switzerland, big hero of—Nicholas
Von Flue

Tactful in the extreme—Thomas
of Villanueva

Tatars, told Prince Dmitry to go fight
the—Sergius of Radonezh

Tatars, treated with the—Alexander
Nevsky

Taxed his clergy to pay for missions—
John the Almsgiver
Teacher of other saints—
Adrian of Canterbury
John of Beverly
"Teacher, the Universal"—Albert the Great
Teachers:
Adrian of Canterbury
Albert the Great
Dunstan
Jean-Baptiste de la Salle
Teaching, wrote the book on—Jean-
Baptiste de la Salle
Te Deum, wrote the—Nicetias of
Remesiana
Thieves and moneylenders, Patron of—
Nicholas of Myra
Thought about picking up the Gospels—
Augustine of Hippo
Tipped the headsman—Cyprian
Tongs, grabbed the devil with his—
Dunstan
Tour guides, patron of—Bona of Pisa
Translators & Alphabet Innovators:
Cyril and Methodius
Mesrop
Stephen of Perm
Travel by water, especially afraid of—
Frances Cabrini
Treasury, found it full, left it empty—
John the Almsgiver
Tree, had the man hang his cardinal's
hat on a—Bonaventure
Tree, once mistaken for—Gregory the
Wonderworker
Tree, was chopped up and hung on
one—Oswald
Triune nature of God . . .
explained by shamrock—Patrick
revealed through pebbles—Augustine
of Hippo
simply explained—Irenaeus
still explaining at her death—Cecilia
Truce of God—Odilo of Cluny

Truth people didn't want to hear—
Marcella, Euphrasia
Truth no matter what:
Anselm
Justin and Blandina
"Twentieth Century Saint"—Maximilian
Kolbe
Ugly, too, to be queen—Joan of France
Underground Eucharist service—Julie
Postel
"Universal, Teacher, the" —Albert
the Great
Universities, oldest in Europe—Albert
the Great
Valdocco, Milan, started a shelter in—
Joseph Cottolengo
Venice, Doge of—Peter Orseolo
Vipers, had pet—Godric
Visigoths pestered her to death—Marcella
Walk, Echternach, special sacred dance—
Willibrord
Wallis and Futuna, patron of—Peter
Chanel
Walked five miles holding his head—
Denis the Cephalophore
Wamba, converted king—Giles Aegidius
War, Hundred Years', helped to end—
Joan of Arc
War, went to it reluctantly but well—
Alexander Nevsky
War, tried to make it more civilized—
Adamnan, Odilo of Cluny
Washed dishes—Bonaventure (among
many others)
Wendy and the Lost Boys, a bit like—
Paulinus of Nola's wife Therasia and
her husband's friends
Wife, angry former, had him killed—
John de Britto
Winaman, Unaman, Sunaman, nephews
of Sigfrid
Wise Women:
Hildegard of Bingen
Lioba

"Wizard's duel," had one with a pagan—
 Stephen of Perm

Wolf, had a "seeing eye"—Harvey/Hervé

Wolf, had his severed head guarded by
 a pet—Edwin

Wolf, mother dreamed she had given
 birth to a—Andrew Corsini

Wolf, tamed a—Francis of Assisi

Women, led a bunch of "well-
 domesticated"—Lioba

Wreaths of roses and lilies, saw an angel
 with two—Valerian

Youths, concerned with the plight of—
 John Bosco

Zyrians of Komi, converted—Stephen
 of Perm